This book is about Black girl magick, queer girl magick, straight girl magick, trans magick, bisexual magick. It's about giving yourself the power to be fierce.

Authentic and unapologetic, this guide to magical spirituality empowers you to take back the power to heal and shine under your own strength. Written by an accomplished Hoodoo practitioner, *Conjuring the Calabash* features spells, recipes, and rituals that help you rise out of the constrictions around you.

Mawiyah Kai El-Jamah Bomani shows you how to bless your calabash (sacred womb) with love and reawaken your fullest potential through folk traditions, personal stories, and her favorite songs and pop stars. An inclusive and intersectional voice in contemporary Hoodoo, Mawiyah will help you become your fiercest self.

Praise for *Conjuring the Calabash*

"*Conjuring The Calabash* is not derivative nor is it tethered to tradition. This book is bold in its contemporary, eclectic, and visionary outlook. In its pages you will learn to address issues that are of today ... Bomani is a gifted Hoodoo and a modern-day wise woman." —**Stephanie Rose Bird, author of *Sticks, Stones, Roots & Bones* and *365 Days of Hoodoo***

"Bomani is the first to concretely compile the religious practices surrounding the use of the Calabash as a sacred vessel and symbol of femininity, fertility, and ancestry, putting together centuries of oral folklore, spiritual tradition, and religious practice in a clear way." —**Elhoim Leafar, author of *Dream Witchery***

"As Bomani shares her encouragement, experience, and wisdom with the reader, a sense of strength and compassion shines through. It's loaded with magickal workings for spiritual and practical livelihood." —**Granddaughter Crow (Navajo Nation), author of *Belief, Being, and Beyond***

"Bomani is why women of color are finally leading the conversation surrounding sex magic. She makes the world a better place through her thrilling yet relatable writing." —**Sophie Saint Thomas, author of *Sex Witch***

"One of the most authentic books on Hoodoo that I have read ... Speaking directly to people of color not only makes this book a must-have to help navigate the hardships we face in this world, but also inspires a rekindling of magic that lives deep within our bones." —**Juliet Diaz, author of *The Altar Within***

"*Conjuring the Calabash* is full of practical advice, tips, tricks, recipes, and folklore. Mawiyah truly understands and shares her lineage and has vast knowledge of this history, the stories, and African traditions." —**Yvette Wyatt, owner of The Motown Witch**

"Bomani does not disappoint in her endeavor to celebrate wombmanhood, weaving stories of her family into the tapestry that is the calabash ... She shares the ancestral wisdom and culture held fiercely in the hearts of those who live it. Though written for women, there is something in the book for anyone looking for empowerment through the art of conjure." —**Denise Alvarado, author of** *The Magic of Marie Laveau*

"*Conjuring the Calabash* fills a blank space in American Witchcraft Literature. This book reveals the mysteries of Hoodoo, making it accessible to understand, practice and incorporate magic in our everyday lives with plenty of exercises, spells, and rituals to experience time and again." —**Laura Gonzalez, CSNP station manager, host of** *Lunatic Mondays*

"A powerful book that unlocks the secrets of African-American hoodoo traditions for modern women … With clear, step-by-step instructions and practical examples, Mawiyah guides readers through the intricacies of hoodoo spellcasting and helps them unlock their full potential." —**Mat Auryn, bestselling author of** *Psychic Witch* **and** *Mastering Magick*

"A well-written and insightful book…It is much needed information on folk magicks of the Caribbean, working with the Calabash. It is a book I will be recommending to my students and colleagues alike." —**Starr RavenHawk, HPs founder of WFT Academy of Pagan Studies**

"A call to all levels of magickal practitioners to embrace the enormity of the powers that lie within us and to enliven and express that power through magick, spellcraft, and ritual … Bomani has created a rich and searingly honest go-to resource." —**Rhonda Alin, founder of Black Women of Magick & Conjure**

About the Author

Mawiyah Kai El-Jamah Bomani is an award-winning writer, educator, and spirit woman. Mawiyah is an eighth-generation Witch, Egun Medium, and Priestess of OYA in the Yoruba system of spirituality. She is also editor in chief of the culture and Afrikan Traditional Spirituality e-zine, *Oya N'Soro*. Mawiyah is the host of *FishHeadsinRedGravy*, a podcast dedicated to celebrating marginalized people of the esoteric/occult world. Her writings have appeared in numerous magazines, including *The Crab Orchard Review*, *Dark Eros*, and *Catch the Fire*. She has written several plays, including *Spring Chickens*, which won her the Southern Black Theatre Festival's 2012–2013 Playwright of the Year Award. She is also the Critical Mass 8 Literary Award winner and a KAT Artist Residency recipient. Mawiyah currently lives, writes, and conducts Orisa rituals, spiritual consultations, workshops, house cleansings, and divinations in both northern and southern Louisiana. Visit her at www.MawiyahKaiElJamahBomani.com.

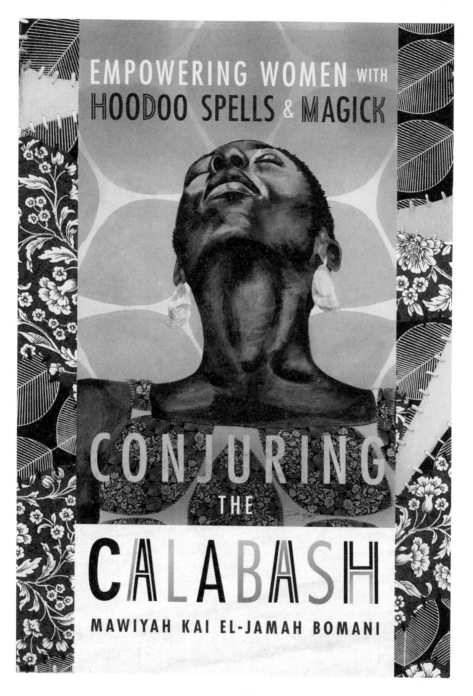

EMPOWERING WOMEN WITH
HOODOO SPELLS & MAGICK

CONJURING
THE
CALABASH

MAWIYAH KAI EL-JAMAH BOMANI

Llewellyn Publications
Woodbury, Minnesota

First Edition
First Printing, 2023

Book design by Christine Ha
Cover art by Delita Martin
Editing by Anitra Budd
Interior illustrations by the Llewellyn Art Department

Photography is used for illustrative purposes only. The persons depicted may not endorse or represent the book's subject.

Llewellyn Publications is a registered trademark of Llewellyn Worldwide Ltd.

Library of Congress Cataloging-in-Publication Data (Pending)
ISBN: 978-0-7387-7371-1

Llewellyn Worldwide Ltd. does not participate in, endorse, or have any authority or responsibility concerning private business transactions between our authors and the public.
All mail addressed to the author is forwarded but the publisher cannot, unless specifically instructed by the author, give out an address or phone number.
Any internet references contained in this work are current at publication time, but the publisher cannot guarantee that a specific location will continue to be maintained. Please refer to the publisher's website for links to authors' websites and other sources.

Llewellyn Publications
A Division of Llewellyn Worldwide Ltd.
2143 Wooddale Drive
Woodbury, MN 55125-2989
www.llewellyn.com

Printed in the United States of America

Dedication

This book is dedicated to my husband, Nadir Lasana Bomani, who can never let a day go by without reminding me my stews, brews, and witchy ways "keep women out my face." (All I got to say to that is sure you right!) To my daughters, the weird sisters, Nzingha, Camara, and Naima, my most beloved coven of revolutionary witches, I truly love you. May this book liberate you, your lovers, your children, and their children for eons to come. To my sons, spirited craftsmen of words, Kambui and Sekou, I see the mugwort in your eyes—now go set the world on fire. To my grandmothers, grandfathers, and mother, Patricia Ann Coulter Dean, I thank you for your wisdom. I'll cherish your stories of salvation and magickal evenings beyond the veil for many lifetimes to come. Lastly, this book is dedicated to YOU, dear reader, for deciding on this day to name yourself healed, whole, and divinely liberated. Ase!

Disclaimer

This book contains advice and information detailing both the usage and formulation of herbs specifically for spellcrafting and rituals. This book is not intended to diagnose, treat, or prescribe for any illness or disease. Readers using the information in this book do so at their own risk. The author and publisher accept no liability for adverse effects. No portion of this book is meant to be used as a substitute for the advice of a licensed/board-certified therapist or physician. If you have or suspect you have a medical problem, do not attempt any of the spellcrafting listed in this book. Consult a health care provider before beginning any herbal regimen.

Readers are cautioned: to achieve maximum results, follow each work as it is written.

Contents

Foreword

I was honored to be asked by Mawiyah Bomani to write this foreword to her engaging and inclusive book, *Conjuring the Calabash: Empowering Women with Hoodoo Spells and Magick*. You see, we're both Hoodoo workers and conjurers first before writers. Hoodoo workers by their very definition have changed over the years. We're at a crossroads of justice and what it means to be in or out in the intersectionality of female, spiritual workings, and political activism. Hoodoo, in my mind, is personal, political, and social. Before I knew anything about the word *Hoodoo*, I just knew my family.

The women in my life were my teachers. Some were just doing the best they could with limited education and support. Some were very successful for their time, meaning they were mothers and wives. Others were different, weird, shunned. Shunned because they chanted to God and Universe at midnight. They consulted bones, black-eyed peas, cowrie shells, and ancestors before making choices. They wore white on some days, washed their hair and clothes on others, and bathed themselves in knee-high stockings full of herbs and roots. They had reverence for Spirit and Angels and numbers and photographs on their altar. These were the women who held and taught me and made me a Hoodoo worker when I knew nothing of the word. I watched and learned their ways and now, with many years of fasting, praying, spirit work, rituals, writing, reading, and trial and error in the Universe's ways, I'm a Hoodoo worker and woman. I can do with water what others need an entire metaphysical store to accomplish.

This personal and practical book gives you Mawiyah's way of Hoodoo so that one day you can integrate it into your Hoodoo. For those of you just starting your journey into Hoodoo, this book will teach you. For those who are already Hoodoo workers, this book will teach you more. For those who doubt Hoodoo can and should be inclusive, Mawiyah's personal story, rituals, and methods will be a balm to heal those wounds. Join Mawiyah as she gives you a key into her personal Hoodoo world. She will be a firm and gentle guide—she won't sugarcoat nor chastise.

Once you've devoured every page, I dare you to look back at the person you were when you began and who you are when you finish the last paragraph. Good books are read; great books touch your spirit and soul. *Conjuring the Calabash* is a great book, and a reference for women of all kinds, Hoodoo and conjure, and the BIPOC experience.

—*Sherry "That Hoodoo Lady" Shone*
Author of *Hoodoo for Everyone: Modern Approaches to Magic, Conjure, Rootwork, and Liberation*, and *The Hoodoo Guide to the Bible: Advice from a Real Hoodoo Worker*

Introduction

You're probably wondering why you're being asked to conjure the calabash, and even more who the wild, witchy woman imploring you to do so is. Let me explain by weaving our journey through the vines of the calabash itself.

The calabash is a sacred vessel in Yoruba cosmology. It's said to represent the energies of man at the top and woman at the bottom. As the two halves are suspended in space, we witness the glory of sky meeting earth in an eternal yet sacred kiss. It's through the power of Ase (the energy to make life happen *for* us as opposed *to* us) that these two remain forever intertwined in a perfect mating dance.

To me, the calabash is the womb of womankind. Even if we've never given birth, it is the heartbeat residing at the depths of our spiritual womb space. The calabash expresses itself as a feminine knowing. It's an instinctual blessing bestowed on every person greeting us with a calm patience. The calabash grounds us to our purpose, spanning every and all life experiences. It's the portal to the ancestral council, those who decide what sacrifice must be paid from each life's toll. The calabash is our reminder that we are sacred, and no amount of trauma can stop us from honoring the drive it took to be born, to smell, to taste, to touch, to exist. The calabash is where we go to recuperate after battles. It's where we return to when we seek camaraderie from those survivors who have been where we are, those living reminders, those calabash women who are too stubborn to die. Calabash women multiply infinitely. Taste their fruit sprouting, reaching toward the sun, reaching toward a collective salvation.

Wherever sistahs congregate is their personal calabash. It might be a book club. It might be movie night. It might be a literal club outing, dancing to house or reggae music as a release. It might be the beauty salon, a day spa, or a girl's trip to an all-inclusive resort. It might be a sistahs' all call for magickal

1

work at midnight, butt naked, in the backyard of the homegirl with the least distractions. It might be at the gym, the yoga studio, pole dancing, or a burlesque class. It could be a hike in the woods far away from civilization and cell towers. The calabash is wherever you and your girlfriends find a deep communal healing for the mind, body, soul, and spirit.

❀ ❀ ❀

I grew up with my grandfather telling me the story of Oduduwa and Obatala sealed inside the darkness of a gourd. As his telling goes, Obatala was nestled at the top while the blind Oduduwa made her home at the bottom. As time went on, both grew impatient with the thought of remaining in the gourd's darkness for eternity. Oduduwa began to complain. Her tongue grew wicked with insults and taunts. As the days trickled into weeks, Oduduwa blamed Obatala for their predicament. With each new insinuation she cut him to the bone. One day his rage boiled over into putrid venom, and Obatala tore out his wife's eyes with his bare hands. Not to be outdone, Oduduwa cursed him with an appetite to eat only raw snails.

Seeing my tears and anger at the story, my grandfather would add, "Eventually they forgave each other and made the darkness their salvation, not their adversary." As I grew up, I placed my ear next to gourds, any gourd, hoping to hear Obatala and Oduduwa either quarreling or soothing the intense pain from each other's aura. Even today, as a grown woman, I can still press my ear against gourds, eagerly waiting for whispers in the dark.

In time, I saw the gourd as a representation of something beyond my grandfather's story. It became the ultimate emblem of fertility, like the uterus it so closely resembles. Gourds have earned the right to be seen as powerful symbols of femininity, and they're often used in fertility rites of passage. Their ritual roles ensure that girls are imbued with the power to conceive as they pass into womanhood. Hollowed and cut, gourds serve as bowls to carry offerings to goddesses, gods, and ancestors.

The calabash gourd represents a generational container cradling the blood of each woman's lineage. The gourd reminds us that for as long as there are women who are heard, there will be women who are loved. What lies in the hollow darkness of the gourd is the potential for life.

The idea of conjuring the calabash is embedded in the reality that a woman who loses her agency to the will of patriarchal mandates has blocked her womb. She no longer possesses the knowledge to free herself from the role of sex slave versus feminine icon.

The offerings in this book will help call forth a woman's self-worth. By performing these rituals, you'll find your sacred voice while reawakening your fullest goddess potential. Isn't it time to bless your gourd with love?

❀ ❀ ❀

But what about Hoodoo? What is it? Hoodoo is the African American's cathartic release. It combines African conjure magick, indigenous Native practices, and a sprinkling of western spirituality in the forms of roots, herbs, and lore to creatively alter, annihilate, and transform inhumane conditioning in our favor. Over the years, Hoodoo has afforded me and my clients the unadulterated freedom to rewrite our stories, fashioning ourselves as we see fit. No longer are we the victimized do-gooders who never get a break. Now we're magical artisans, reconfiguring the void for eternity. And if we want a lover to park his or her feet under our coffee table? Then please believe me when I say, we got a spell for that too. There are more methods to Hoodoo than you can shake a switch at.

Growing up in New Orleans, I came to understand Hoodoo as a gumbo of Indigenous beliefs and practices stirred together in one engorged melting pot. See, Hoodoo differs from Black person to Black person depending on their region and other cultural influences that intermingled in their specific roux. Where I'm from, there's a mixture of Africans from the Senegambia region of West Africa, the Bight of Benin, Congo, Ghana, and Sierra Leone. Then, as the roux thickened through the knowledge of Louisiana staple herbs and roots, it incorporated Indigenous healing knowledge from the Atakapa, Bayogoula, Natchez, Choctaw, Chickasaw, Taensa, and Alabamon peoples.

The more Christianity was forced on Afrikans, the more they channeled their spiritual traditions into a deeper understanding of rootwork; in this way elements of Indigenous botanical knowledge became a staple of Afrikan retention. As offspring of the first Afrikans to the region became devout Christians and Catholics, Hoodoo remained an unwavering yet unspoken fixture in many households.[1]

❀ ❀ ❀

In writing this book, I hope to share a fragment of the spellcrafting that has shaped and continues to shape my life, as well as the lives of folks I hold dear. I'm an educator, eighth-generation witch, Egun medium, priestess of Oya in the Yoruba system of spirituality, and lifelong practitioner of conjure cloaked in the splendid attire of Hoodoo. For eleven years I served as editor in chief of the culture and Afrikan Traditional Spirituality e-zine, *Oya N'Soro*. For fifteen years I've divined for women and men alike. Over the years, these people have reiterated how potent my readings were in helping them recharge their life's goals. Not only do I point out parallels between their present and future, but I also offer a look into past lives with a specific emphasis on healing through the use of herbs, roots, baths, powders, candle work, crystals, and satchels.

When a querent leaves me, I want them to have so much more than a simple set of emailed words on a screen. Rather, I want folks to walk away wielding the power to build a new beginning from the ruins of a once-debilitating past.

This book is intended for those who don't want to devote their time and energy to the dogma of religion, with all its prejudices and fire-and-brimstone hurdles on the path to emotional salvation. This book is for those of us who've decided that the Goddess and God's abode is everywhere, and no one's rendition of scripture is more sacred than the autonomy of our own voice.

....

1. I use the letter *k* in the word *Afrikan* instead of a *c* because the *k* sound aligns with rules of Afrikan vernacular throughout the diaspora. The *c* is believed to have been used because the sound pattern fits European language rules. I interchange the *k* and *c* so readers can immediately identify whether I'm discussing an idea derived from Afrikan or European constructs.

This book is for all women of color, whether they be African American, Native, Asian, Latino, lesbian, bisexual, nonbinary, transgender, or any other identity—honey, I accept you and love you fiercely no matter what! And when I say "women," I mean any person of color who identifies within the realm of the divine feminine—even if you're wielding a divinely masculine body, this book will uplift you and provide an avenue toward connecting with the feminine perspective sashaying within us all. Most of all, this book is for women who seek to liberate themselves by healing from the outside in and the inside out.

All that being said, I'm a cis woman, meaning the sex I was assigned at birth matches the gender I identify with. I'm also in a heterosexual marriage and have been for years. This book's insights and workings are drawn from my lived experience because I can only share with authenticity from that vantage point. Likewise, only you know your vantage point: your lived experiences as a woman and what being a woman means to you. I invite and encourage you to use your unique vantage point to modify the techniques in this book as needed. Make it authentic to your life.

Women are often told to temper our expectations. We're told that being strong willed will leave us unmarried, childless, and excluded from important circles. This book is about Black girl magick, queer girl magick, straight girl magick, trans magick, bisexual magick. This book is about giving yourself the power to be fierce. This book is about allowing magick to set the record straight once and for all: Black women are hierophants, magicians, empresses, and high priestesses, and sometimes if you catch us right, we can even unleash the Devil.

Chapter One
Crescent City Hoodoo

You've probably heard some version of the following: When a man cheats, he's simply "being a man." But when a woman cheats, she's a whore, or worse. And if this same woman is killed by her lover or husband, the thinking is, *well, she shouldn't have been stepping out in the first place.* I'm strongly against this sort of brainwashing. I wasn't born with instructions attached to my toe telling me to listen to men because all men are always and forever right. My belief in the woman-as-goddess concept stems from my resistance to the idea that women should be treated like children—spanked into submission either verbally or physically. Yet I hear from women who've been brow beaten by church into letting their husbands decide how their lives unfold. As a result, many of these women feel they don't even have their own thoughts. I don't need a man or a religion to teach me my worth as a woman. I know I deserve a cherished existence.

Women can choose to follow a god, goddess, both, or none. We can vocalize our disdain at our underrepresentation in the clergy and fight to stand at the pulpit, not filling the chalice of a male adept who blames what lies between our thighs for humanity's exile from utopia. We women are fully capable of paying our own bills, deciding to have or not to have children, leading ourselves in prayer, and maintaining our homes, cars, and, most important, our bodies. We're also more than capable of finding our sexual sweet spot every time, no questions asked.

As a living, generational practice, Hoodoo is important to include in the lives of women. Hoodoo uses blood, bones, spit, shit, hair, urine, semen, plants, roots, and shoots to conjure forward the spirits of the Nether Region, those ancient figures from our lineage who may be unknown, but are highly beneficial to our survival. When we feed these spirits, we nourish the void. This spiritual intervention impacts our physical realm, making the world an easier road to travel. In this way, Hoodoo gives women the means to control their spirituality. It provides women an equal opportunity to voice their ideas and desires, and to create the consequential themes that will forever define their lives.

Jena Street

My own connection to spirits came when I was five and living in uptown New Orleans on Jena Street. The spirits who floated aimlessly throughout the shotgun house called to me by name. They could appear on any given day at any hour. Some forty-three years, later I still vividly remember one encounter with the spirit of Ms. Odessa, my father's second wife. That night, she and her prickly nails scratched at my heels as urine streamed down my legs. I ran from my bedroom, vaulted over a cedar trunk, and leaped into my mother's bed, where she calmed my hysteria with whispers and soothing kisses. I latched onto her fuchsia nylon gown, hiding my face between her gardenia-scented breasts. I had made it to my safe zone.

But while I'd escaped Odessa's scratches, I couldn't outrun the multicolored fluorescent balls of talking lights that had followed me from the bedroom and now hovered above my mother's bed. I took the only course of action I could think of: I jumped up and began hurling objects from my mother's nightstand into the congregation of gurgling bubbles. But they refused to shush. I tossed a hairbrush, a Bible, a *TV Guide*, Linda Goodman's *Love Signs*, an O.E.S. (Order of Eastern Star) handbook, a *JET* magazine, a deck of tarot cards, even a stack of eight-track cassettes. As I reached for my mother's quartz crystal ball, she finally screamed, "Stop and put that down! They won't leave you alone! They have a purpose, and they will stay here until you reconcile their reason for choosing you. They chose *you*; there's no denying it! Sorry, Charlie, but you have to help them close their chapter way before you write your own."

Mama and I were both born with a veil of flesh covering our eyes. It was the caul's fault that we were four-eyed seers in worlds both physical and metaphysical. That skin over our eyes was a sign to the world that we were as close to superheroes as our family would ever know.

My mama taught me to relax my anxiety over the spirits with breathing techniques. She taught me to listen to the loudest voice in the room—spirits rarely wait to be called on, so asking them to play nice and speak one at a time is out of the question. "Focus," Mama would tell me. "Drown out the others, choose the one, solve that spirit's problem, then cross them over. As for the others, you'll have to fade them to black until you're physically and emotionally strong enough to tackle the next situation."

Over the course of fifteen years, I met more than a hundred spirits in that house on Jena Street. Some still visit me in my dream space to this day. The most vicious and spiteful spirit was Ms. Odessa. Her residual impressions lived in the walls and floorboards. The entire house was a shrine to her refusal to go in peace; this would forever be Odessa's house. Her lavender scent strained the lining of my nostrils. With every swallow, I tasted the foliage on my tongue. I could hear the sour, raspy tone of a woman who had forgotten how to laugh, a woman hell-bent on sucking the air from the house so that all that remained was turmoil and internalized self-doubt.

My mother told me Ms. Odessa had dabbled in Hoodoo. By "dabbled," I mean Ms. Odessa procured spells to keep her longshoreman husband employed and to encourage his ascent to foreman. She later used Hoodoo to convince an Irish Italian realtor to sell a barroom in an upstanding part of town to my Black no credit or collateral–having stepfather for pennies on the dollar. By "dabbled," I mean she lived a life filled with jewels, shoes, stockings, wigs, the best cuts of meats, imported champagne, and cartons of femme fatale cigarettes. By "dabbled," I mean she paid good money to beauticians for hair clipped from the freshly hot-pressed heads of any young woman who might interfere with her till death do us part.

It was common knowledge that my stepfather had a roving eye. He was thirty-five years older than my mother when they fell in love, and he was still very much married to Ms. Odessa. She died before they could be found out. My mother said it was the mojo bag and juju she carried in her bra and purse that kept Odessa off her scent. "Odessa barked daily but never up the right tree," Mama said. And my aunt, who hot pressed my mother's hair, made sure any fallen split ends were torched in an ashtray and flushed down the toilet. My mother also took extra care to ensure her nail and hair clippings were never left out in the open where women like Odessa could use them against her.

After marrying my stepfather, my mother inherited Ms. Odessa's queen-size bed along with a host of other antique home furnishings—a cherrywood French provincial nightstand, dishes from Hong Kong, a Zenith Allegro stereo with eight-track console, and an elephant carousel music box from New Delhi. My stepfather thought it was a good idea to avoid splurging on a new way of life until my mother felt emotionally and physically comfortable enough to view his house as a permanent home for herself and her children. When that day came, everything that once belonged to Odessa was hauled off to the Goodwill, everything except for a checkboard blanket. Mama was planning to burn it.

After getting in bed that night, I learned why. I watched as that blanket crawled from the floor and onto my bed, slithering up my legs and traveling to my throat before stretching the length of the bed. I tried to scream, but the blanket tightened around my throat. That's when I ran to my mother's room.

That next evening, we put the blanket in a heavy metal trash can before setting it ablaze. The howl that blanket made was like a tornado screeching across a tin roof. As we topped the can, smoke escaped from the dented left side. The smoke's silhouette looked like a woman exhaling her sins into the air for the last time. We watched the blanket burn to a crisp. Afterward, Mama spat on top of the can and tossed in salt, holy water, and a small Bible. Then she made me take a vow. "Never repeat what happened here tonight to anybody at that catholic school," she said "This is ours to keep. Going around talking about possessed blankets wouldn't make sense to most people. They either wouldn't believe you or worse, they would think you were born with loose screws. Either way, they'll try to take you from me." Mama was sure the White nuns would look for any reason to commit me to a mental institution.

That night I started a serious study of magick and how to properly determine if someone had evil eyed me or crossed me up. Dolls became my first familiars, and my life from that point forward became a whirlwind of shad-ow-people, with bumps in the day and most assuredly in the night.

Hoodoo as Black Justice

Hoodoo has long been the displaced Afrikan's response to surviving the psy-chological and physical violence of the New World. Hoodoo is the Black per-son's justice in the face of untrustworthy White doctors, police, governing bodies, educators, and store owners. Hoodoo also transforms the Black-on-Black adversities of divorce, infidelity, miscarriage, rape, murder, depression, mental illness, poverty, death, sexual dysfunction, and deplorable socioeco-nomic structures.

Survival in the New World relied on knowledge extrapolated from Old World experiences. As our colonizer enemies became more heinous, we infused satchels, herbs, roots, and powders with the power to heal, kill, or protect. At the same time, we needed an accessible way of translating this knowledge to folks with little to no memory of their Afrikan story. This is why Hoodoo needed to be free and open to all, void of both initiatory cri-teria and sovereign leadership. Hoodoo would speak to and for all people of color adjusting to life in America.

Over the years, most Whites and well-to-do Black people feared Hoodoo rituals. They considered it a discipline of black magick practiced by heathens clinging to the archaic imagery of bush Afrikans. As a result, Hoodoo was labeled an occult practice and shunned in many circles as a form of "radical occultism" riddled with political implications.[2]

My grandfather used to tell me this story about *The Green Book*, first pub-lished in 1936. He told how it wasn't enough to have a travel guide detailing which motels, gas stations, salons, drugstores, and restaurants would service Black people or what cities you would have to haul your butt through, with

2. Gilbert Osofsky, ed., "Introduction" in *Puttin' on Ole Massa: The Slave Narratives of Henry Bibb, William Wells Brown, and Solomon Northup* (New York, NY: Harper & Row, 1980), 31–39; Zora Hurston, "Hoodoo in America," *Journal of American Folklore* 44, no. 174 (1931), 317–417, https://doi.org/10.2307/535394; Philip D. Curtin, in *Two Jamaicas: The Role of Ideas in a Trop-ical Colony, 1830–1865* (Westport, CT: Greenwood Press, 1968), 29–31; Maya Deren, *Divine Horsemen: The Living Gods of Haiti* (London, UK: Thames & Hudson, 1953).

a quickness. That's where clutching your flannel came in handy. He'd say, "Sometimes, Hoodoo was all that stood between you, a lynching tree, and safety. If it wasn't for the juju around my neck, I might not have believed I was as brave as I had to be traveling through Mississippi. I can remember staring down the moon while hunting for work with no more than fifty cents to my name, but my Hoodoo kept me sane and untouchable."

Is Hoodoo an Open Practice?

People often ask me if White people can practice Hoodoo. My answer is always the same: Whenever you tell someone they can't do something, their lust for doing the unthinkable tends to grow. And really, after saying Hoodoo has no governing body, I can only tell you that Hoodoo's direct connection to Afrikan ancestry is a slippery slope one should tread lightly over. Hoodoo was made for people of color by people of color coping with insurmountable odds. It wasn't made with White folks in mind, so enter at your own risk.

That said, if you're White and choose to jump down this rabbit hole, I ask that you follow the same steps I would ask anyone new to Hoodoo to practice. Ask the spirits of the Hoodoo ancestors if they would be willing to allow you entrance as a humble servant, not as a cultural appropriator. Stepping into another culture can be done respectfully, but only if the Spirits allow it.

Playing Judge and Jury

No matter who you are, the best way to ask the spirits is to feed them with food—literally. The following ritual will help get you started.

The key to feeding spirits, now or at any time, is to remember that this isn't about you. Don't try to put the spirits on a diet or restrictive eating regimen. If you want a better chance of Spirit granting your desire to practice Hoodoo, prepare the food as listed for the ritual. Remember, we're talking about enslaved people and their earliest descendants. These ancestral spirits lived in human form at a time when no one diagnosed them with diabetes, high blood pressure, or heart disease. They wouldn't have consulted a dietician to streamline their meals even if one had existed during their day. These

Black folks made do with what was provided, harvested, and stolen from the plantation's fields or kitchens. Their diet is what they're familiar with, accustomed to, and what they'll respond to.

Another important note: spirits only need enough food to fill a saucer; the rest you can share with a homeless person, neighbors, or even your coworkers. Trust me, you'll have no problem getting rid of the excess. I sometimes even take a paper plate of food and leave it under a tree in a cemetery. The more often you perform these feedings, even after being granted permission, the more adept you'll feel in your abilities.

Cooking for the Spirits

For this work, you'll need to prepare the meal yourself; don't buy anything precooked. I recommend preparing a bowl of gumbo or jambalaya, especially if your ancestors loved those dishes; any recipe will do. If you're feeling less inclined to go the gumbo or jambalaya route, you'll need to prepare a Cornish hen with your choice of greens (e.g., collards, turnip, dandelion, poke, or mustard) as well as some cornbread and sweet potatoes.

If you're short on time or you feel your cooking skills might set off a fire alarm, here's a quick substitute: Wash, cut, and slice three to six fresh okra into small, circular pieces. Season with salt and cayenne pepper, then fry the okra using vegetable oil. I call this Pinch Okra because it does just that—works in a pinch! However, if the spirits accept you into their fold, I strongly suggest learning to prepare the meals mentioned above. Learn them one at a time, and work at your own pace. Spirit will thank you for the soul-filled love.

RITUAL FOR ASKING SPIRIT

Once your meal is ready, move on to this ritual to ask Spirit for acceptance.

Needs:

For the altar:

* 1 piece of cloth, at least 2 x 2 feet
* 1 glass of water
* 1 white candle
* 1 stick of frankincense incense
* 1 stick of myrrh incense

For the ritual:

* a saucer of your chosen prepared food
* ½ cup water
* ½ cup Florida water (see pages 31–32)
* 1 photograph or drawing of two Hoodoo ancestors, such as Jean St. Malo, Lala Hopkins, Black Hawk, or Mother Catherine Seals (*Note: It's important to have one male and one female image to balance the energies. If you can't find an image, tear off two pieces of a brown paper bag and write the names of any two ancestors of African spirituality on them, one on each piece of paper.*)

Instructions:

First, set up a basic altar for the work: Lay the cloth over a clear flat surface. Place the candle, incense sticks, and the glass of water on the cloth.

In a small bowl, mix the water and Florida water. Bless the mixture by whispering your name, date of birth, and intention over it. Place the bowl and saucer of food next to the candle. Light the incense sticks and candle, then stand the ancestral images up behind the candle. If using slips of paper with

names, form a cross, symbolizing the crossroads between humans and God/Goddess energy.

Ask the spirits of these Hoodoo ancestors if they would be willing to serve as your guides. Ask them to slap your hands or mouth if you slip into appropriator mode. After fifteen to thirty minutes, extinguish the candle. Leave the items in place.

Sit with the spirits this way for fifteen to thirty minutes daily for nine days. If at any point during the nine days you feel the spirits saying a definitive no to your request, stop and don't continue. If the spirits send you the energy of yes, you can begin, but start your practice small.

Continue to Feed Spirit

The spirits you petitioned will be your guides, so you'll continue to work through them and them alone. Feed them once a month as before, adding a slice of bread pudding if desired, and refresh the water each morning (you can toss the old water out your front door).

When it's time to feed them, leave the chosen food out overnight. In the morning place the food at the foot of a tree, thank the spirits, then walk away. This is reciprocity paid to the spirits and their defendants.

Remember, prepare the food yourself—don't buy anything precooked!

Get to Know the Orisa

From time to time throughout this book I'll mention the Orisa. The Orisa are forces of nature in the Yoruba pantheon of spirituality. These deities exist within God but are individually charged with reigning over different elements of our lives and Universe. Following is an abbreviated look into the world of the Orisa.

The Supreme Being/God Force is Olodumare or Olofin (the Law Giver). Olodumare rules over many Universes, not just ours. Since the Supreme Being can't be expected to listen to the trials and tribulations of every man, woman, and child 24/7, the Orisa use the powers given to them by Olodumare to help us govern our own lives through sacrifice, and by accepting the consequences of our actions and oftentimes our reactions.

There are 401 Irunmole/Orisa, but you'll find when most folks mention Orisa, they're referring to the most popular of the selected heads. Here are a few:

- *Esu* is the guardian of the crossroads (not the Devil, as some mistakenly claim). You make a choice and Esu tosses you a sackload of consequences; deciding whether the consequences are good or bad is up to the beholder. Esu is fed first in rituals.
- *Ogun* removes obstacles from our lives.
- *Obatala* helps us discern with the wisdom of a trusted elder and encourages us to use our third eye when facing turmoil in our life.
- *Yemaya* teaches us to nurture ourselves, family, and community with tough love and a swift tongue.
- *Osun* teaches us how to better ourselves with the tools provided by the ancestral realm and the knowledge we've acquired living through many lifetimes.
- *Shango* is the fiery one who convinces us that with heightened passion we can fight through any turbulence hurled into our lives, both warranted and unwarranted.
- *Oya* reminds us that changes happen whether we see them on the horizon or not. She says to our teary eyes, *whatever I remove you no longer needed.* She jerks our burden from under us and doesn't care if we spill our bellowing heart across the floor. What's done is done.
- *Ochossi* is the truth within our hearts that says no one is above reproach.
- *Olokun* is the spirit of those ancestors whose souls season the murky depths of the ocean floor. They're the ones who in their refusal to remain captive journeyed to the depths of sorrow.
- *Babaluaiye* teaches us how to protect ourselves from situations that could cause sickness or debilitation.

- *Osayin* is the power of herbs and the understanding that every herb bears both the power to curse and heal.
- *Orunmila* is the reason we possess the know-how of divination. It's because of Orunmila that we speak to deities and ancestors and know the means to propitiate them to great heights of happiness.

This interpretation is necessarily brief in the interest of saving space. I strongly encourage you to research the Orisa further, especially if you're just learning about them for the first time. Look for books written by people of color on the subject.

Juju on the Fly

It's no secret that there are days we feel rushed and ill-equipped to fit into our skins, spirits, or souls with ease. On those days we need to know our Hoodoo is working for us even if we don't have time for elaborate workings. We need to know as we sip our morning latte, apply eyeliner, or nibble that breakfast bar that our backs, fronts, and all areas in between are spiritually covered. I can't tell you how many days Juju on the Fly has saved me from taking off my earrings, applying Vaseline to my face, braiding my locs back, and proceeding to lose my proverbial sheesh.

Case in point: the birthing of this book. There were days during its conception that I heard this voice telling me that even if I wrote the book, it would never get published. No White person would put it out unless I catered to White people. I would cry, tear pages up, cry, burn pages. Finally, I took my fight to the streets, figuratively. I sat myself down and laid out the facts: I'm a writer. It's what I was born to do, not to dance or sing, but to write. Any publisher worth their company's name and reputation would see that. Then I did a Juju on the Fly working, and it gave me immediate peace and allowed me to experience the labor and delivery of this book baby.

Magick in Plain Sight

Hoodoo has several divinatory systems. Playing cards are one of the most popular. Playing cards can be used to inconspicuously work magick in plain sight and on the fly. A testament to this fact is the Great Ancestress Caroline Tracy Dye, remembered as Aunt Caroline. This Hoodoo matriarch was born into slavery in South Carolina around 1843 and she would go on to become one of Hoodoo's greatest card readers.

Aunt Caroline refused to give readings about love or war. Instead, she used her cards to help unravel the mysteries of missing persons, stolen livestock, and in determining the homes where jewel thieves roamed. Day in and day out folks would clamor into her home for readings. It was even said that a well-to-do White businessman didn't make any decisions without first seeking out Aunt Caroline's guidance.

Aunt Caroline died on September 26, 1918, and is buried in Gun Grove Cemetery in Newport, Arkansas. Even though she was illiterate, she's remembered as both a thriving fortune teller and real estate mogul, owning eight farms. In addition to her rental properties, she invested in Liberty Bonds to support the war effort during World War I. Now tell me Aunt Caroline didn't know how to diversify her earnings!

Each chapter of Conquering the Calabash ends with a Juju on the Fly work, a quick meditative exercise that uses playing cards not for divining, but more as an energy pull. You can do them in five minutes tops, and even better, you can do them on the fly—you could do a card pull while cruising out the front door and never miss a beat. These exercises are that extra spice to get you pumped up for the next chapter of the book, or better still, the next chapter of your life.

The pull won't use your standard deck of cards. Instead, we'll be using a mini deck, which is easier to manipulate. These decks, which can be purchased online, are 2 x 1.5 inches (as opposed to the standard 3.5 x 2.5 inches). Try to keep two or three fresh decks of cards on hand at all times. That way when a particular card gets worn, you can move to the next deck and pull the card needed.

EXERCISE: WORKING THE ACE OF HEARTS

In this work we're using the Ace of Hearts to call home our desire for affection. We could be feeling the need to affectionately birth a child into a calm environment; we could feel like it's time to reinvent our affections from the inside out or the outside in. Or maybe we've outgrown our romantic relationships, friendships, acquaintanceships, jobs, living situations, or even hairstyles. All that new growth comes with the need to be seen through loving, self-affirming eyes.

Whatever this call to love with affection looks like for you, it's time to accentuate your strong suits. It's also time to update any character traits that have outlived their usefulness. The Ace of Hearts is an awakening. It says, "Girlfriend, once upon a time you were unappreciated, but from this day forward know you're an oasis of affection." This is the card that wants to be carried into your day as a reminder that you're not a finished product but a constantly evolving masterpiece. Those fools who thought they knew you had better recognize.

Needs:

* 1 Ace of Hearts playing card
* 1 red satchel big enough to hold the card (fires up the work)
* ¼–½ teaspoon Hoyt's cologne (adds luck and points the work in the right direction)

Instructions:

The night before the work, pour the Hoyt's cologne into your satchel. Use just enough to leave a smell but still have a dry satchel come morning. Leave the satchel on a towel overnight to help it dry out.

In the morning, take the Ace of Hearts into your hands and vigorously rub the card between your palms for three minutes.

Feel the heat transfer from your palms to the card. As you rub, repeat: *I am open to new beginnings in personal relationships, love, money, all creative exploits, and to the birthing of abundant joy into my life. I deserve pleasure at the very deepest level. I appreciate my story and the enduring legacy it took to mold me in the image of a goddess. I intend to fulfill my obligations to my soul contract by ensuring that I look, act, and walk in truth. I am the sistah, mother, lover, and friend you and I have been waiting for.*

Place the card inside the satchel and tie the satchel, by its cord, to your bra strap. You can also place the satchel in your pocket or purse. To put even more pep in your day, take a picture of the card before placing it in the satchel and gaze at the image from time to time. This working can be repeated anytime you feel unappreciated.

That's it, go forth in truth. You, my sistah, are love brewed from the home of sweetly spiced intentions.

Chapter Two
Tools of the Trade

Hoodoo is adaptable to our fast-paced lifestyles because, in most instances, you already have the necessary tools at home. When I work with clients, sistah friends are amazed at how their pantries possess much of the required accoutrements to immediately dive into working their Hoodoo. That's part of the reason I champion Hoodoo. Just think about the resourcefulness of our ancestors making New World substitutions for Old World conjure modalities. The body, in many instances, was enslaved, but not the mind.

With Hoodoo, you don't need special initiations or overpriced mystical products. The seasoning for my workings begins with simple, focused intent. I tell folks, you have to want your outcome to manifest with such an innate desire that you see it with your mind's eye as well as your physical eye. You must feel your devotion to the process deep within your soul before you lift a finger to assemble tools. If you don't, that oil will be just oil; that candle will just be a candle; that soil will be just dirt; and those herbs will be just flavoring. Once you season your mind, you season your heart, allowing everything you touch to become magick. My advice is to get your mind right first. Believe in your power, and believe that powerful magick exists all around you, waiting for you to tap into its essence.

I can't tell you how often I run into folks who expect me to teach them how to pull magick from between their butt cheeks and solve their generational trauma in two seconds flat. There are no cheat codes to magick. An ongoing relationship with those beyond the veil requires you to be a well-oiled machine, and that, dear hearts, comes with practice. The spirits have to get acquainted with you before they trust you enough to bestow blessings. They need to hear your sincerity and not get beat over the head with your desperation. Just because they lack a physical body doesn't mean they're crazy or easily manipulated. You're not all that and a bag of chips to them. They will always have the upper hand—remember that.

21

Spirits know when you're just playing nice to achieve an outcome. The spirits need you to come correct, or don't come at all. Plan on sitting down over your preferred beverage, dimming the lights, lighting a white candle, and speaking out loud for fifteen minutes to an hour. Ask your ancestors, your first line of defense, whatever is on your heart. Take the time to get to know what motivates these spirits before asking for their blessing of protection. Treat them with respect and they'll stand firm in your defense for an eternity.

Altars

I always encourage folks to begin any serious magickal undertaking by creating a sacred space or altar. You can build your altar on a piece of furniture or on the floor or even outside in a garden area, wherever you find value. It doesn't need to be rigidly sculpted or forever confined to a certain space; in fact, being able to put up and take down an altar in minutes is a must for me. Just like us, Spirit loves movement. I find that transferring an altar from one location to another can be an offering by itself, shedding light on the efficacy of our journey. I might start with an altar in my communal living area then move it my bedroom, or take it with me on a visit to my daughter. Don't worry about knowing when to move your altar. Spirit will guide you through dreams, feelings, and sensations. As you find yourself moving past the current location, the urge will settle in your third eye to travel elsewhere.

On paper, draw out exactly how you want that movable sacred space to manifest in your reality. Draw it in pictures or in words or both. Be flexible with the items you include, and let them dictate how you place them. Later, as you get used to your altar, you can acquire more items to make the space even more sacred in your eyes.

Altar Cloth

An altar cloth covers the surface underneath your items and should fit the size of your chosen working area. I've used altar cloths that were a foot long and others that were as long as six feet. A good starter size is two feet square, but make it work for you.

Some more structured spiritual traditions and their followers will tell you to only use white cloth on your altars. For our purposes as Hoodoo practitioners, we can bend a whole lot. Remember, Hoodoo isn't a religion, and because of that we have a lot more room to dismantle dogma. Besides, a lot of younger folks have relayed to me that they don't have white fabric laying around, so they put off setting up their altar until they can buy some. You don't have to do this—use any kind of fabric that aligns with the spellcasting you're about to complete. It doesn't matter if the fabric has birds, flowers, school buses, emojis, runes, adinkra symbols, kente patterns, tie dye, laughing children, wine, witches, or skeletons. If it speaks to your working, use it.

For my altar cloth, I use clothing from an ancestor (a deceased relative) that I cut into strips and squares. If I have time, I sew strips of fabric together until I have the length and width I want; I've even sewn ancestral fabric into a full tablecloth. If I'm using a deceased relative's clothing, the fabric's color or pattern doesn't matter to me because the fabric harnesses the Spirit energy regardless of the color. I want and need that ancestor's spiritual energy to send my magick into the next stratosphere.

Altar Tools

What tools go on the altar? The staples should be water, a candle, your altar cloth, and photos, but all else is open to your knowledgeable discretion. Include whatever makes the space sacred for you. On my altar, you'll usually find a glass or mug of water, a saucer for food, and a shot glass for gin, rum, or whiskey (if I'm in a pinch I substitute beer or wine for the liquor). I always keep a white candle there and bells of various shapes and sizes, along with an assortment of jewelry, lipstick, and nail polishes. I might include incense, a cigar, fruit, photos of my ancestors, and a picture of my Hoodoo hero or heroine. I also enjoy using fresh flowers, perfumes, my shekere, and other different gourds on my altar.

From time to time, you may find that what you place on your altar changes. Along with the items above I've been known to place money, playing cards, dice, dowsing rods, and chewing tobacco on mine. I'm not a smoker, but we give Spirit what Spirit wants so they can grant us success in our workings. This isn't the time to ban substances our ancestors enjoyed in life like alcohol or tobacco. We aren't the health police; we're seducing their service.

Travel Altars

Travel altars are easy to make. I use makeup bags to carry a basic set of altar tools, or you can use a small shaving bag or men's travel bag.

When using a travel altar, you can set it up, sit with Spirit, then put it away when you're ready to close the space. You don't need to keep the altar up for the duration of your travel, especially if you're in a hotel or staying with a host who isn't open to your practice. Stashing your altar can also bring you peace of mind that your tools won't be manhandled by a curious hotel worker or friend.

Candles

When it comes to candles, I make it a point not to discriminate—whatever I find, I use. Some people make distinctions between candles based on their burning time or other very specific magickal properties. Not this witch. For many people, the only option for candles is the corner dollar store, and you can't walk into a dollar store and ask for a fourteen-day half-blue / half-white home protection candle. But you *can* find candles in basic white, blue, yellow, red, brown, pink, orange, and, depending on the season, black, gold, and even silver candles.

Two lessons to take from this: one, check out dollar stores and craft stores to stock up on seasonal candles whenever they're available, making sure to note clearance days. (Here's a thrifty witch tip: seasonal candles are usually at their cheapest the day after the close of the previous holiday.) Second, when you're stocking up on candles, go cheap first, then choose the color to fit your intention.

Color Associations

Speaking of colors, white is your staple. No matter what your goal, when there's no other colored candle at your disposal, you can always go white and be all right. White candles are synonymous with the energy of healing, meditation, peace, new beginnings, and calling down Spirit. They can also stand in for any other color. Because of this, and because they're so widely available, I recommend keeping lots of white candles on hand.

Here are the other candle color associations:

- *Black*: protection, absorption of negative energy, banishings, hexes, and unblocking obstacles
- *Blue*: creativity, focus, inspiration, and dreams
- *Brown*: connecting oneself to the earth and its animal impressions
- *Gold*: success and confidence
- *Gray*: peace and the sharing of spiritual wisdom and understanding
- *Green*: abundance, luck, and money
- *Light Blue*: patience and mental stamina
- *Magenta*: the intensity of lust and unbridled passions
- *Orange*: joy and playfulness
- *Pink*: romantic love, affection, joy, self-love, and friendship
- *Purple*: divination, wisdom, self-awareness, and the pursuit of esoteric knowledge
- *Red*: fast-moving energy as it pertains to your workings; also increases potency/vigor and passion
- *Silver*: intuition and increasing telepathy
- *Yellow*: easing mental confusion and increasing logic while maneuvering through new beginnings

Candle Safety

When extinguishing candles, I place a fireproof stopper—my mini cauldron lid—over the candle's flame, pressing down to keep any air from escaping. If you have a candle snuffer by all means use it, but never blow the candle out; this is like spitting in Grandma or Grandpa's face. Use only fireproof pot bottoms, saucers, plates, cauldron tops, or pot lids to extinguish flames. Never leave flames unattended or in an area where they could be knocked over.

In a child's room, battery-operated candles are your best bet. These candles are safe to leave on through the night and you don't have to worry about children or pets knocking them over. Battery-operated candles are also excellent for use in travel altars. If you're spending the night away from home and need to do a candle spell, try this method: Sprinkle a teaspoon of herbs and three drops of oil into a Styrofoam cup. Write a one-word intention on the cup, then breathe over it and repeat your word nine times. Turn on your battery-operated candle and place the cup next to the candle before you go to sleep.

Satchels

Hoodoo satchels—often called flannels, mojo bags, or juju bags—are drawstring bags that can be made of any cloth you have available, though they're customarily flannel, felt, or velvet. Satchels are used to house elements of our magick that we want to keep close to the body or carry with us from place to place. Satchels can be put in pockets, tied to our bra straps, or worn on a leather cord around our necks (recall the red satchel used in the Juju on the Fly ritual in chapter 1).

You can purchase satchels from online stores, fabric shops, or you can even download a template or pattern to create your own drawstring bag. There are many tutorials online.

The color associations of satchels are the same as those listed above for candles. As with candles, keep plenty on hand when choosing to add a little extra manipulation to your magick. I have a drawer of different satchels so I always have the right color and size on hand to keep my magickal recipes brewing.

Incenses and Oils

Incenses are resin grains mixed with spices or plant material that, when burned, release aromatic smoke that infuses the soul space and can put one in a meditative state of release. Essential oils are a highly concentrated hydrophobic liquid that can take on the scent of spices and plant materials. Both have a long history in human society. Resin balls were once used to repel evil spirits and kill pesky insects. People quickly learned that incense had other valuable uses. It killed pungent odors and aided in the creation of meditative states. Essential oils date back to Egypt, when aromatic plants such as thyme, lavender, and aloe were cultivated into oils and used in mummification rituals alongside cedar and myrrh. The combination of these oils was believed to protect the soul of the deceased from errant energies on their journey to the afterlife.

I burn incense even when I wake up late and don't have time for a full-blown morning ritual. The smell of incense has the power to realign my focus from anxious to calm. In a sense, it depressurizes my mood while invigorating my aura. Spritzing the air with a mix of essential oils and water as incense smoke rises is a slice of heaven no amount of money can buy.

Carrier Oils

Essential oils are highly concentrated. They can cause skin irritations and burn you something awful if you apply them directly to your body without a carrier oil. Carrier oils like sesame, jojoba, and avocado oil dilute the strength of essential oils, making them less harmful to our skin.

For magick purposes, each carrier oil can be used alone or with essential oils using an incantation that correlates to its listed metaphysical properties. For example, if I wanted to repel psychic vampires, I would whisper a healing chant or phrase into a cup of sesame seed oil, something like *Never again will (named person) be able to cause me harm as I lie awake or in my dream space. I send your attack back to your gates. Suck the life out of your own dreams. From this day forth I am free. Suck this sesame seed oil and get back, get back, get back and get lost, and feel this attack.*

Here are the top invaluable carrier oils and their properties:

- *Almond*: aids in the transference of wisdom and prosperity
- *Apricot*: softens our emotional stability
- *Avocado*: ideal for love and fertility

- *Coconut*: purifies the spirit and transforms anxiety to calm
- *Grapeseed*: promotes abundance and mental clarity
- *Jojoba*: stimulating love base
- *Rosehip*: used to summon spirits
- *Sesame Seed*: heals psychic ailments and past life trauma
- *Sunflower*: aids in wish magick

When adding essential oils to carrier oils, start with three to thirteen drops of essential oil per one-quarter to one cup of carrier oil. If you want to use blends to build on a work, start slowly with two different oils. Once you feel comfortable, add a third. Limit your blends to no more than three oils; that way you can study how the intermingling plays out in your spiritual life and on your body.

For example, if I were a high schooler trying to get my principal to listen to students protesting the denial of an LGBTQ club, I might use a quarter cup of sweet almond oil for the prosperity of my goals, combined with six drops of lemon essential oil (so the spirits of my family can guard me against scrutiny) and six drops of rue essential oil (to break generational curses stemming from the idea that homosexuality is best left closeted). I would then swirl the mixture toward me with my finger nine times and let it sit on my altar overnight. In the morning, I would massage the blend over my entire body and rub a small amount on the inside of my shoes. Thus spiritually prepared, I would engage the principal in a discussion. It might take several meetings, but in time the transformation would work in my favor.

How Long Do Oil Blends Last?

I usually keep my spiritual oils and blends between four and six months. They're still potent up to six months as long as they don't have a funky medicinal smell or metallic stank. If they cause a skin reaction or if the color turns a pale yellow or takes on a reddish orange tint, get rid of them. Those are all sure signs your oil is on its last leg. If you want to be even safer, create a new batch of your blend every one to two months.

Top Essential Oils and Incenses

I combined these two topics because in my life, they often go hand in hand. In my cupboards you'll find incense and essential oils that bear the same fragrance. For example, if I want to heighten a particular work, I might use both patchouli incense and patchouli oil. That double dose of patchouli heightens my magick and focuses my intent.

Here are some of my favorite standalone incenses and essential oils (remember, blend the oils with a carrier oil before use):

- *7 African Powers*: opens and clears roads (*Note: 7 African Powers is extremely potent because it harbors the energies of the Orisas Esu [crossroads messenger], Oshun [Creativity/dream expansion], Yemaya [growth and fertility], Sango [power and passion], Obatala [eases legal strife], Oya [transformation and rebirth], and Ogun [protection activism].*)
- *Allspice*: gives an energy boost
- *Almond*: generates money
- *Anise*: aids in clairvoyance
- *Basil*: soothes lovers' quarrels and protects the home and its inhabitants from violations
- *Bergamot*: aids in quick luck
- *Camphor*: increases psychic strength
- *Carnation*: solidifies good health
- *Cedar*: eases misery and deep bouts of sadness
- *Cinnamon*: ignites sexual vigor
- *Citronella*: increases a business owner's revenue
- *Eucalyptus*: eases depression
- *Frankincense*: removes spiritual energy left by the death of unsavory individuals
- *Gardenia*: creates a peaceful vibration
- *Geranium*: brings love to you, and no one will be able to resist your charm
- *Ginger*: increases passion
- *Heliotrope*: prevents psychic attack after dissolving a relationship

- *Jasmine*: opens your heart center to love
- *Juniper*: heightens meditative states
- *Lavender*: increases a man's lust and insatiable appetite for sex
- *Lemon*: calls protective spirits
- *Lotus*: blesses a space
- *Myrrh*: reverses hexes
- *Neroli*: harmonizes the energy of groups
- *Nutmeg*: opens the third eye
- *Orange*: transforms stagnant vibrations
- *Orris*: excellent for attracting the opposite sex
- *Patchouli*: excellent at grounding and a powerful oil/incense to use when warding off malevolence
- *Peppermint*: relaxes an anxious temperament
- *Rose*: transforms affection to love
- *Rosemary*: increases confidence and self-love
- *Rue*: breaks generational curses
- *Saffron*: increases telepathy
- *Sandalwood*: opens you to the astral plane
- *Tuberose*: acts as an aphrodisiac
- *Vervain*: increases creativity
- *Wisteria*: aids in passing between worlds
- *Ylang-Ylang*: keeps lovers faithful

Colognes and Water

Colognes are alcohol-based combinations infused with essential oils and flower petals. They're typically used to protect one's physical body from psychic overload and attack. Colognes can also be placed on your altar as an offering. You can buy most colognes at any botanica or online.

Hoodoo water is mostly made of tap water, but it can also contain alcohol and one or more of the following: herbs, flower petals, Epsom salt, red brick, or pine or orange oil. Hoodoo waters are used to clean floors and wash walls, porches, steps, and tools. You make most of these waters yourself.

Here are a list of the colognes and waters I can't live without. There are plenty to choose from, so it's easy to keep two to three types on standby. From trial and error, you'll decide which one work for you. (*Note*: If a working calls for water without specifying a type, feel free to use any kind of water you have on hand.)

- *Hoyt's Cologne*: This cologne lives alongside my favored herbs and is part of my regular spiritual rotation. It protects your finances from thieves and increases luck in life. It also brings good luck and power to gamblers, risk takers, and anyone in immediate need of quick satisfaction. I use a nickel- or quarter-size amount on my shoes, hands, pens, computer bag, wallet, and phone case.

- *Lavender Cologne*: Lavender cologne increases peace in the home by keeping negative waste from accumulating. I especially like spritzing it in the corners of rooms.

- *Orange Blossom Cologne*: This cologne strengthens any partnership, platonic or romantic. It also improves fidelity and sexual desire. I wear it as a perfume or pour a few capfuls into my bath.

- *Palo Santo Cologne*: This cologne is used for its potency in stomping out haters. It's an excellent cleaner against all entities malevolent and downright foolish. We should also burn Palo Santo sticks instead of white sage for cleansing, because the latter is nearing extinction from overuse.

- *Rue Cologne*: Rue cologne keeps negative influences and impressions from invading your space, especially in crowded places. Jealous folks won't be able to bat their evil eye at you if you combine a capful of rue cologne with a quarter cup of water in a spray bottle to spritz your outfit before showing out in public. This is also a good one to spray on a child's backpack if they're dealing with bullies.

- *Florida Water*: You might recall this water from the ritual in chapter 1. Florida water is used as an offering to the spirits and to cleanse sacred tools or items you buy at garage sales or thrift stores. It's also great for dressing herbal satchels. In a pinch, if there is just no time to make Florida water from scratch, I like to use a store-bought brand, adding a teaspoon of raw honey and 13 drops of orange essential oil. For a carrier oil, I like olive or almond oil. (All recipes that mention Florida water will assume the addition of the honey, orange essential oil, and carrier oil.)

- *Kananga Water:* Like Florida water, Kananga water can be used for both ritual cleansings and offerings. It can also clear neg-ative energy from a room and add a protective element to your workings.

- *Rainwater:* Use collected rainwater for banishings and libations. Collect your rainwater in a pot covered in muslin, which prevents leaves, branches, and bugs from contaminating the water. Store the collected water in mason jars.

- *Rose Water:* Rose water is used to center yourself during med-itation. I also love to spray it on my clothes because its effects in glamour magick are amazing. It has the power to seduce the opinions of others, transforming an unfavorable review to a more favorable one.

- *Storm Water:* Storm water is collected during thunderstorms. This water is good for restoring vitality after a long day. (You can do this by adding it to bath water.) Storm water prevents night ter-rors when placed under a child's bed with a calming herb. Sprayed over door sills, it protects the home from messy people. Spritzing your clothes with it makes you a fierce opponent against a cruel, cold-hearted world. I keep storm water in a metal thermos with a clear quartz crystal inside. The crystal helps guide the water's focus during my spellwork.

- *Van Van Floor Wash:* This wash can be spritzed in a car or office space to clear stagnant energy.

Tarot

The work week can be full of unexpected surprises. Getting the upper hand on situations before they unfold can be hugely helpful, which is why the tarot is one of my favorite tools. Tarot lays it *all* out. I can see who's bringing the drama and how to deflect it before it becomes a crisis. Tarot is such a large part of my practice that I place a three-card spread on my altar every Sunday without fail.

Tarot comes up in several of this book's rituals, so you'll want to have at least one deck on hand. Any local or online metaphysical store will have a plethora of options to choose from. Buy a deck that suits your spirit. When choosing one ask yourself, does the story of the artwork speak to you? Does the deck make you feel balanced and eager to jump into the interpretation of each story? Does the guidebook resonate with you? Can you easily feel the alignment between the author's interpretation and your vision for each card? If you run across a particular deck and answer yes to all these questions, quite possibly you've found a lifelong friend, the kind who will cut no corners when telling it like it is. Here are a few of my current favorite decks in no particular order:

- The Melanated Classic Tarot
- Melanade Stand's Tarot
- Dusk II Onyx: A Melanated Tarot
- Santa Muerte Tarot: Book of the Dead
- The Light Seer's Tarot
- The Hoodoo Tarot
- The New World Tarot
- Simplicity Tarot
- Akamara Tarot Deck
- The Tarot of the Orishas
- The New Orleans Voodoo Tarot
- True Heart Intuitive Tarot
- Neo Tarot

EXERCISE: TAROT MEDITATION

If you're a newcomer to tarot or an infrequent user, start by pulling one card and meditating on it. Don't use the guide book that comes with the deck for at least the first three months; this will sharpen your intuitive interpretation skills. It's okay to glance at the book. I just don't want the author's words to become your mantra every time a given card appears.

The following is a practice exercise.

Needs:

* tarot deck
* journal
* pen or pencil

Instructions:

In your mind ask the Universe to show you what is to unfold in plain view or beneath the surface. Then, do a one-card pull and study the image. Take three to five minutes to carefully examine the card.

Next, in a journal devoted exclusively to your spiritual work, date the page and write the name of the card pulled. Describe the image in one paragraph. Formulate a story as if you're the main character in the card's scene. If you're feeling really gung-ho, you can turn the story into a short story or poem.

Discuss how your interpretation of the card could manifest positively in your life, then interpret the card with a less favorable result (this allows you to see all possible consequences). Take a few moments and sort through both viewpoints. You can also write out some ways you can recover if the day takes an unexpected turn for the worse. Do self-checks in your journal throughout the day.

I do my card pulls at night to give me time to choose between writing a short passage, poem, or story. After a month you can advance to pulling two cards and in three months pulling three.

  With every added card allow the story to build, jumping from one card to the next. Once you're comfortable with three-card pulls, you can pull as many cards as you want or have time for. Listen carefully as the story of your life is foretold. Consider this your cheat sheet to cosmic truth.

Bluing

Bluing is another spiritual tool you can find at your local dollar store. Bluing (I use Mrs. Stewart's Bluing) is used to whiten clothes, human hair, and pet hair; to soothe ant bites; and when added to your pool's filtration system it colors the water a beautiful shade of turquoise. You also can keep a mixture of one part bluing and one part Florida water in a spray bottle near your front door to spritz your hands, head, and feet before heading out each day.

In spiritual work, I've added a capful or two of bluing to a glass vase filled with water to create a focus point for meditation. I sometimes add shells to the water to simulate an ocean bottom, or I'll google an ocean scene and enlarge that image or video on a screen next to the vase. When I meditate like this, I sometimes turn off all the lights, allowing myself the freedom to sit in quiet darkness for as long as I need.

You'll find that working with bluing in this way relieves stress and helps center your third eye and heart space. But don't attempt it unless you're ready to devote your undivided attention to the exercise. It won't work if you're thinking about the next bullet point on your to-do list. You must set aside the time and focus to meditate at the bottom of the ocean.

EXERCISE: BLUING MEDITATION

I always keep a bottle or two of bluing in my pantry. It's one of those ritual necessities that can help you feel better than a trip to the spa.

Needs:

* 1 vase, preferably clear
* 1 teaspoon bluing
* 1 blue candle
* 3 drops each ylang-ylang, bergamot, eucalyptus, lemon, lavender, and geranium essential oils (combination mimics the scent of the beach)
* Optional: recording of ocean wave sounds

Instructions:

Pour the bluing into the vase and fill with water. Place the vase and candle on your altar, positioning the candle behind the vase. Sit and stare into the vase, focusing on the tranquility of the blue color. Try to clear your mind and remain present in your own shell. Meditate like this for fifteen to thirty minutes before extinguishing the flame. You can keep the water and repeat this exercise for nine nights before tossing the water into the street.

EXERCISE: BLUING BATH

After your meditation, run a bluing bath. This ritual further releases stress.

Needs:

* 1 vase
* Sand, enough to fill the vase
* 1 blue candle
* 3 tablespoons bluing
* 3 tablespoons spirulina flakes

* 3 drops each ylang-ylang, bergamot, eucalyptus, lemon, lavender, and geranium essential oils (combination mimics the scent of the beach)
* 1–3 teaspoons sea salt

Instructions:

As you run a bath, fill the vase with sand; set aside. When the tub is full, add the bluing, spirulina, oils, and sea salt to the bathwater. Light the candle and place it in the sand, then step into the water. Allow the water to flow over your entire body for ten to fifteen minutes. Tell the water what you need released from your spirit/soul. Afterward, you can bathe and let the water drain out as usual.

EXERCISE: BLUING FLOOR WASH

Bluing rids your home of psychic nuisances. It also opens your home's vibration to spiritual success so not only will you be pleased but your ancestors will be too.

Needs:

* 1–3 tablespoons bluing
* 1 cup Florida water
* 3 tablespoons red brick dust
* 1–2 gallons warm water in a bucket
* A mop

Instructions:

Add the bluing, Florida water, and red brick dust to the bucket. Leave the mop soaking in the bucket for three minutes before mopping. As you mop, tell the water what you're trying to rid your home of in a firm voice. Mop as usual, but be jovial about what's leaving—sing or listen to music that brings a sense of relief as you work. Once finished, toss the water into the street. Spritz the mop and bucket with Florida water before putting them away.

Handkerchief Magick

Another tool to add to your arsenal is a handkerchief with a lipstick kiss and your signature scent. I was talking with a sistah recently about how women in our mother's and grandmother's era would tote handkerchiefs with lace edging in their purses. We reminisced about having a runny nose in church and watching as the elder women opened their patent leather purses, hands diving inside to retrieve the lacy cotton square. Sometimes they were monogrammed, and other times they had lipstick imprints or even rouge. If you were lucky, sometimes a peppermint fell out when the deaconess was folding it into a square just the right size to cover a six-year-old's nose.

I remember a time my stepfather told me to lay his suits on the bed. He was going to take them to the cleaners after the wrestling match on TV ended. I was ten and in a hurry of my own to play with dolls across the street at my best friend's house. She had the Barbie Dream House, and every time I played with it, my doll became a wealthy socialite who chained up my brother's action figures. She was an Amazon who despised men. She gave elaborate parties and never ran out of food, drinks, or couture. But before my adventure, I had to lay out my stepfather's suits and check the pockets for keys, candy, or loose change.

I found the handkerchief in the third and final suit. It was tied in a familiar bunching and fastened with gray twine and black ribbon. My grandmother had come to me in my dreams to warn me about women who find dead things tied in a handkerchief. She warned me of the impending doom to any marriage when the handkerchief was unwound and the elements were allowed to breathe. "You ever see it, you pick it up with an old rag and don't allow it to touch your skin. Do not allow it to touch nothing that matters, or else you'll have to throw what matters out too. You'll cry about it, but at least you'll have the life to cry about it." Grandmama told me to take the wrapping to the catholic church at my school when nobody was looking. Her orders were to "leave it behind the virgin Mary; she's woman enough to handle that devilment. I mean, she was woman enough to hold a god in her belly and that didn't kill her." I did as she instructed. Like any child I wanted to know what was inside the bundle, but I was smart enough to understand it wouldn't be wise to cross myself with bad luck.

Over six Saturdays I found six of those handkerchiefs before the other woman just phoned my mother and filled her in on my stepfather's insatiable appetite. In return, my mother decided to send her a present. In the bottom of my stepfather's closet, Mama had found a cocktail dress that wasn't her size tucked under blankets, cigar boxes, and whiskey. Mama stitched a handkerchief to the inside of the dress's flared skirt in between the organza and lace. She infused this handkerchief with her words, scent, and determination to keep her man until the day she decided he didn't deserve her hand in marriage. In two weeks that woman was nothing but a memory, smoke in the wind.

Handkerchiefs are an easily adapted form of Hoodoo that you can use in plain sight. If you want a lover to have that "can't wait to see you again" feeling, take a beautiful cotton handkerchief, lay it flat, and sprinkle your usual scent on it. The scent must be one you wear regularly. If your lover doesn't recognize the scent as yours, this spell won't work. Also remember not to oversaturate the cloth; the idea is to leave an impression that wafts across the air without overpowering.

If you wear lipstick, gloss, or even Vaseline, apply it. Then kiss the handkerchief as if you were kissing your lover (hold back on the tongue). Next, take the handkerchief into your hands. Whisper *Miss me, miss me, you will never forget me. Where you go, I go. You want my loving, then follow your nose.* Place the handkerchief somewhere inconspicuous that your lover uses daily, like a work bag. You can even place it in their car under the seat or in the glove compartment. Be creative—your lover shouldn't know the handkerchief is there. If it's too large to hide easily, just cut it up and do your thing.

You can do the same work with a scarf. And get this, you can leave your scarf out in public on purpose! Pretend to leave it in the car or on the bed, or tuck it in his briefcase or gym bag. See the cunning? You can always say static electricity must've made it to stick to your clothes, bae. Or blame it on multitasking: "Honey, that's just the price of doing too much with just two hands."

Juju on the Fly

Live long enough and you'll run into your share of narcissists. They're the people who judge their importance by how many disjointed situations they can place themselves smack dab in the middle of. They're the folks who discard others whenever a more impressive character enters the picture.

Sometimes we mess around and allow these narcissists to take up residence in our heads and our hearts. The narcissist's misfortunes become our problems to solve and sulk over. We place them on a pedestal and at the same time label them unlucky and in need of our constant coddling. All the while, we struggle with their lack of empathy. Years may pass before we realize our blurred vision of friendship or love has come at the price of our sanity.

I was friends with a narcissist back in undergrad. At first, I enjoyed our friendship—she was full of jokes and knew how to make her life seem like a never-ending sitcom, one I was happy to be a part of. But I learned that when life got real, she got real vicious with her words. Case in point: She was poor and hoped to find a rich man in college. But she flunked out before that could happen. She quickly shifted her line of attack to me, specifically my goals and my hue. For example, she would remind me, often right at the moment I was overcoming a hurdle, that I was only smart enough to double major in journalism and English literature because I was dark-skinned, and what else can dark-skinned girls do except be smart when pretty has eluded them?

How did I end the relationship? Simple—the Four of Spades walked in, and I walked her butt right out of my life.

The Four of Spades is the card of hardworking, stable, and protective sistahs who refuse to allow their unhealthy and unhealed alliances to block their life's inheritance. This sistah believes in therapy and mindfully working toward healing each and every day. This sistah with the Four of Spades believes graduating to better health means giving her traumas—every last one of them—a death date. She knows you can't heal standing still. Her legs must walk into tomorrow and the next day and the day after that, dedicated to moving as far away from catastrophe as possible.

The Four of Spades also says, "Listen here, Boo, don't *be* a narcissist." If you think you're on the verge of becoming one, evaluate where you are right now and who got you there—I bet you didn't do it alone. It's up to you: would you rather spend your life as a character in a narcissistic soap opera or do you want to reclaim your time, grow with stability, and truly *live* in whatever way you see fit?

The day I cut off my so-called friend my whole life widened. I could feel myself breathing regenerative breaths again. Her toxic hold over my self-image was no more. That's the power of the Four of Spades.

EXERCISE: HARDWORKING FOUR OF SPADE

Needs:

* 1 Four of Spades playing card
* 1 red satchel big enough to hold the card (fires up the work)
* 1 teaspoon Hoyt's cologne (improves luck)

Instructions:

The night before the work, pour the Hoyt's cologne into your satchel. Use just enough to leave a smell but still have a dry satchel come morning. Leave the satchel on a towel overnight to help it dry out.

In the morning take the Four of Spades into your hands and rub it vigorously between your palms for three minutes. Feel the heat transfer from your palms to the card. As you rub, recite the following:

> *Abundance is my birthright. I welcome the peace of mind*
> *it takes to create sacred peace in my life. I can love my*
> *sistahs and not be in perfect alignment with their pain.*
> *Meaning, I don't have to create drama in my own life*
> *to show solidarity with yours. If we live long enough*
> *trauma will find us; no need to go hunting for it. I don't*
> *need to blow up my life, my family, or my stability to*
> *be accepted in any group. I recognize the people who*

have loved me the longest and the hardest. I intend to
thank them for their love and devotion even when I didn't
deserve it. I didn't live life in their shoes, nor will they
live life in mine. Because they breathe, they are champi-
ons; because I breathe, so am I. None of us are perfect,
and I accept that the past will never be forgotten, even
with therapy. I take ownership of my rights and wrongs.
I won't pass the blame for choices I made—I did what
I did because I wanted to and not under duress. Today,
I choose not to carry my past into the relationships of
tomorrow. I release all narcissists from my life. I release
all narcissistic thoughts from my third eye. I move from
this day forth, building a shrine of genuine happiness.

Place the card inside the satchel and tie the satchel, by its
cord, to your bra strap. You can also place the satchel in your
pocket or purse. To put even more pep in your day, take a
picture of the card before placing it in the satchel and gaze at
the image from time to time.

Chapter Three
Sexual Evolutions

In 1986, when I was a high school sophomore, I was part of my school's Army Junior Reserve Officers Training Corps program, or JROTC. I knew a girl who was also in JROTC for a short stint before her sexuality became a problem for the group's adult sponsors. I'll call her Evangeline.

Evangeline, a junior, was on the JROTC's color guard, a special team responsible for handling the American flag at different events. A few months before parade season (the drill team's busiest time of year), Evangeline came out as a lesbian. The news of an openly gay girl on the color guard spread not only throughout our school but to neighboring schools as well.

One day, our two sergeant instructors called a mandatory meeting after school. They ordered us cadets into formation before going on a rant about how we were never in a trillion years going to be the laughingstock of Mardi Gras season. They didn't say her name, but all eyes fell on Evangeline. She slithered out of the room, slamming the door behind her. The instructors dismissed us thirty minutes later after reassigning us spots to accommodate Evangeline's absence.

On my way home, I searched for Evangeline, not wanting to be complicit in her pain. I ran for blocks until I found her walking near the Foucher streetcar tracks. Her eyes were puffy and red from crying.

Evangeline and I were friendly but not friends. On this day, though, she was my sistah, and she didn't deserve the treatment the world was forcing her to swallow. I reached for her hand and invited her to grab a burger.

On our walk and at the burger joint, we talked about why it mattered in New Orleans of all places that she was gay. We also talked about why she told everyone—Why didn't she wait until she graduated and went off to college? I wondered. She was tired of hiding who she was, she said, so she emancipated herself. She laughed often and stood her ground always.

She told me about her father, a religious zealot of a Baptist minister. He had thrown her in the streets when he found her masturbating to one of the nudie magazines he kept under the bathroom sink. She was living in a group home and had been for over a month.

Over two hours, Evangeline and I talked and ate crinkly fries and cheeseburgers heavy with onions and jalapeno peppers. We drank root beer sodas and dared each other to smell our breath. Evangeline dipped her fries in mayonnaise and kept begging me to try one, but I always made the most disturbing gagging sound.

Evangeline told me about her next moves: She was a straight-A student who had already begun taking college-level courses. She planned to run away to San Diego with her lover—a girl she met while at the group home. Once there, they'd go on to college and get an apartment; they'd already made plans to take their GED test in a few weeks.

I had never met somebody as daring as Evangeline, never known someone as strong willed and determined. She reminded me of the sheroes we only talk about during February. At the end of the night I wished her well and gave her my address and phone number so we could keep in touch.

By parade season, Evangeline was gone. It was as if nobody beside me noticed, or worse, as if nobody cared. Evangeline and I kept in touch for years, though. She eventually became an AIDS activist. Last I heard, she was living a happy grassroots life with her lover from the group home and their two kids. I think of her often when I'm home in New Orleans and I pass the Foucher streetcar stop, or when I see someone dip their fries in mayonnaise. I've still never tried it, though—to this day it's just too gross for me!

Inspiring Voices: Janelle Monáe

In a 2018 *Rolling Stone* article, Janelle Monáe stated, "Being a queer Black woman in America, someone who has been in relationships with both men and woman—I consider myself to be a free-ass motherfucker."[3]

....

3. Brittany Spanos, "Janelle Monae Frees Herself." *Rolling Stone*, April 26, 2018, https://www.rollingstone.com/music/music-features/janelle-monae-frees-herself-629204/.

I chose Monáe to represent this chapter of rituals not only because she's my sexmagickal shero, but because she epitomizes a badass attitude of *I don't care what you think about who or how I fuck.* Her life, like her song "PYNK," is one long, voluptuous ritual gushing with excitement.

Owning our sexual orientation, inclinations, and desired activities allows us to fully embrace who we are without shame, without the fear of being ostracized, and most important without the fear of being labeled a deviant. It's time to take back our sexy. It's time to embrace our inner sex goddess, the stiletto-wearing slut sistah covered in Adinkra tattoos, burgundy lips, crimson rouge, amethyst waist beads, ylang-ylang scented areolas, and coconut-oiled limbs. It's about damned time we invest in elemental power to increase our odds of finding the lovers we need and the sensual compliments we deserve.

Before we can ride off into the night ready to conquer our next sexual adventure under a waxing moon, we should make perfectly sure we don't leave it up to a significant other to define erotic pleasure for us. We need to be fully aware of what forms of play bring us to ecstasy and what shit irks the living daylights out of us. It's time to flush those strict religious ideologies around having somebody eat your pussy or plug that ass down the toilet for good. If you open your mind, you might find a host of deliciousness to feed your appetite. Remember, you can't rightfully say you don't like something if you ain't tried it. Get some rope and get tied up, or play dominatrix and submissive, or give him some head in the car. Whatever you do, just go on and get in the game!

Courting the Yoni

Yoni is a Sanskrit word defining the vagina as a source of divine creation. It describes the sacred passageway leading to the divine temple of our womb. The following spell, "Moscato Me, Baby," is about working our way toward earning our orgasm while recognizing that each orgasm brings forth the power of our life's mission. To do this, you must seduce the clitoris to erection. Don't get me wrong, there's a time and place for the old "my day went to crap, I need to release all the BS of my day onto this dildo." I've been there. But let's envision for a minute the many ways a yoni steam and yoni egg might benefit you.

Vaginal steams help ward off painful periods, nourish and tone the uterus, and prevent painful intercourse and dry vaginas. However, avoid steams if you're pregnant, experiencing heavy menstrual flow, have an infection contributing to vaginal sores or blisters, or if you've had trauma associated with your vagina or feel you can't or don't want to try it or for any reason. Keep in mind that steams can be viewed as a facial for your lower region. There are even yoni spas available. So don't shy away from the steam just because you've never done it before.

A yoni egg is an egg-shaped gemstone designed to aid in toning the vaginal muscles, much like Kegel exercises. It's believed that the gemstones' healing qualities help release properties that spiritually heal from the womb center throughout the body. When choosing an egg, choose a size appropriate for your level of experience: larger for less experienced users to smaller for advanced users.

If you've never used a yoni egg, don't worry. It can't and won't get stuck inside you; your body will release it when it's ready. You'll feel it slide out naturally, or you can push it out as if trying to have a bowel movement. Laughter and urination can also work, but if you use the latter, be careful to have your hands ready to catch the egg—you don't want it floating in your toilet, or worse your work toilet!

After using your yoni egg, rinse it thoroughly with warm to hot water and body wash to eliminate any vaginal secretions and prevent bacterial build-up. Dry it thoroughly and store it in a cloth drawstring bag until the next time you use it.

EXERCISE: MOSCATO ME, BABY

This ritual consists of two parts. Read the instructions all the way through before beginning.

Needs:

* * 9 drops ylang-ylang oil diluted in a ¼ cup sweet almond oil (promotes irresistibility)
* * 1 old flat sheet
* * 6–8 cups water
* * 6 tablespoons each, dry:
    - basil (love and protection)
    - calendula (prophecy)
    - hibiscus (dream magic, love spells)
    - lavender (happiness, peace, chastity)
    - marigold (prophetic dreams)
    - motherwort (clears bad luck and curses, bonds lovers)
    - oregano (financial security, popularity)
    - rose petals (enchantment)
    - rosemary (lust, healing, sleep)
* * 1 cup rose water (romantic luck)
* * 2 large pots (*Note: These pots will only be used for yoni steams, not for cooking. You'll use one pot to brew the herbal mixture, the other for the actual steam. The steam pot should fit comfortably in your toilet.*)
* * 1 rose quartz yoni egg (brings love and romantic luck)

Instructions:

Before beginning the work, clean and disinfect your toilet thoroughly. Rub the seat with a bit of the diluted ylang-ylang oil, then put the rest in the toilet pot. With the seat up, place the pot inside your toilet, then lower the seat.

Next, cut a hole in the center of the sheet; this will be the neck hole of your steam robe, so make sure your head fits through it comfortably. Put on the robe to make sure the sheet is long enough to drape past your knees. Set aside.

Fill the brewing pot with the water, herbs, and rose water. Bring to a boil, then remove from the heat and let steep for ten to fifteen minutes until the blend is warm to the touch but still steaming.

Pour the contents of the brewing pot into the toilet pot. Hold your arm over the pot to see how the steam feels on your skin. If it's unbearable, close the bathroom door and recheck in three-minute intervals until the temperature is satisfactory (not cold, but still steaming).

Put on the steam robe and remove your clothes from the waist down (you can keep your socks if you like). Sit over the steam for ten to fifteen minutes while repeating this incantation:

Dry herbs from Mother Earth
Calendula, motherwort
Marigold, oregano
Basil, hibiscus
Rosemary, rose petals
Soothe my pussy
Juicy is the portal of life
Juicy is the doorway to futures unknown, yoni sacred
pathway
Drench my thighs
Drench my legs
Hear my moans
Uterus
Cervix
G-spot

Rock me to sleep
Rock me to ecstasy

When the water has cooled and the steam has subsided, you're ready for the second part of the ritual: Lying down, insert the yogi egg into your vagina and inhaling to the count of four and exhaling to the count of four. Place all of your focus on the egg sliding up and down inside you. With each inhale, squeeze your vaginal muscles. With each exhale, release your muscles. Do six to twelve reps. By the end of this ritual your whole inner core should be enlightened and more open to receiving loyalty and love.

When you've finished the work, don't forget to clean up. Dump the steaming water out. Clean and dry your yoni egg and pots thoroughly before putting them away. (*Tip: I store my pots in the bathroom so they don't get mixed up with my cooking pots.*)

Massage Oils and Lubes

The work I've just described brings me to the next topic: massage oils and lube for masterful yoni massage. Massage oils can be made or purchased, and are specifically designed to free the body from physical or mental imbalances by inducing an altered state of focus that promotes relaxation and harmonizes the totality of the body. Like spiritual oils, which work on a metaphysical level to invoke divine intervention from otherworldly beings, massage oils need to be handled with care.

Before using massage oils, do a patch test to determine if you have any allergies to them. To do this, choose a small patch of skin in an inconspicuous area of your body, such as the underside of your arm, thigh, or triceps. Place a small pea-size drop of the oil on the area and allow it to sit for three to five minutes. Monitor the area for any redness, itchiness, or swelling. If any reactions occur, immediately rinse the area and apply a cold compress and hydrocortisone cream. You may also need to take an over-the-counter antihistamine tablet or liquid. Discontinue use of this particular oil. If there are no reactions after five minutes, repeat the patch test a second time on the same day. Repeat the test for two more days after that to ensure you can physically tolerate the oil's chemical makeup.

Remember, if you're making your own essential oil blends, you must use a carrier oil. Go back to the section on essential oils in chapter 2 for instructions.

Bang for Your Buck

When buying oil, I always look for deals. I'm not a cheapskate, but I prefer to get a bang for my buck. Some massage oils are as cheap as $12.00, and some are as expensive as $70.00. Lubes run about the same range. I suggest you seriously study what you want against what's offered. Don't go cheap just for the purpose of cutting corners. You will be using this oil in a multipurpose way. I recommend buying a masturbation massage oil that can also be worn out in public as a come to me oil. It will make you more open and receptive to the pheromones of your ideal lover.

You also want an oil that relaxes your muscles and creates a sensation of longing while allowing for ease of penetration. If you must spend a little more to feel erotic pleasure and not traumatic pain, then by all means spend lovingly.

EXERCISE: THE TURNED WAY UP MASSAGE OIL

Nobody has time for sandpaper skin. Use this recipe to create a massage oil for your feet, elbows, and neck. For the chocolate girls out there who struggle with ash, this joint is right up your alley.

Needs:

* ¾ teaspoon lotus oil (attunes the mind)
* 1 cup sweet almond oil (intoxicating personality)
* 1 plastic bottle or lidded container
* 1 funnel
* 6–8 cups water in a large pot

Instructions:

Pour the oils into the plastic bottle or lidded container using the funnel. Close and shake vigorously for five to seven minutes.

After it's thoroughly mixed, you can use your oil immediately. But if you're like me, you might like to add a little heat to your massage: Bring the water to a boil, then remove from the heat to cool until it's warm to the touch. (If you can see steam rising from the water, it's still too hot.) Let the bottle soak, lid off, in the warm water for a few minutes.

When the oil is ready, massage your feet, hands, neck, and ankles. Wear socks to ensure the silky-smooth oil stays put and doesn't wind up on your floors. In the morning, your skin will look and feel like a new pair of twenty-dollar hose.

EXERCISE: HONEY, SUCK MY NARCISSUS BATH

This is an oil blend that will make your bath divine.

Needs:

* 10 drops each:
    - lily of the valley oil (cheers up the heart)
    - narcissus oil (boosts confidence)
    - neroli oil (protection against creepy people)
* ¼ cup each:
    - brown sugar (sweetens our desires)
    - dried flowering honeysuckle (protection)
    - dried flowering jasmine (love opens)
    - dried flowering orange blossom (luck in love)
    - witch hazel (adds divine guidance)
* 1–2 cups whiskey (fires life up)

Instructions:

Place all the ingredients in a large mason jar, seal tightly, and shake for five to seven minutes. Turn the jar upside down and let sit for twenty-four hours before use. To use, add half a cup of the blend to your bath. Make sure to include some of the herbs with the liquid (a small scoop can help with this).

CBD Oil

CBD (cannabidiol) products are a great option for massages and spiritual work. Scientists have discovered that CBD, a component of marijuana and hemp, possesses extreme pain-relieving benefits. CBD oil has the potential to ease muscular tightness while releasing tension. The human body contains an endocannabinoid system, or ECS, that regulates sleep, appetite, pain, and immune system response. CBD reduces chronic pain by impacting ECS receptors to reduce inflammation while also treating pain related to arthritis and sclerosis.[4]

What about using CBD oil for sensual pleasure? When used in massage, CBD oil supports blood flow to those delicious regions, lubricates for ease, heightens orgasmic sensation, and enhances sexual comfort. Please don't get all bent out of shape over CBD's connection to cannabis. You can't smoke CBD oil, and it isn't addictive unless intentionally abused. Try to find CBD oils with a mixture of kava kava extract or botanical blends—together they enhance tactile sensations, decrease tension, discomfort, and dryness. The best part of CBD oil is that it stimulates your natural lubricants and increases your g-spot circulation.

Although the following rituals use CBD oil for self-pleasure, you can use it with a partner too. But remember to choose an oil or lube that doesn't include coconut oil, which can cause condoms to break. Nobody got time for that!

....

4. Midland Health, "7 Surprising Benefits of CBD Oil," Midland Health Testing Services, August 26, 2018, https://www.midlandhealth.com/General-Health/7-Surprising-Benefits-of-Cbd-Oil.

EXERCISE: CHILD PLEASE, MY LOVE CAN BRING YOU TO YOUR KNEES OIL BLEND

This is a ritual massage oil that will bring you love and make you irresistible.

Needs:

* 19 drops each:
    - CBD oil (opens your third eye)
    - kava kava oil (luck)
    - orange essence oil
    - rose oil (irresistible love)
    - tuberose oil (sweetens your disposition)
* 1 cup jojoba oil (attraction)

Instructions:

Pour all of the ingredients into a large mason jar, seal, and shake vigorously for five to ten minutes. Unseal the jar and whisper into it:

Child please, my love can bring you to your knees.
Follow the scent to my home, in my bed, under my sheets.
Come to me, lover. Open your heart, mind, and soul to me.
Child, please let my love bring you to your knees.
Child, please let my love bring you to your knees.
Love me, love me, love only me.
Come to me, lover.
Come bring your love home to me.

Seal the jar and store it in a cool dark space. The oil is ready to use immediately.

Sexual Psyche of Women

Monáe reported to *InStyle* magazine in 2019, "If my mother had let me have a vibrator at a young age to be in touch with my body more, I could have saved myself from so many poor decisions."[5] Now I'm not advocating that mothers rush out and purchase vibrators for their teen daughters as a rite of passage to sit alongside their first package of sanitary napkins. Hell no! I'm saying that because of our Judeo-Christian backgrounds, so many of us grow into adulthood falling victim to laws dictating how we own our sexuality. We grow up inundated with ideas like sex toys are taboo, kink requires repentance, and oral and anal sex are ungodly. Our biblical upbringing even dictates how we honor ourselves as sexual beings. You've seen it: women condemning other women for being overly sexualized in their dress, in their decisions to be sex workers, in their liberating lyricism expressed through songs about kissing girls or their spicy rap mantras about fuckboy groupies. Christianity has screwed over the psyche of women and messed us up. We're taught that women are born to be passive bodies of spread legs, allowing our men the courtesy of crawling on top of us to do their business. All the while our entrepreneurial business stocks plummet, leaving us with the only viable solution: shutting our doors (mouths) permanently without any recourse.

If you saw the 1985 movie *The Color Purple*, you might remember when Celie referred to sex with Mr. as "him climbing on top of her and doing his business." Shug's retort is, "You sound like he going to the toilet on you."[6] Celie is a classic example of a woman never taught the ins and outs of her sacred yoni. She was a sensual goddess vibrating throughout life as a woman void of sexual prowess. She was a human blow-up doll for men. She wasn't supposed to express her needs or desires. She was a means to an orgasmic end, a fill-in for the "makes her own money" succubus sistah too independent to cater to any man.

....

5. Maiysha Kai, "'I'm Exercising My Freedom': Janelle Monae Talks Liberation in Instyle's Badass Women Issue," *The Root*, July 11, 2019, https://www.theroot.com/i-m-exercising-my-freedom-janelle-monae-talks-liberati-1836256843.

6. "Celie and Shug," *The Color Purple*, directed by Stephen Spielberg, (1985; Burbank, CA: Warner Bros. 2011) Blue-ray Disc.

To me what Monáe was saying in that article is that her sexual journey of exploration was left completely up to lovers, fellow explorers and conquerors who sought to earn notches in their pubic hairs, or thrill seekers hoping sex would magickally eradicate their pain, or even worse, label them as cool. That needs to change.

Yoni Massage

Yoni massage is one way to help women and their partners better connect with the female body. The aim isn't sexual exploration or even foreplay; it's about this connection, which allows women to discard notions that their yoni is nasty or simply a sexual tool. Yoni massage can also help women work through sexual trauma. It puts you in control of your sexual representation, needs, and desires. If you like, you can even pamper yourself with a yoni massage to build sexual excitement.

First, however, you want to release your baggage from your life. You're free to orgasm alone or with a partner after that, but not right now. The masseur, whether that's you or a friend, should focus on awakening the healing energy of your erogenous zones. The sheer magnitude of sensual touch is life altering and earth shattering but in a "hell yeah" kind of way.

I've divined for countless women between the ages of eighteen and sixty, and very few are unwilling to try a yoni massage. If you're familiar with tantric massage for your nether regions, a yoni massage is pretty much one and the same. I've shared a yoni massage ritual to get you started. Again, let me repeat—the intention of yoni massages isn't climax! You don't have to reach an orgasm. It's about connection.

The following ritual makes use of a yoni wand. "What the freak is a yoni wand?" you ask. Well, they aren't the stuff of Harry Potter's Hogwarts. Think of them as ergonomically correct dildos made from medical-grade, lead-free borosilicate glass. They can also be made of crystals like clear quartz, amethyst, rose quartz, red jasper, and obsidian, to name a few popular materials.

Yoni wands are intended for internal massage, pleasure, and healing. A large majority of sistahs are well versed in the positioning of their labia majora, labia minora, and clitoris. Yet many are baffled when it comes to sailing down the vaginal canal to their g-spot. Wands are designed to make it easier to reach this region.

As with the yoni egg, make sure you rinse your yoni wand thoroughly with warm to hot water and body wash to eliminate any vaginal secretions and prevent bacterial buildup. Make sure to thoroughly dry and store the wand in a cloth drawstring bag until the next time you need it.

EXERCISE: CONJURINGS OF THE HOLY HOLE

Make ample time for this ritual, and remember, it's about connecting to your body. Read the instructions all the way through before beginning.

Needs:
* any lube oil you prefer
* 1 glass or crystal yoni wand

Instructions:

First, set the atmosphere by taking a bath. Once finished, lie on your bed and state your goal. Remember to hold that goal in your mind the entire time, repeating it over and over in your head. Do you want to open the Universal flow so you can get a better or different job? Do you want to make yourself more glamorous for a potential lover? Do you want to realign your chakras and free yourself from stress, anxiety, and self-doubt? Cosmic regeneration through yoni massage can liberate your whole body while also liberating your soul space.

Continue to lie in stillness. Ground your earth element by practicing the tattva mudra. This pose reminds us that we are pure transcendent beings worthy of extending love and being loved. As you hold this pose, touch both hands to your forehead, heart, pelvis, and clitoris. Continue to breathe as you recite this incantation:

Sweet, juicy pussy with the slippery center—awaken and bring me peace.
Teach me to accept truth, to change direction when necessary, to love my kinky.
There is no shame attached to this sacred snatch.
Today I welcome all with an open mouth and willing tongue.
Come get some of this yoni snack.

Using your lube, massage your vulva with one finger (your nondominant hand is usually gentler than your dominant hand). Use one finger to penetrate yourself and the other hand to gently stroke your clitoris. With your finger, tap the deep canal to increase vaginal fluids and heighten your horniness. Then, stroke in whatever motion you like. Listen to the rhythm of your body and pay close attention to the amount of secretion. Engage in sound therapy: moan to ignite your inner wild woman. As you find yourself crossing the threshold of climax, stop and invite your yoni wand to come play.

There are sistahs who report squirting fluid, or amrita, from their vagina as a result of wand play. While squirting is sexy as hell, don't get fixated on it. You weren't put on this earth to reach another woman's happy place. You're here to experience your own bliss. Don't sweat it if you don't squirt your first, second, third, fourth, fifth, sixth… get the point? Don't let the OnlyFans girls fool you.

The physical dexterity needed to achieve this release requires constant and focused g-spot pressure. To help with this you can purchase a curved wand, which can reach more uncharted regions than a straight wand. While you might not squirt, who says you can't slobber? Remember, the goal is always to allow intentional healing to transport you to the next level of pleasure and consciousness.

When you're done, don't forget to clean and store the wand properly.

Love Mojos

Often when sistahs think of love spells they have this idea that a magick potion is going to hypnotize a potential lover and have them worshipping at their feet like a brain-dead zombie. Trust me, that's not what you want. It's what you *think* you want, until someone comes into your life with an Armani disposition and quickly becomes some knockoff lover with an Ormane attitude. My grandmother used to call it "cute for nothing," meaning you look good, hell, you may even smell good, but your disposition is on life support and fading fast.

My idea of love magick is more concerned with creating a sense of erotic appeal inside you. You'll then project this appeal outward, affecting the energetic fields of everyone you meet. Love mojos aren't about impairing a person's ability to choose whether or not they want to love you but rather about granting you the ability to love through acceptance of the skin you're in. Once this is achieved, you'll connect with lovers who share an appreciation for your remarkable beauty and sensuality.

When Armani Becomes Ormane

I knew this gorgeous older sistah born and raised in Egypt. The sistah was stunning. Her skin had a hint of bronze, like grains of sand. She carried this gargantuan cloth bag full of candles, salves, strips of cotton, parchment, dragon's blood ink, patchouli, nag champa oil, and she even had a skull wrapped in black cloth. There were items I never saw exit that bag, but the mysterious shapes they made protruding from each side made me wonder, who was this woman with a skull companion?

She said it was the skull of the man who had violated her mother as a child. When her mother died, the skull passed on to her so she could continue his torment. In life the man wasn't a fan of music of any kind. To him, all music was noise, and the sounds enraging. The sistah carried a tiny drum, finger cymbals, and a kazoo tucked inside a fanny pack. She played these instruments at midnight with the skull as the only listener in attendance.

Also in the deep, dark recesses of the Egyptian sistah's bag was a toddler's shoe box. Inside the box was the waistband of a withered pair of men's underwear; toenail clippings; a braid of hair, each end tightened with twine; and a ripped t-shirt with bloodstains. In the corner of the box was a small, scraggly cloth doll whose insides had been ripped out. She told me that everything in the box—the underwear, the nail clippings, and the braided hair—had lived inside the crawlspace of that doll's hollowed-out soul.

As the story goes, the sistah met a man at a park concert. She felt tingly all over and thought it was intuition telling her to do whatever it took to make him hers. "Whatever she needed to do" turned into a binding spell. She decided to bind him to her forever, and she was quick about it.

In the beginning it was sunsets and pussy kisses. Armani. She was with a man who was everything she could've ever imagined, until the day he wasn't. He became the classic case of Dr. Jekyll and Mr. Hyde. It was during his Hyde episodes that he beat this woman so badly she would lose consciousness. He broke her ribs and dislocated her arm; he even broke her nose. The day he found out her period was two weeks late he kicked her in her stomach until blood spewed from her vagina. The flow indicated to him that if there had been a pregnancy it was now terminated, free of charge.

You get where this is going? That spell was working like a muthafucka. She had been taught how to love bind, but never how to undo a binding that obviously wasn't serving her highest good.

One night after her lover lost too much money on a football pool, he beat what my mama would call the daylights out of her until he was too pooped to go on. He dropped to his knees and slumped over, falling asleep in her arms. Somewhere around 3 a.m. she managed to pack that gargantuan bag with the toddler's shoe box flanking a damp, bloodied corner. Blood streamed from her eyes, her nose, and her mouth as she guarded the doll sliding from corner to corner of the box.

It had been her child's shoebox, a child that drowned three years before meeting him. The baby was in her sister's care while she worked a twelve-hour shift as a paramedic. Of all nights, her sister decided to shoot heroin for the first time while lounging alongside her apartment complex's pool. Unattended the baby slipped off her floaties and slid beneath the deep only to be retrieved by the apartment supervisor the next morning. Losing her child broke the sistah, she thought, until the day he walked in.

On the night she decided to leave, she went to the drawer where she kept the binding doll—the doll she had become afraid to touch over the years She had thought in time he would work on his issues and see how much she loved him, and instead of beating her he would make love to her more. She had sworn on the lives of her parents that the sex was the only reason she stayed. It could be so medicinal after a beating, and in her mind, she could count on both hands the sistahs who never took a lick upside the head and averaged one orgasm a month. Sex also kept her from dismantling the binding doll still stuffed into the box under girdles and period panties and loose tampons. Maybe a spell to keep his fist from going upside her head would fall in her lap one day, but that night her ancestors were the ones who were sick and tired of being sick and tired.

Into the dark she ran until she came to a bus station. Before she knew it, seven states separated them. Then, in seven years, she had a new life, a new love, and even an adopted daughter. When she ran into her past love while vacationing on a beach in Florida, he was taking a break from an educational conference. He stood at the water's edge in rolled-up sleeves, bow tie, khakis, and wing-tips, contemplating what happened to his angelic sweetheart, the only woman he would ever love. It was all because of that doll.

When he spotted her tossing a beach ball back and forth with her daughter, he rolled on her in his quirky way, and they talked for about an hour. She wasn't afraid of him anymore. Instead she pitied how absent he seemed inside his own body. He kept apologizing and asking her to be all right so he could get her off his mind. She lied to him about how insufferable their relationship had been, the broken ribs, the dislocated shoulder, the eye that stayed swollen shut for a month. "Incompatible," was all she kept saying. They were on two different wavelengths which made them incompatible idiots destined to fail.

After a month of trying to find her with no luck, he had checked himself into a rehabilitation program for domestic abusers. He was proud to tell her his faith in love had been renewed. He swore he was a new man now, free of sin and the demonic force that had made him a monster. But she knew where this was going, so she lied and told him she needed to retrieve a bottle of sunscreen from her car. Standing at the trunk of her SUV, she felt that she was at a safe enough distance to peer over her left shoulder. He was now seated, wrapped in a blanket, at the edge of the beach, where the water kissed the sand.

She reached for the child's shoebox, ripping away at her past until the innards of the doll lay strewn at her feet. In one deep sigh she not only freed her tormentor, she finally stepped into her own awakening, making space for the sweet satisfaction of joy. By the time she and her daughter walked back to their blanket, he had vanished into the crowd of beachgoers, never to be in her physical space again. Freed from her web, the man no longer longed for her or possessed the desire to be loved by her. A year later the woman's sister emailed her a scanned image of her former lover's wedding notice. A month later the sistah was expecting her own new beginning—a baby boy.

Hopefully, this story is lesson enough to convince you that you should never force feed your love to someone else. It isn't emotionally or physically safe, for you or your intended significant other. It also isn't fair to take away a person's free will.

EXERCISE: HOYT TO HOYT (SATCHEL)

The purpose of the mojo is to make it known to the world that you're a free agent in the pickup game of love. It will attract *exactly* what you ask for, so be specific!

Needs:

* 1 teaspoon Hoyt's cologne (provides you luck in all things)
* 1 copy of the Lovers tarot card
* 2 High John the Conqueror roots, about 1 ounce each
* 1 copy of a photo of you
* 1 teaspoon dried clove (drives away hostile potential lovers)
* 1 teaspoon dried sweat pea (aids in making you more attractive)
* 1 red satchel big enough to hold all the ingredients

Instructions:

Before engaging in this work, write out the type of lover you want. Detail all your negotiables and nonnegotiables, and be firm about character—I think folks get so caught up in describing their lover's outward appearance that they forget to consider a person's emotional stability, until that stability proves to be *in*stability.

Lay a towel over your work area. Place the High John roots inside the satchel, then pour the Hoyt's cologne inside. Let the satchel sit on the towel for twenty-four hours to dry.

The next day, place the copy of the Lovers card and your photo inside the satchel. Add the cloves and sweet pea. Whisper into the satchel your desire to find love, and be specific about the type of love you desire. Tie the satchel, by its cord, to your bra strap. You can also place the satchel in your pocket or purse.

Conscious Quickies

In *Urban Tantra*, author Barbara Carrellas refers to twenty minutes of orgasmic release as "conscious quickies."[7] These are times spent making us artists of love. Erotic awakenings don't just happen in a vacuum. I personally didn't have sex until the age of twenty-three, and the man who popped my proverbial cherry is my now husband of twenty-six years. No, he wasn't a virgin; I know that would make this story a Black fairy tale. And no, I wasn't one of those God-fearing young women who viewed sex before marriage as a sin. I was deathly afraid of pregnancy even more than AIDS, gonorrhea, or syphilis. Pregnancy and the thought of not getting my degree was my boogeyman. Learning to navigate my own body through conscious quickies has helped me accept my fupa, my yam thighs, and my fat labia. Baby, I own the beauty in my breasts even with the psoriasis, and I rationalize it as all part of what makes me a turn-on. Navigating your sexy should never come with shame or fear or hatred. Strut all your stuff because it belongs to nobody but you.

Pleasure Principles of Tarot

Using tarot as part of our pleasure principles produces a deeply meditative event that enhances our understanding of what it means to be a whole-ass human being, requiring all the freedoms that love entails.

....

7. Barbara Carrellas, "Chapter 4: Wake Up Your Mind, Calm Your Body, and Free Your Spirit," in *Urban Tantra: Sacred Sex for the Twenty-First Century* (New York, NY: Ten Speed Press, 2017), 57.

The next ritual uses the Magician, the Lovers, and the Sun cards. Before doing the ritual, study each image and consider how they might relate to intimacy. If you find it hard to interpret the tarot's relationship to intimacy, here are some ideas to generate insight:

- The Magician is about sensual mysticism, and he says that you're divine because you not only have a rose quartz yoni wand, you know how to use it.

- The Lovers remind us that falling in trust is much more important than falling in love. I'm talking in the initial stages of any relationship. We must grasp the idea of loving ourselves enough to make a personal pact that no matter how cute, or fine, or how wealthy a person is or isn't, they aren't worth loss of our sanity. You deserve to be more than liked when building the foundation of your relationship; you deserve to be understood and heard.

- The Sun is about rejoicing in the fact that the Universe will allow for only what we truly need. Nothing penetrates our safe zone that's unnecessary. When we let the sunshine in, we linger in the spirit of release. The past is the past; what we called a failure was really a moment of adding another brick to our strong resolve. The sun says it's okay to be vulnerable; it doesn't mean you're weak. The sun is resilient in the way it warms our heart and provides sustenance for our soul.

After meditating on the cards, imagine how they relate to intimacy as it looks in your own mind, heart, and erogenous zones.

EXERCISE: YOU'RE JUST TOO GOOD TO BE TRUE RITUAL

This ritual is designed to help you become sensually appealing. Before starting, decide which of your attributes you want to heighten as you step into the world. For example, I might say, "When folks see me, I want them to notice my almond eyes and become not just hypnotized but mesmerized. I want them to gravitate to my gap-tooth smile and think, *She got a sugar*

bowl below. I want folks to view my hue and wonder if I taste like chocolate."

Needs:

* 1 red penis candle
* 1 red pussy candle
* 60 stick pins
* 2 saucers
* 1 pair of female underwear
* 1 pair of male underwear
* 1 Adam and Eve root, about 1–2 inches (promotes love and happiness)
* 2 lodestones (represent male and female, draw love)
* 1 High John the Conqueror root, about 1 ounce (attracts powerful love that never bends or breaks)
* rose water in a spritz bottle (powers glamour magick)
* Hoyt's cologne in a spritz bottle (attracts a financially stable lover)
* 3 yards red satin or nylon fabric
* 1 roll of twine
* 1 shot of whiskey
* 1 each of the Magician, the Lovers, and the Sun tarot cards

Instructions:

First, puncture your penis and pussy candles with thirty stick pins each. Place a saucer on top of each pair of underwear, then place a candle on each saucer.

Next, take the Adam and Eve root, lodestones, and High John root and spritz them heavily with rose water and Hoyt's cologne. Wrap all the items in the red cloth and tightly fasten the ends with twine. Liberally sprinkle whiskey on the wrapped items. Touch them to your head, heart, womb, and pussy. Whisper the attributes you chose to heighten into the bundle and place it near the candles.

Touch the inside of your vagina. If you aren't moist, masturbate yourself to moistness. Rub the juice from your fingers onto both wicks, consecrating them. Wait for fifteen minutes. During that time, meditate on what each tarot card symbolizes in this work.

After fifteen minutes, place the cards in an arch around the candles and wrapped items. Light the candles and play music that inspires you; I like to listen to Janelle Monáe's "I Like That" and "Q.U.E.E.N." for this ritual. Dance and sway; with this ritual you're moving into a rhythm where the law of attraction will call love to you. Listen to the Universe and let love have its say. Claim love and love will claim you.

Carry the wrapped root on your person or in your purse daily. Sit with the candles for fifteen minutes each day for six to nine days (the candles should be extinguished after each fifteen-minute seating). How long your candle lasts will depend on its size. Continue to meditate on the tarot cards.

Sacred Sex

Sex magick isn't as ceremonial or difficult a concept to add to your magickal repertoire as it sounds or as folks would imply. The hardest part for me has been (and still is) figuring out what pressing need deserves to share my orgasmic space. Orgasms are potent energy.

Here's your crash course in sex magick, so take notes. First, sex magick involves setting an intention—a deeply rooted desired outcome. Make sure you truly believe in the outcome. Take your outcome and create a mantra or incantation for it. An example is as follows: *My manuscript will be complete by the year's end, and it will generate positive publicity once published.* Be firm by phrasing the outcome in a way that indicates it will manifest.

Next, repeat your mantra for thirty minutes to an hour. Allow yourself to feel the sensation sprout from your mind's eye to your heart, then to all erogenous zones. Once you feel the energy flowing throughout, it's time to go on and get that orgasm. As you feel yourself heighten to climax, envision your outcome manifesting. To continue with the earlier example, the manifesting might look like a published book reaching the hands of many as you're happily engaged in book signings.

You might feel a bit awkward your first time out and question if you're doing it right. Growing up on a diet fortified with pornography may've made you feel disconnected from your yoni. I get it—we need to awaken your yoni maiden.

EXERCISE: AWAKENING THE YONI MAIDEN

Warning: you might fall in love with this ritual.

Needs:

* 1 clitoral stimulator
* 1 g-spot stimulator
* 1 tablespoon Aloe Cadabra Natural Personal Lube
  (*Note: This lubrication is made with organic aloe. Among other benefits, aloe increases your sensation of beauty, moisturizes the vagina superbly, and makes you feel more glamourous from the inside out. If you're older, it restores your vagina to its youthful brilliance.*)
* 1 recording of rain falling in an open field
* 1 tarot card deck

Instructions:

Turn the lights off and set your intention. Speak into the Universe the blessing you want manifested. When you feel the intention is set, begin with the g-spot stimulator. After you're near the point of orgasm but not yet breaking down the dam, switch to the clitoral stimulator to finish the job. The heavens

will open, and sex will become more than a social exercise, it will become magickal.

Lay those hardworking babies aside. Your worker bees have blasted your intent into the next stratosphere. Get ready to meet your destiny.

Practice this ritual for nine nights straight, kicking it into an even higher gear each time. Don't forget to clean and store your stimulators every day. You're now a woman more inclined to use her pussy power to invoke the change she wants to see and be in the world.

EXERCISE: THE MORNING AFTER REJUVENATION RITUAL

Here's a ritual to start your day. You can do this after the last one or on its own. Once again, your tarot deck will come into play.

Needs:

* 1 each of the High Priestess, the Emperor, and the Fool tarot cards
* 1 black seven-knob candle
* 1 white seven-knob candle

Instructions:

In the morning, lay out your tarot cards in this order: the High Priestess, the Emperor, and the Fool. Place the candles at the top of the card setting.

First, pick up the High Priestess card. The High Priestess represents where you're headed as you complete this work. You've chosen to put past traumas behind you and to allow magick to be your emissary. You've decided to trust your instincts and intuition. You've awakened your inner mysticism and will be guided by the knowledge; you've straddled two worlds and

lived to tell the tale. Pick up that card and kiss her. Thank her for awakening your soul.

Next, take up the Emperor card. It tells you you're in charge of your life. You make the rules, and no one has the right to sentence your voice to a dungeon. Your life is no medieval torture chamber. Kiss this card and tell him you'll determine the boundaries from here on out. Thank him for his service and banish him behind the High Priestess card.

Last, take up the Fool card. Here lie uncharted waters. The future is unknown but vast. It's always scary to step forward, but those of us who manage to step out on faith to find our fate are the ones who laugh best. There are no gold stars for being miserable, just time wasted, memories unmade, passions unfulfilled, and dreams scattered. Shall I go on? The Fool knows that to look back is to open yourself to stagnation.

Harriet Tubman carried a gun, and she was known to point it at any person who was too afraid to carry on and say, "Move or die." She didn't want a scared fool to get everybody killed, including her. The fool is moving into an unknown abyss, unafraid and willing to find out what lies beyond the veil. Thank the Fool for allowing you the courage to move. Kiss the Fool and take the card with you as you leave for the day.

When you return, right after work or before bed that night, light the candles. Place the entire tarot deck with the Fool on top in a stack in the center of the candles. Sit quietly for ten minutes, thinking back on the lessons gained from this work, and close with this incantation: *I am back! The Queen! The Emperor! The Majestic Fool! I was born to rule! I was born to laugh! I was born to love! Welcome back, Queen! Welcome back, Emperor! Welcome back, Fool! You are worthy! You are worthy! You are celebrated!*

Carry the Fool with you for nine days to complete the work.

Daily Glamour Magick

A final concept I want to incorporate here is the use of glamour magick in our daily lives. It's another way to embrace the magick you're inviting into your life. Before work, if I know the day is going to be highly volatile, I psyche myself up. To come out unscathed, I indulge in a snippet of glamour magick. This work heightens areas of your appearance and attitude so folks see you as engagingly pleasing.

Glamour magick also gives you an extra layer of protection. While it makes you irresistible to those you want to find you irresistible, it also can make you invisible to those you want to move in the shadows against. I read somewhere that a woman uses glamour magick on her makeup compact so that every time she goes to redo her makeup, she's gifted with a hint of magickal empowerment to counter her day. This woman uses rose quartz to conjure love with each brush stroke.

There's no limit to what you can glamour: your car, lipstick, lotion, perfume, and yes, even your purse. I wear my glamoured objects with ease and go out to greet the world in my gemstone suit of invisible armor. My feeling is always one of "World, you better beware. This sistah is about to misbehave."

EXERCISE: GLAM SQUAD 9 TO 5

This is a quick glamour magick ritual.

Needs:

* 1 outfit with shoes
* 1 black tourmaline (lightens your vibrations by blocking negative and errant energies from causing psychic attacks)
* 1 lapis lazuli (stimulates creativity, allowing one to speak honestly but with compassion)
* 1 apatite (alleviates stress and emotional overload, quiets shyness and encourages self-confidence and courage)
* 1 rose quartz

Instructions:

Lay out your outfit, from bra and panties to slacks and shoes. Rub your palms together until you feel a nice heat flow. Pick up the gemstones and glide each one over every clothing item as if caressing them. Ask the stones to glamour these items so that you may go undetected as a threat to anyone and your enemies won't see or hear you. May these gemstones protect you from errant energy both conscious and subconscious, and may all your undertakings be granted success, love, and tranquility. The next morning, put on your clothes and see how the day goes.

Juju on the Fly

The Queen of Hearts is the card that recognizes our sexual liberation is just as important as our emotional liberation. How we view ourselves psychosexually often directly correlates to how our religion, social media, family, and friends convey and instruct us in the their values and beliefs around which sexual behaviors are acceptable and which are questionable. This card should be used when we're feeling oversexed, undersexed, confused about whether sex has been clouding our rational decision-making processes, or even when we feel too embarrassed about our desires to get a little kinky with our freaky.

Overcoming Hurdles

Several years ago I spent a long time doing internet research for a book on sex magick for people of color. While researching I noticed that squirting was quickly becoming all the rage across social media platforms. Many of the discussions even became a battlefield, labeling Black women as frigid and uptight when it came to reaching the so-called most satisfying orgasm in the world.

Women of color I spoke with felt as if squirting was just another hurdle we had to jump through. The message seemed to be "squirt, or risk men feeling like they can't satisfy us in comparison to White women." Some of my clients were beginning to believe that an absence of squirting meant they had been experiencing mediocre sex. White women had bested them, and if their bodies weren't equipped to spray vaginal fluids all over the place, these same White women would wage a full-fledged assault on Black love. Many felt as if they were being shut out of a closed society. But as I noted earlier, not everybody squirts, and working with this card helped my clients understand this. Pointing them in the direction of tantric experts of color also helped many dismantle claims their pussies were inadequate or broken.

I had a sistah come to me for divination who had allowed the Bible to dictate what her sexual relationships included. She would talk for hours about how masturbation was sinful and how it could do only one of two things: make you sterile or a prostitute. She also felt the best sex could only be achieved through the missionary position. She was thirty-six with six previous lovers. She came to me for a reading hoping to find out why she had become a revolving door to men, a casting couch on their way to marrying their forever lover.

After a long discussion about how growing up the daughter of a strict Southern Baptist preacher had left her with a wealth of ideas to unpack, she decided that tarot, Lenormand, and black mirror sessions were exactly what she needed. The revelation led her to an understanding that she needed to work through deep-seated sexual phobias with a therapist. In our ancestral work, we learned she had been a preacher's wife in a past life. The preacher was uncomfortably older than she was and often demanded sexual control over her body, including inflicting pain because it aroused him. Very rarely did he engage in penetrative sex with his penis. Instead, he would defile her with objects from his toolshed. He told her sex was unclean unless a child sprang from the act, and that it should be performed in silence. Afterward he made her kneel on dry rice and pray to God for her sins, which included his erection and orgasm.

In addition to her therapy and tantric studies, this sistah and I worked on freeing her spiritually. Her test was to begin accumulating sex toys. She would have three months to become acquainted with each toy. She would write a letter and a story about the specific sexual anxiety each toy would heal. Over time, she purchased ten toys. And throughout it all she kept a

Queen of Hearts on cardstock in an eight-by-ten frame. It was her centering image, the image that let her know it was okay to explore her nether regions. She didn't need anyone else's permission but her own.

Within a year she had become proficient in how to bring about her own arousal and with that knowledge she became the choosey lover. In time she shifted from one orgasm in six years to learning how to live a multiorgasmic life.

EXERCISE: MY PUSSY AIN'T BROKE

Here's a quick Juju on the Fly ritual to take control of and delight in your sexuality.

Needs:

* 1 Queen of Hearts playing card, 8 x10 inches (print out an enlarged image or enlarge a photocopy of a standard playing card)
* 1 pink womb, vagina, or pussy candle
* 1 pink satchel big enough to hold other items
* 3 drops ylang-ylang oil (*Note: Undiluted is fine for this work.*)

Instructions:

Place the oil inside the satchel, followed by the card and candle. Tie the satchel closed and hold it as you repeat the following incantation: *I own my sexuality. I determine what feels good. I determine what I will and will not indulge in. I won't be forced to partake in sexual acts that belittle me, abuse me, or cause me to jeopardize my self-worth in my own eyes. If I want to try something new, I will without fear, and I don't care who judges. This is my body, and when this life comes to an end I'll laugh, knowing I squeezed every bit of satisfaction out of each and every delicious orgasm.*

Tie the flannel to your bra strap or place it in a pocket. Carry it for nine days. Each morning add three new drops of oil and repeat the incantation. On the ninth night burn the candle and sit. Breathe in and out, allowing the breath to travel across your body. As you exhale, moan lightly and increase the crescendo. Do this for fifteen minutes with three-minute breaks for every five minutes of orgasmic breathing. Close by going to bed. Repeat this exercise once a month as needed.

Chapter Four
Love Me or Leave Me Alone

The spellwork in this chapter is specifically dedicated to helping sistahs heal from relationship trauma. These magickal workings will serve to heal your spirit and declutter your soul so you can make peace with your need to transition into a newly improved you. According to the National Sexual Violence Resource Center, 81 percent of women and 43 percent of men in the US have experienced sexual assault or sexual harassment.[8]

At sixteen, I was punched in my chest by a cute Ralph Tresvant-looking guy. My handsome boyfriend's blows landed so hard I plummeted down a flight of stairs. At twenty-one, I was drugged and had to fight my way out of a gang rape situation. My college boyfriend at the time invited me to dinner at his group home job, where he intended to allow three of his colleagues to enjoy my body as well.

It doesn't matter these guys' reasons for assaulting or trying to assault me. It doesn't matter what I was wearing, or if I said no loudly enough to be taken seriously. What happened shouldn't have happened to any of us. There's never a justification for assault or abuse—*ever*. That trauma lives within me but no longer consumes me. That's the difference I've chosen to make in my life.

Trauma as defined by the American Psychological Association is "an emotional response to terrible events like an accident, rape, or natural disaster. Afterward individuals usually experience shock and/or denial. Long-term effects can manifest as unpredictable emotions, flashbacks, strained relationships, with physical symptoms such as headaches and nausea."[9] In some instances, people find it difficult to move on with their lives and should most

....

8. Holly Kearl, "81% Of Women and 43% of Men Have Experienced Sexual Abuse in USA," Stop Street Harassment, February 21, 2018, https://stopstreetharassment.org/2018/02/newstudy2018/.

9. "APA Dictionary of Psychology," American Psychological Association (American Psychological Association), accessed April 17, 2023, https://dictionary.apa.org/trauma.

definitely seek out the assistance of a board-certified therapist to assist them in realignment. I cannot repeat this sentiment enough.

The following magickal workings will help in your healing process. When engaging with any of the rituals listed, don't be afraid to first study this chapter and use the rituals you find most therapeutic in your hour of need. Don't be dogmatic about working in sequential order. There's no wrong way to live magickally.

Inspiring Voices: Beyoncé

Beyoncé is the Queen B of not only inviting us into a high-powered billion-dollar Black marriage but also blessing us with songs detailing the perils of infidelity and how women can be portrayed as "jealous or crazy." My twenty-seven-year-old daughter, Nzingha, is a Beyoncé superfan. She's watched Baechella over ten times! Nzingha can sing every Beyoncé song word for word and regale you with a synopsis of what was happening in Queen B's life when she penned those lyrics to paper. Nzingha would say, "Beyoncé is the sistah who wasn't going to lose. She was and is willing to do whatever is necessary to keep her man in line. She manages her career and her life like a goddess! That's bad witch energy. That's what makes her Queen B."

As you begin to work your mojo, try choosing Beyoncé songs that resonate with you and blast those rhythms loud enough so you feel the beat tickling your spine. For instance, to get me in the rumble mood, I might start with an oldie but goodie by Beyoncé such as "Irreplaceable." Feel the music in your spirit, let it transpose you to a heightened vibration of healing. Song and dance are integral parts of magick, and the soundtracks of our lives serve as potent forms of medicinal escapism. Dance, twerk, get your groove on, and shake what yo mama gave you!

Sistahs, I want you to rid your space of any material reminders of the traumatic breakup. When removing items related to the demise of a tumultuous relationship, you don't have to become as "high octane" as Angela Bassett's character Bernadine Harris in *Waiting to Exhale* when she set her cheating husband's personal effects on fire. I honestly can watch that scene at least once a day. Afterward I walk away feeling like my own life has had a bowel-freeing moment, feeling like I dumped that fecal matter with a quickness and came out on the other side, not only alive but satisfyingly revived.

May the following workings tide you over the rough waves of turmoil. May they guide you back to shore as a diva draped in a sparkling cowrie bikini with sand tickling your gorgeously manicured toes. Know you're a Divine Queen B in your own right. Be prepared to own your agency in this world, and never ever give away your truth.

Gaslight Stoplight End That Ish

The most traumatic issues sistahs come to me seeking divination and spiritual guidance for involve toxic relationships. Usually these women find they've become victims of severe gaslighting on the part of a lover or spouse.

What is gaslighting? *Encyclopedia Britannica* defines gaslighting as "elaborate and insidious techniques of psychological deception and manipulation, it's usually performed on a single victim over an extended period."[10] The goal is to prevent the victim from confidently distinguishing their truth from their gaslighter's falsity, thereby placing the victim's ideas of right and wrong solely in the gaslighter's control. The victim becomes the puppeteer's emotional and intellectual slave with depleted self-esteem and a confused sense of self-worth. Victims are unwilling to accept until too late in the game that the truth—their truth—is unravelling right before their eyes. Victims grow used to blaming themselves and apologizing for wrongs enacted against them while slowly losing their purpose and equal footing in the relationship.

....

10. Brian Duignan, "Encyclopedia Britannica," in *Encyclopedia Britannica* (Chicago, IL: Encyclopedia Britannica, 2002).

EXERCISE: UNREQUITED LOVE BOXING RITUAL

The following ritual is a practical and spiritual way to help you make a break from a toxic relationship, or any relationship. You'll be getting rid of physical items from the relationship.

For some women, detaching from material things brings up deep-seated emotions surrounding, what else, separation anxiety. The moment you realize this is really it, you're changing the locks or even changing the metaphorical address, your life may become a tug of war between soul and spirit. I get it. I've included breathing methods to help you, no matter how hard it gets.

The memories will take time to fade, and you may find yourself tempted to return to the thrift store to buy back everything you gave away. But you've got to cut the cord to set your fierceness free. Physical reminders lying around the house will make resolving the past that much more painful, maybe even impossible.

Needs:

* 1 large cardboard box (*Note: If you need more than one box, bring it on!*)
* 1 roll of packing tape
* 1 permanent marker
* The remains of the relationship

Instructions:

First, box his or her things up. Write the following on the box(es) in big, bold lettering (or type, print, and attach a copy to the box): *I am taking back my voice! I am taking back my sight! I am acknowledging what I hear as truth that I can and will trust! My voice is my right to sing, scream, cry, and laugh as often as I damn well please!*

Next, travel by whatever means available at least nine blocks away from your home. It's fine to travel more than nine but not less. Nine is the number of Oya, the Orisa of change and transformation. Since you're in the process of transforming your life, you need to move in accordance with Oya's space. Oya's energy will allow a spiritual death to take place the moment you cart these items off to a dumpster or thrift store.

Once you've left the items behind, sit in your ride or walk at least a block away before taking a deep breath in and out. Do this deep breathing technique nine times; go slow and don't hyperventilate. This breathing represents the beginnings of our cord-cutting work. If you need to breathe more than nine times, use multiples of nine such as eighteen, twenty-seven, thirty-six, or forty-five.

Once you've settled your spirit, repeat to yourself: *I am taking back my voice! I am taking back my sight! I am acknowledging what I hear as truth that I can and will trust! My voice is my right to sing, scream, cry and laugh as often as I damn well please!*

Return home, taking comfort in the knowledge that from this second on your life will experience contractions. You're on the verge of birthing a new awakening, a new dawn, a new you.

Repeat the following incantation daily until you feel emotionally healed enough to laugh through each line (change the pronouns as needed):

> *there was a knock*
> *at the door*
> *her breath fogged*
> *the keyhole*
> *he could smell her jollof rice and oxtail stew*
> *he said*
> *honey I'm home*

she said
try if you will
but this here body
it ain't got no
open door policy
the day you walked out
I changed
all the locks

Corner Hustlers

I find that anytime we try to cleanse our physical bodies in a need to rid ourselves of trauma, we often overlook the true starting point: clearing out our environment. Most times this oversight leads to a reinfection of our aura. We allow the very psychic doodoo we're trying to wash down the drain to hide in the crevices and corners. They lurk there, waiting for the moment we're horny enough or lonely enough or desperate enough to say, "Maybe this is as good as it gets for me. Who am I to even question deserving more? You get what you get, so don't throw a fit."

EXERCISE: GONNA SWEEP THAT JACKASS OUT OF MY HAIR

The way I have clients avoid corner hustlers (aka dust divers) is by beginning all cleansings with a thorough spiritual sweeping, wall spritz, floor wash, or carpet wash.

Needs:

* 1 all-white outfit (including underwear)
* 1 white head wrap
* myrrh incense sticks, enough for each room of your home (calls forward your ancestor guides to serve as protectors of your emotional state)

* 1 new natural-fiber bristle broom (Swiffer or dust mops aren't acceptable)
* cinnamon (for healing and protection)
* cayenne pepper (removes obstacles)
* red brick dust (protects the home from negative energy)
* 1 brown paper bag

Instructions:

Put on your all-white outfit and head wrap. Begin burning the incense in the first room of your home. Next, sprinkle your broom generously with the cinnamon, cayenne, and red brick dust. Recite this mantra into the broom's bristles three times: *I am taking back my voice! I am taking back my sight! I am acknowledging what I hear as truth that I can and will trust! My voice is my right to sing, scream, cry, and laugh as often as I damn well please!*

Sweep the room, starting with the corners. Pay close attention to the walls and the ceiling. Knock down any cobwebs or dust mites. Sweep all dust, trash, insects, and so on into the paper bag and move to the next room, repeating the ritual beginning with burning the incense. Once you've swept the entire house, close the bag tightly, write your mantra on the outside, and place the bag aside to be discarded on the following day.

Remember the nine blocks or more rule when discarding your residual doodoo. You aren't required to do the deep breathing technique when discarding the bag, but do get the hell out of there without looking back once the deed is done.

EXERCISE: GONNA VACUUM THAT JACKASS OUT OF MY HAIR

If you have carpet instead of hardwood or linoleum floors, I'm not leaving you out. This working makes a carpet powder that can be easily vacuumed and used for healing and protection. (*Note: This recipe can be doubled, depending on the space you need to cover.*)

Needs:

* 1 cup cornstarch or arrowroot powder (improves your future)
* 9 drops each:
  - patchouli oil (separation)
  - rue oil (exorcise past love from the heart)
  - hyssop oil (purification)
* tobacco from 1 cigar (for healing)
* ½ cup fresh coffee grounds with chicory (remove obstacles)
* 1 pestle and mortar
* 1 funnel
* Optional: 1 paper bag if you have a bagless vacuum

Instructions:

Place the cornstarch or arrowroot in a medium bowl. Grind it with the pestle to an even finer texture. Place your tobacco and coffee grounds into the mortar and grind them down until they look like sand. Add the tobacco and grounds to the cornstarch/arrowroot mixture.

Continue grinding and mixing with the pestle. Once the mixture is well-mixed and has a fine consistency, add the oils in succession. Keep mixing as you transition between oils. When the mixture feels evenly blended (remember, you're the Hoodoo woman, you decide), use the funnel to pour the mixture into a large mason jar, seal tightly, and shake for ten minutes.

Unseal the jar and recite the following mantra into it three times: *I am taking back my voice! I am taking back my sight! I am acknowledging what I hear as truth that I can and will trust! My voice is my right to sing, scream, cry, and laugh as often as I damn well please!*

Reseal the jar and voila! Your Hoodoo carpet clearing is ready when you are. Sprinkle and vacuum the past away. When you dump the accumulated carpet trash, follow the same rules as with the previous ritual: Bag it up if you have a bag-less vacuum, write your mantra on your vacuum or paper bag, then drop it off nine blocks away. Then get the hell out of there without looking back.

EXERCISE: YOUR FOOTSTEPS DO NOT MOVE ME NO MORE (FLOOR WASH)

If you have linoleum or hardwood floors, here's a floor wash for you. It removes any residual imprints made by your ex-lover's trek throughout the home. It also opens a path so a new love can find their way to you. This wash also declutters the speedway between where you now are and where you want to be.

Needs:

* 1 extra-large pot (*Note: Use the largest in your home, or borrow a gumbo pot from Grandmama.*)
* 1–2 gallons spring water
* 9 drops each:
  - frankincense oil (protection, uplifts the spirit)
  - myrrh oil (creates peace)
  - orange essence oil (luck in walking toward new love)

* 1–2 spritzes Florida water
* 6 tablespoons each:
    - ground cayenne pepper (heats up your movement toward a new direction)
    - black salt (see recipe below) or 1 ground charcoal disc (prevents you from traveling back into dying relationships)
    - cinnamon (offers success in future lust)
* 2 cups Pine Sol (offers you sexual protection so you won't fall into a fertility trap with a played lover)

Instructions:

Pour the water into the pot, leaving one to two inches of space at the top. Cover and bring to a boil over medium to high heat. Watch the pot closely so you know exactly when it reaches a boil (anywhere from seven to fifteen minutes). When it does, remove it from the heat and add the remaining ingredients. Stir slowly while reciting your mantra three times.

You now have a floor wash you can use immediately or save in a reusable plastic jug for a later date.

EXERCISE: BLACK SALT FROM SCRATCH

You'll find that several of my workings call for black salt like in the previous working. It's easy to make it from scratch and keep on hand.

Needs:

* 3 charcoal discs
* 1 pestle and mortar
* 3 tablespoons white sea salt
* 1 tablespoon soil from a graveyard

* Optional: 3 drops rosemary oil for protection or 3 drops cayenne oil drops to transport negative energy back to the sender

Instructions:

Place the charcoal discs inside the mortar and begin breaking them apart with the pestle. Once the discs are crumbled into smooth grains, add the sea salt and begin mixing them in swirls with the pestle. Add soil and swirl again. Keep swirling until the salt's color is to your liking. For a darker hue, you can add another charcoal disc. Allow your salt to sit outside under the moonlight to charge, or on your ancestral altar. Store in a mason jar.

The Kundalini of Hair

Hair is a creative, lifeforce energy. A yogic belief states that spiritually nurtured hair "helps to raise the kundalini energy (creative lifeforce), which serves to increase our vitality, intuition, and tranquility."[11] Another long-held belief is that the bones of the forehead transmit light to the pineal gland, a pea-size tissue located behind the brain's third ventricle. This gland is responsible for secreting melatonin, a necessary ingredient in keeping our sleep regulated while aiding in proper sexual development. The pineal gland is also responsible for converting nervous system signals into endocrine system signals. This conversion allows us to be better equipped emotionally when handling daily stressors. In other words, we become adept at deciphering when to take flight versus when to fight.

The light transmitted from the forehead bones to the pineal gland medicinally affects our brain growth hormones as well as hormonal changes within our thyroid. In this belief framework cutting bangs as a means of showcasing aesthetic beauty actually impedes the vital transmission of one's life force

....

11. Deva Kauer Singh, "Improve Your Vitality and Meditation with Long Hair," MrSikhNet, September 4, 2007, https://www.mrsikhnet.com/2007/09/04/improve-your-vitality-and -meditation-with-long-hair/.

energy. Yogic belief further states that when the hair on your head is allowed to attain its full, mature length, phosphorus, calcium, and vitamin D are produced. They then enter the lymphatic fluid, and eventually the spinal fluid through two ducts on the top of the brain. This known ionic change creates more efficient memory and leads to greater physical energy, improved stamina, and patience.[12]

Some people view hair as our antennae to the world. These antennae are conduits of cosmic energy. When we cut our hair, it takes eight years for new sustainable antennae to form. These antennae also channel the sun's energy, which aids our brain in meditation, visualization, and in reconfiguring alternative realities that help us channel our way out of depressive episodes. When brushing your hair, try to use wooden combs or brushes to better circulate lifeforce energy. Wooden combs and brushes don't cause or create static electricity like metal combs and brushes or encourage stagnant energy as with plastic combs and brushes.

Hair DNA

Hair contains DNA, which makes it a desirable accoutrement in the hot hands of a jealous rival, ex-lover, estranged spouse, or two-faced relative. In other words, loose hair can be used against us. Once dropped into a cauldron, hair has enough spice to run our asses crazy, make us ill, or cause accidents so severe they send our carefree asses to the emergency room quicker than we can say, "Hell no, that mutha wouldn't!"

Hair, fingernails, toenails, blood, urine, and fecal matter all possess a potent life force energy. Our life force energy makes us who we are both physically and spiritually. As a child I was admonished never to leave hair stuck between the teeth of my mother's bush comb, especially not out in the open for all to see, touch, and manipulate as a weapon against me. Have you ever heard of folks taking your hair, wrapping it around chicken wire, and setting it inside a box along with a curse to cause physical harm or frequent bouts of insanity?

....

12. Alexander Light, "The Spiritual Strength of Hair - Yogic Perspective," Humans Be Free, last modified February 19, 2018, https://humansbefree.com/2018/02/the-spiritual-strength-of -hair-yogic-perspective.html.

My grandmother and mother would place any hair refusing to slither down the rounded innards of beaded cornrows into an ashtray. Then they would use a cigarette to set the hair on fire. The sizzled hair turned to orange then black then gray then ash as the women chanted something along the lines of, "This hair belongs to this child. This hair isn't for sale. No one will twist and turn and bludgeon the life from this child's bones. To the earth goes the ashen hair. To the past goes what was. This hair is ours, hers, the ancestors to own."

There are four ways to dispose of hair, fingernails, blood, saliva, urine, semen, or fecal matter: flush, fire, trash, or bury. Only trash it as a last resort, and do the following: First, wrap the item in newspaper, then place it in a grocery store plastic bag, then inside a plastic zip-top bag. Place the zip-top bag inside a durable garbage bag. Sprinkle a quarter cup of cayenne pepper into the garbage bag, then a quarter cup of ammonia. Finally, tie the bag and trash that ish nine blocks from your home.

EXERCISE: SHAMPOO THAT LOSER RIGHT OUT OF MY HAIR

Our hair also houses remembrance. The best way to separate from those unwanted remembrances is to spiritually cleanse your hair.

Needs:

* ¼–1 cup liquid black soap (amount depends on the thickness, length, and texture of your hair)
* 9 drops each:
  - chamomile oil (calm your nerves)
  - neroli oil (makes you a magnet for joy)
  - jasmine oil (brings prophetic dreams)
  - tea tree oil (heals troubled spirits)
* 9 teaspoons apple cider vinegar (promotes self-love)

Instructions:

Mix or shake all the ingredients in a bowl or plastic squirt bottle. Uncover the mixture and whisper this incantation three times:

> *Hair on my head, release all that bad juju, you got brewing through and through. I'm talking the misguided kundalini, the emotional trauma, the physical strain. Let that muck run down the drain. Hair on my head let this queen live a beautiful life from the top of her head to the soles of her feet. Let my alignment begin with my crown. I wear it well with diamonds, rubies, and pearls; all eyes on me! I am a bad, bad girl! The queen has entered the throne room. Time for all you witches to bow down. You can look but don't even think about touching this crown!*

Work the shampoo into your hair naturally. Let it sit for ten to fifteen minutes, rinse, and move on.

EXERCISE: RECONDITIONING MY HAIR

Here's a follow-up conditioner to the previous shampoo ritual. It will help your hair and further power your intention.

Needs:

* ¼–1 cup shea butter, melted (amount depends on the thickness, length, and texture of your hair; shea butter should be warm, not hot)
* 9 drops jasmine oil
* ¼ cup coconut cream (prevents rebound sex and promotes chastity)

Instructions:

Follow the same mixing instructions for the shampoo and recite the same incantation three times, then use the conditioner

as you normally do. Let it sit for ten to fifteen minutes before rinsing. Cover your head in a white cloth or scarf after you dry, roll, braid, or plait.

The Convenient Art of Spritzing

How many of us have walked into a room after either being in an argument or by happenstance and traveled through a battleground of off-the-cuff expletives and heinous insinuations? In these instances, how many of us have felt the asphyxiating contempt ready and able to knock you off your feet? I have, and trust me, it isn't an easy experience. There are times I've become unhinged, succumbing to and feeding off this haze of indignation with such voracity that I slice through the flesh of every person in the room until all that remains are blood-stained walls and carcasses I happily used as toothpicks. (I do mean that figuratively.)

On more than one occasion, I've found myself in an erratic state of crying, laughing, and screaming for Oya to please cut the cord on this whack BS. In these moments, my spritz bottle was my saving grace. It contains an herbal solution in a holy water base that realigns my chakras and brings much-needed calm back to my daily grind.

"Spray first, ask questions later" is my spritz mantra. Usually before I cross the threshold of any room, I pull my juice gun from my purse and let the atmosphere have three squishes. I wait for a count of ten, then freely walk into the space without a care in the world. If I'm going to spend a lot of time there, I spritz the walls, corners, and doors too. I spritz where I sit. If I need to touch the phone, I spritz that too.

A word of caution: there are folks with allergies, so be careful how much mist you spritz into the air. In lieu of spraying objects directly, you can also spritz a napkin and wipe down objects like public phones, bathroom stalls, and water faucets; restaurant plates, cups, knives, forks, and spoons; communal writing utensils; and so on. These objects all hold the residue of every person that comes and goes, but more important, these objects hold every emotional state the wielders of these objects introduced into the terrain, knowingly or unknowingly. It's up to those of us who know better to be about the business of doing better with the lives we were given.

EXERCISE: IF THESE WALLS COULD SPLIT, THEY WOULD RUN FROM MY SPRITZ (ROOM/WALL SPRITZ)

The following exercise is specifically for use at home on walls, doors, windows, or furnishings as part of your healing process. But the method can be used at work to achieve the same intent. You can even use it in hotels for spiritually clearing the atmosphere of your secluded getaways.

Needs:

* 1 funnel
* 1 plastic spray bottle
* 3–4 cups spring water, sea water, or rainwater, enough to fill a medium to large pot halfway (*Note: If you use rainwater, collect it after a thunderstorm.*)
* 6 tablespoons dry parsley (calms and protects)
* 6 tablespoons dry basil (cleans the vibrational energy vortex)
* 1 tablespoon dry mint (mental rejuvenation)
* 9 drops vetiver oil (soothes the mind)
* 9 drops sandalwood oil (enhances transformation)
* ½ cup grapeseed oil (mental power)
* ½ cup whiskey (banishes stale energies and fires up concoction)
* Optional: 1 strainer

Instructions:

Fill a medium to large pot halfway with the water, bring to a boil, then remove from the heat. Add your herbs, oils, and whiskey. Cover the pot and let it sit for fifteen minutes untouched.

Meanwhile, move your hands in a counterclockwise motion as you recite the following incantation three times: *Boiled water, herbs, and oils. Trauma be gone from my life. Wash these walls, these nooks and crannies. Holy water, purge the lies, tears, and vanity lusting from wall to floor, to door, to tools scattered around this witch's room. I banish you. I banish your tormented energy. I'm not your host, and you, you repugnant muthafucka, won't become my ghost.*

After the fifteen minutes have passed and you're done with the recitation, uncover the pot and stir the concoction in a clockwise motion. Repeat the incantation three more times.

Now you're ready to portion the water into the spray bottle using the funnel. You can strain out the herbs or leave some floating throughout solution, whichever you prefer. As you fill the bottle, leave two to three inches of space at the top.

Now go on and spritz away! Spritz your walls, doors, windows, or furnishings. The remaining concoction can be saved up to a month in an airtight plastic jug. You can place it in a cool dark cupboard area near the floor or freeze it if you have the space.

Your Peace Belongs to You

Now that you're done ridding yourself of what you don't want, you'll want a sense of peace in return. You want to feel tranquil enough within your own skin before venturing out to give this love thang another try. Dissolving a relationship can make you feel yucky, icky, and maybe even like your flesh—at least the top layer—belongs to somebody else. Think about the intimacy you and your ex-lover shared. Think about all those intense moments of pleasure still taking up residence in your pores. That was once a titillating idea to mull. Now it feels just plain ole yucky. A good bath is exactly what you need to emotionally disrobe from the residue lurking within.

EXERCISE: CANNOT STEAL MY ZEN SPIRITUAL BATH

Needs:

* 1 bar of black soap (spiritually tears away at the layers of trauma)
* 1 plastic zip-top bag
* ¼ cup each:
    – pink Himalayan sea salt (keeps you faithful to yourself above all)
    – Epsom salt (breaks the curse of choosing wrong lovers)
    – baking soda (releases debris and protects the heart space)
* 9 drops each:
    – patchouli oil (creates separation from negative vibrations)
    – rue oil (breaks hexes and curses)
    – hyssop (purifies the body's aural temperature)
* 3 cups goat milk (turns bad luck into good luck)
* 1 cup pink and red carnation petals (soothes heartbreak)
* 2–3 Nag Champa incense sticks (creates a meditative healing environment)
* 1 blue seven-day candle
* 1 all-white outfit (underwear included)
* 1 black obsidian yoni egg (*Note: Obsidian helps cut the cords of traumatic experiences by absorbing any unsettling vibrations that have accumulated in our womb space. See* chapter 3 *for more information on buying and caring for yoni eggs.*)
* Optional: 1 index card and permanent marker

Instructions:

Take the bar of black soap and carve the following sigil into it.

This is the Hye Won Hye, an Adinkra symbol that means "that which does not burn." If you're into carving, you can also carve the phrase into the soap. If you don't feel comfortable carving, you can write the phrase or draw the image on an index card and place it inside the plastic zip-top bag with the soap. Seal the bag closed.

Place the soap under your pillow for a night. You can do this step ahead of time and even if you don't need a spiritual bath. If you do, store the sealed soap in a drawer until you need it.

On the night of your bath, mix the salts, oils, goat milk, and petals in a bowl or plastic container. Draw a bath. When it's ready, sprinkle the herbal mixture into the water. Use your hand to swish the water around, ensuring the ingredients are evenly distributed. When finished, chant:

Body, body, sexy body, wake up and soothe this wise woman warrior. Do not let the world steal my joy! Do not let the words or actions of fools ruin my mood. Queens do not bow to mere mortals. This is my sovereign right to be gloriously revered and to flaunt my assets around, as the world is my pedestal. My mind and my will must heal. I was born to endure! I was born to rise out of the flames, majestic, intelligent, ferocious, and sensually satisfying. Bye-bye, drama. You have no place in my domain. See

you again never, heifer, now crawl your ass down the drain.

Next, light all the incense and the candle. Get into the bath. Lather your soap and wash your hands first, then face, then work your way down to the soles of your feet. Scrub as if you've just come from mud wrestling. You can use a loofah or a towel, but soap to body works fine. Rinse and wash two more times.

Sit for fifteen to twenty minutes more until the incense sticks are completely infused into the air, then step out of the water and dry off. Leave your soap out overnight to dry. Sprinkle water on the candle's flame but don't blow it out. Remember, blowing it out blows your blessings away.

Proceed toward your bedroom. Dress in all white from head to toe. Pop in that yoni egg with the fat end first and push it as far up as you can. Close your eyes and go to sleep. This closes the ritual and seals your transformation.

In the morning allow your egg to come out on its own, or you can push down as if you're having a bowel movement and the egg will plop out. Remember to keep a towel under you to catch it and prevent the egg from chipping. Wash and dry your yoni egg before storing it away as previously instructed. Store your soap, which should be dry, inside the plastic zip-top bag somewhere it won't get mixed with other soaps.

Spiritual baths are highly purposeful, so try not to become addicted. Knowing when to use these baths is half the battle, but knowing when *not* to is being an empathic empress. A good idea for new witches is no more than twice a month. Once you become proficient in identifying human and inanimate situational stressors, you'll grow more adept at avoiding burning buildings while wearing a gasoline thong, and you won't need the bath as much. Even when life is on point, I'll only do a spiritual bath at most once a month. This covers me against lurking negative attachments that may go on out of sight, or even out of my mind's eye.

Yoni Exercises for Survivors of Sexual Assault

It may be difficult for victims of sexual assault to connect with their yoni spirit, especially when sex magickal journeys feel particularly intense. Luckily there are other spiritually therapeutic methods that can help. We live in a society where sex trafficking, child pornography, and rape are rampant visuals in the news, on television, in newspapers, and in major motion pictures. Sexual trauma can make it difficult to engage in sexual intercourse and may lead to years of trying to reclaim one's sexual identity. Survivor stories of the Me Too Movement and celebrity allegations of high-profile television and motion picture actors and executives are forcing society to acknowledge that there's a real problem when *no* isn't enough. And despite this, *no* is often portrayed as a joke, a sign of weakness, or a lack of commitment to sealing the deal. Victims are left wondering how they become more than the sum of their experiences.

Post-Traumatic Stress Disorder (PTSD) decreases a person's libido exponentially. Sex happens in both the body and the brain. When the brain views sex as dangerous, the brain determines it's better to seek flight over arousal. It's important for survivors to seek professional therapy along with any spiritual work.

EXERCISE: HOLDING SOUL SPACE FOR THE YONI OR LINGAM

This ritual can bring forth a calming effect on the brain and yoni soul space. If you're a male-bodied person wanting to connect with lingam (penis) spirit, you too can benefit from this working. It can be performed as often as you like and at any time of the day or night.

Needs:

* 1 blue candle (opens the mind, heart, and soul to strong healing)
* a recording of the 396 Hz solfeggio frequency (reduces fear and guilt associated with trauma; *Note: To find a recording of the frequency, search for "396 Hz" online. You'll find many options to choose from.*)
* 3 tarot cards:
    - the Star (instills hope)
    - the Two of Cups (calls forth healing)
    - Temperance (ensures healing for the future)
* 3 cotton balls
* 1 saucer
* 9 drops lemongrass oil, divided (reduces depression)
* 1 orange incense stick (reduces the deepening effects of PTSD)

Instructions:

Light the candle, start the frequency, and lay the cards in front of you, either on the floor or on a table. Place the cotton balls on the saucer and drop three drops of oil onto each one. Light the incense. Sit with your back against a chair or a wall (if you're sitting against the wall, sit on a pillow or yoga mat).

Place both hands, one on top of the other, over your heart space. Inhale with your mouth closed. As you inhale, extend your abdomen. Hold for five seconds. Exhale and release your stomach. As you release, create a low guttural, sound, like a heavy sigh.

Repeat ten times, making sure not to hyperventilate.

Repeat the inhale and exhale ritual. This time as you breathe in instead of extending your stomach, grip your pelvic muscles. (These muscles support your bladder by controlling

your urine flow—think of the gripping as if you were stopping yourself from urinating.) Repeat ten times.

As you breathe, stare at the cards, envisioning them cleaning your aura of emotional pain. Take in the smells of lemon and orange. Feel your heart beating out love for your survival.

Sit for as long as you like after completing the breathing, then extinguish the candle and deposit the cotton balls in the corners of your room. Allow the incense to do its thing. You can vacuum the cotton balls up later.

The Two of Cups is an excellent card to take with you when you visit the therapist to aid in healing. Just tuck it in your pocket or purse.

Juju on the Fly

The Queen of Spades card allows you to witness the power of manifesting your divine right to change your own mood, attitude, and emotional reaction to situations you believed to be going one way but that turned out to be adversely affecting your life. The card's energy demands that you spend less time getting bent out of shape over other folks' decisions and keep a closer eye on your own journey. In addition, this card makes folks pay for making your journey a painful lesson in unrequited love. People will forever be people.

When I was in high school, I was desperate to find a boyfriend. All my friends had one and were having sex, so they said. I was tired of being the virgin in the crew and the girl who had never been kissed. Then, in my junior year, I had my first best friend–approved boyfriend. I was over the moon in love, so I thought. One weekend day early in our relationship my sister saw him out at the grocery store with his hand down the pants of another girl. Their lips were so tightly interwoven he didn't notice my sister stepping up to him and calling his name. When he regained his consciousness, he double-blinked and took one long gulp before smiling at my sister and playing it off with, "Your sister knows we're just friends. She's saving it, and I'm just not with that." My sister shouted profanity at him and then threatened to run him over if he didn't get out of the store by the time she checked out.

The following Monday, I confronted him at school. It was around 7:20 a.m. and we were standing on the staircase preparing to deliver invitations to the JROTC ball. He was standing at the top of the stairs when he began screaming at me about how he could do whatever he wanted. Then he punched me in the chest, and I fell down a flight of stairs. He walked out and left me blacked out and bleeding. The last thing I remembered was him stepping over my body and snatching the invitations from my hands. In the nurse's office I remember trying to process what had happened. I remember my best friend's sister checking me out to take me to the doctor's office. My best friend had convinced her to pretend she was my sister. She had told her the situation was a dire one, and that it had to be handled in secrecy.

This was a time before school secretaries cared about forms of identification to check a student out. If you showed up and were an adult who seemed to display good character, you could sign out anybody you wanted to. After a brief stint at the hospital to receive stitches and pain pills for my shoulder, I went home to heal. Thankfully I had thought to contort my body at the last minute, twisting to my left so the impact was less severe for my head. I told the same story to everybody: I had slipped and lost my footing. Only my best friend knew the truth.

A week later, a woman I met through my best friend gave me a card: the Queen of Spades. She told me, "Witches heal, they love, they protect, and they get their revenge in life and in death." She explained how this card would allow my revenge to manifest; in time I would witness his failure. Within a month he was dismissed from the drill team. He also wrecked his mother's car, slipped in the shower at his girlfriend's house, and broke his leg. A case of mistaken identity got him jumped and fist-fighting five boys from a rival neighborhood.

I'm not here to celebrate causing havoc for the sake of causing havoc. I'm here to encourage utilizing magickal alternatives to aggression. We are nobody's punching bag, and magick has its own way of soothing our troubles. The better acquainted we are with speaking to the spirits the more open they are to having our back in times of crisis.

The Queen of Spades not only stops you from making other folks' obstacles your burden but also warns that when you see a train derailing, jump off. It ain't good for your physical nor mental health to stay put. Think about how you, now, process your reactions to situations that are in your control versus those that are outside of your control. Which situations proved more fulfilling? Was it managing a situation that adversely affected you or trying to alter somebody else's course as they kicked, scratched, and bit you every step of the way?

I saw a meme recently where a man was on the beach with a mop and a bucket. He was trying to mop the ocean water up every time it crashed against the shore. The caption read something like "This is what you look like trying to control a Universe of constant change. Release folks who invite drama and pain into your life by allowing them to drift off to sea. Stop mopping up after them." Managing other folks' lives is a battle we'll never win, even with a fresh mop straight out of the plastic wrap.

EXERCISE: HARD HEAD MAKES A SOFT BEHIND

Needs:

* 1 teaspoon extra-hot sauce (brings the vexation of pain to a foul individual's spirit)
* 1 photo of the person (*Note: Make sure your target is the only face in the picture.*)
* 3 bay leaves (brings satisfaction and reroutes the course of a life that needs protection and boundaries)
* 1 black marker
* 1 Queen of Spades playing card
* 1 roll of tape
* 1 left shoe (*Note: You'll be wearing it for nine consecutive days, so make sure it's from a pair you adore.*)
* 1 black satchel

Instructions:

The night before the work, pour the hot sauce over the photo. Leave it on a towel overnight to help it dry out.

On each of the bay leaves write a one-word outcome you'd like to see manifest at the completion of this work. Examples might be freedom, healing, or esteem. These should be for you.

The next morning, tape the photo to the bottom of your left shoe. Place the Queen of Spades card and the bay leaves inside the satchel and tie the bag tightly. Keep repeating the words you wrote on each leaf and envision yourself enjoying the outcomes you've set in balance for yourself. Attach the satchel to your bra strap, or place it in your purse near your wallet. Throughout the day, stomp your left foot and scratch it against the concrete to send reverberating pain to your target. As you do, think about what they deserve and how that pain will manifest in their lives.

Chapter Five
Cold Hard Cash

I know you were waiting patiently for the section on money rituals. Make that money, money! I get it. You're ready to hear how one itty bitty spell can have you swimming in Benjamins, lounging in condominiums, strutting on a nude beach, or sipping sangria while nibbling on barbecue shrimp. Well, sistahs, have a seat. Breathe into a paper bag if you must. I'm so sorry to be the full-bladdered witch insistently pissing on your parade, but the key ingredient to money spells as I construct them is talent. Nothing from nothing leaves nothing—you may be familiar with that phrase. You must have something if you want the green to lean inside your wallet.

Finding a way to earn money begins with finding the best way one can employ their talents in service to their individual greater good. This is easier said than sorted through. There are times a person has no clue where their talents lie. This may cause them to run full throttle into jobs and careers that may pay well but end up killing their spirit in the long run. These people often try to play catch up ten to fifteen years before retirement, or they make a serious and purposeful reinvestment in their creative endeavors by channeling their dreams into their second life. Second life is the understanding that at age fifty one will live life doing whatever they've spent the previous forty-nine years putting off. It's now their time to shine, in other words.

Some of you might think it isn't godly to be overly concerned with money. I can remember a time a preacher taught us that money is the root of all evil. Yet those same preachers demanded we tithe 10 percent of our earnings in the name of an omnipotent sky god and his omnipresent son. In her book *The Millionaires of the Bible,* author Catherine Ponder writes, "Religious leaders put down prosperity from the pulpit. Yet burden their followers by calling for increased offerings."[13] Now, I'm not about to go on an antitithe

13. Catherine Ponder, *The Millionaire from Nazareth: His Prosperity Secrets for You!* (Camarillo, CA: Devorss & Co, 1979), 14.

spill. It's your money do with it what you please. However, there are many published books, like Ponder's that speak to the finances of well-known religious figures.

In her book, Ponder aims to expose the net worth of biblical rock stars such as Abraham, Isaac, Jacob, Joseph, Moses, and even Jesus Christ. According to Ponder, none of these biblical icons ever tight-roped near a poverty line, nor did they encourage those who encountered them to accept poverty as a means to spiritual enlightenment. She asserts that "Jesus was the wealthiest man who ever trod the earth. He was a wonder-working mind that could turn ordinary water into wine, multiply bread and fish to feed thousands, raise the dead to life and heal all manner of disease."[14] Through a belief in prayer and the riches in heaven, Jesus recognized that having had his father's power bestowed on him, this same power could also help people achieve their earthly desires. A reading of Ponder's book will lead you to the understanding that neither God nor Jesus wants you to be poor. According to Luke 12:32, "it is your father's good pleasure to give you the kingdom."[15]

Inspirational Voice: Nina Simone

Nina Simone's net worth was somewhere between one and five million dollars in 1965. Whatever your opinion of her, you must admit that's gangsta considering she was an artist who had her ups and downs. She ultimately fought and won the right to do her shit her way, and it didn't matter who resented it. I know there were moments in her life when she struggled. I know about White folks and Black folks behaving badly in her life, bringing the anxiety and the dysfunction as only haters could.

Then there are the ones who unearthed Nina's legacy. I'm referring to the young Black women and men who, on an expedition through a video or a music streaming service, or even traveling through their parents' or grandparents' record collection discovered the incomparable Empress Nina Simone for the first time. They may have felt cheated for not knowing the freedom of such a haunting voice before that moment. Penning noncrossover songs

....
14. Ponder, *Millionaire from Nazareth*, 18
15. King James Version (KJV)

like "To Be Young, Gifted and Black" meant Madame Simone would never achieve the fame of an Aretha Franklin or Diana Ross. Yet her visceral word wizardry is forever a reminder of the sinister murders of Medgar Evers and the Sixteenth Street Baptist Church bombing that killed Addie Mae Collins, Cynthia Wesley, Carole Robertson, and Carol Denise McNair.

Radio stations saw "Mississippi Goddamn" as an incendiary slap in the face of a White America that wanted a tame pianist entertaining a dimly lit stage, classically trained and voiceless. What they got was Nina Simone, whom southern stations banned; in fits of derogatory ecstasy, they even broke her records. As Dick Gregory put it, "We all wanted to say it and she said it."[16] At concerts she was so fueled and outspoken against racism that she was known to ask concertgoers if they were ready to kill if necessary. Who do you know today would do that? Tell me that ain't high priestess energy.

It was Ancestress Nina's voice, her poetry, and her rage that taught me to value the many faces of women who live within me as I've lived within them, taking no part of their emotional, sensual, and spiritual being for granted. We've been victimized by society since our enslavement and forced to do whatever it takes to survive, "by hook or crook," my mother would say, by force or choice—money is and has always been the link to our survival. Yet as women, we've never run from owning our keep. There's no shame in how we choose to feed our children or our dreams, unless we give in to self-ridicule.

As unapologetic as she was with her music, Nina was just as unapologetic in her presentation. Some iconic moments of style in Empress Nina Simone's life are the netted jumpsuit she wore in 1967, her hairstyle in 1968 during that London portrait session, and her Egyptian-style draped headdress. Nina proved time and time again to be just as much a free spirit in fashion as she was in song, blending bold prints with retro classics. From evening gowns bangled earrings and oversized sunglasses Nina flavored our lives for decades. Through her sassy dress she taught us to honor our Black beauty, our inherent intelligence, and the culture we nurture within.

....

16. Aaron Gustafson, "Nina Simone 'Said It' When Others Couldn't," Aaron Gustafson, February 14, 2019, https://www.aaron-gustafson.com/notebook/nina-simone-said-it-when-others-were-afraid-to/.

For me, her energy heightens our money rituals because she teaches us to speak our truth no matter who pays us or how much they consider our talent's worth. We imbue a freedom to live not as slaves to a dollar but as masters of our own financial security.

EXERCISE: BABY, I'M A STAR RITUAL

This ritual will help you connect to your own star power and help you align with your talents.

Needs:

* 1 pair of gold shoes in your size (*Note: You'll be wearing them for nine consecutive days, so make sure it's a pair you adore.*)
* 1 shoebox
* A selection of crafting supplies:
    - 1–2 packs of gold star stickers
    - Any color glitter glue or glitter and glue
    - Various markers of all colors
    - Construction paper or wrapping paper
    - Craft paints
    - Gold material
* pictures that speak to your talents and dreams of success (*Note: These can come from anywhere: magazines, newspapers, websites, etc.*)
* 1 gold candle (brings spiritual attainment and fortune)
* 1 freestanding mirror
* 10 index cards
* 1 piece of carnelian gemstone (increases creativity, motivation and self-expression)
* 1 gold satchel big enough to hold the gemstone

Instructions:

Decorate the shoebox and its lid, inside and out, using the craft supplies; glue down your pictures too. I like to paint the insides of the lid and box and then place stars all over, but it's up to you.

Once you're done decorating, close the box and place the shoes on top. Put the candle near the box and light it. Then place the mirror behind the candle. The candle should be reflected in the mirror.

Take the ten index cards and on one side of each card write the name of a person whose life you admire. It could be any-body—a writer, dancer, singer, actress, athlete, and so on. On the opposite side write what you admire about their will, their grit, their passion in one sentence. If ten cards are too many, use as many as you can.

When done, place the carnelian on top of the stack of index cards. Let the candle burn and the items stay enshrined for an hour. Afterward, read each card out loud, front and back. Once done, tell the shoes they will be your key to unearthing your hidden talents.

When you're done, place the stone in the satchel and tie it to your bra strap, or put it in your pocket or purse. Keep it with you every day. Place one of the index cards in your purse or pocket as well. Take it out and read it throughout the day. Make it a ritual to wear the shoes at least once a week.

Do this ritual in its entirety once a month for the next four months and anytime thereafter when your talent radar needs reconfiguring. In time you'll become the talented diva of your dreams.

Hoodoo Superstar

Years ago, after seventeen years of perms, wash and sets, and braids, my family's regular hairdresser, Mrs. Betty, succumbed to severe leg trauma and deep vein thrombosis, which were accompanied by painful spasms. Standing on her feet from 6:00 a.m. to well past 2:00 a.m. five days a week caught up with Mrs. Betty in the worst way imaginable. When over-the-counter pain killers no longer quelled the tingling tightness, she cancelled appointments more often than not.

In time, Mrs. Betty's cocktail of self-medicated elixirs included two main ingredients: Percocet and Moscato. She quickly became a bedridden, zombified shell of her normal self. Her inebriated stupors left our new growth shedding even more tears than our eye sockets. The women in my immediate family found themselves floundering along with the rest of Mrs. Betty's regulars, scouring the streets of New Orleans for a reasonably priced back-up beautician.

My aunt Cleola Williams was known as the family's bargain hunter. She was a woman famous for never hitching her new growth to the hot comb of any one beautician. Aunt Cleola was a free agent, always on the prowl for a deal she couldn't refuse. When the unfathomable happened—our perms were ten weeks past due—she found just the woman for us: Sharon Delacroix, a fortysomething caramel-colored woman who wore her hair in a jet-black mushroom bob. For twenty dollars, Mrs. Delacroix would not only perm, wash, color, set, dry, and style your hair, she would also read your palms and feed you, a deal she offered every customer who crossed the threshold of her makeshift beauty shop.

Mama, my sister, and I filed into Mrs. Delacroix's haint-blue house excited to finally straighten the crowd of kernel-size follicles congregating one on top of the other, soaking up every drop of Vaseline we put on them. (We used Vaseline on our itching scalps to hold off the urge to tear chunks of hair out by the roots.) Those visits to Mrs. Delacroix were also four to six hours of calm away from my stepfather, who drank vodka and gin like Prohibition was coming back.

Mrs. Delacroix's home was tucked inconspicuously behind a fast-food restaurant. Inside her walls were covered in vision boards and vodoun veve encased behind glass frames. The entire house smelled of pumpkin spice, lavender, and orange blossoms. There were tea light candles guiding anyone who entered toward the kitchen and away from the hall with the beaded curtain separating the living room from her séance room.

I once tried to enter the forbidden séance room. I tiptoed toward the beaded curtain, my fingertips tickling the golden knob. But just when the room was within my grasp, Mrs. Sharon stepped in front of the door, her fingers held in what I now know was a mudra. She smiled. "No, no, that room is for trained spiritualists only. It's not a playground for curious children. You must be ready when it calls again. You must be prepared to devote a lifetime of study to channeling the dead. Maybe when you're old enough the spirits will turn the knob for you—open sesame." She studied my mangled new growth and grinned even wider. "Women come to me for the same reason you here. You just don't know it yet cause you too young. They don't want to have to worship no man's wallet. Listen to what I say and watch everything I do. When you old enough to choose a lover, you'll remember how easy it is to become a man's slave when his money makes the laws for you and, in his eyes, you in no better position than the children you gave birth to."

Vision Boards

It was probably on my third or fourth visit to Mrs. Delacroix's that she first introduced me to the construction of vision boards. She'd caught me running my fingers over the glittery laminated vision boards that lined her walls while my mother, aunt, and sister were safely tucked under her soundproof hair dryers.

At first I resisted, thinking these boards were nothing more than time fillers designed to occupy a curious child. But I eventually learned her home was always full of women who learned how to live a life of abundance and joy through the casting of these vision boards. She assured me she wasn't trying to play grown-folk mind games on me, nor was crafting a vision board another name for scrapbooking. "Don't get it twisted," she said. "This is magick. It's how you'll petition the Universe for whatever you want, and if you feed the Universe, the Universe will feed you." I liked her description of feeding the Universe—it seemed so sci-fi and otherworldly that I closed my eyes and began to envision a real need, my intention.

In time, my mother proved the efficacy of Mrs. Delacroix's vision board recipe. She meticulously ushered in a world of abundance in the form of a j-o-b that made her a financial force to be reckoned with. Mama's vision board abundance wasn't always fashioned in the form of money but rather opportunities that led to empowerment, which eventually led to financial gain. For example, my mother's rise in status at her lodge led her to becoming a grand secretary for the State of Louisiana. This rise in social status led to cross-country travel and networking with powerful people who recognized her vast managerial skills weren't being properly utilized.

This work has never failed me. Anytime I feel my finances require a boost, I go full vision board. The petition on my very first board (which I made while sitting on Mrs. Delacroix's couch) involved a reward: "Spirit of Day, Spirit of Night, make it so my poem wins the contest. Make it so I win the ice cream sundae attached."

A week later, I was walking home from school with a blue and gold first-place ribbon. In my blouse pocket was a twenty-five-dollar gift certificate to a toy store. I giggled for five blocks, singing, "Mrs. Delacroix's a witch. She might be a fairy. She can change your sad face to merry. She got magick on posters and magick in jars. She got magick on leaves and magick buried under trees. Mrs. Delacroix's a witch. She might be a fairy. She might be from New Orleans, might be from Mars. Mrs. Delacroix's a Hoodoo superstar."

EXERCISE: MRS. DELACROIX'S VISION BOARD

I still use Mrs. Delacroix's vision board recipe today with minor adjustments to fit my own Spirit. Give it a try to realize your own abundance and joy.

Needs:

* 1 poster board, 8½ x 11 inches
* 1 pair of scissors
* 1 roll of tape or glue
* pictures from magazines, computer clipart, photographs
* 1 picture of you
* your perfume, or Florida water or rose water in a spray bottle
* 1 aluminum baking pan, 9 x 11 inches *(Note: If you need to use a board larger than any available pan, perform the work outside with a large garbage bag or two acting as the base level for burying.)*
* 2–4 cups graveyard dirt
* 1 marker
* Optional: a few strands of hair or a small amount of blood *(Note: If you add blood to your board, use a sterile lancet. You can purchase these at any pharmacy.)*
* Optional: a laminating pouch and iron

Instructions

Mrs. Delacroix would begin her vision boards by meditating on her intention. You should do the same. Think about what you want to achieve and what it looks like to be successful at it. Mold this in your mind. Allow your meditation to birth a specific set of two to three sentences about your intention.

On the day of a full moon, lay out the poster board and craft supplies. Write out and answer these questions on your poster board: *What do I want to achieve? What do I need*

today, in a month, and in a year to aid me in achieving this
outcome? What would the ultimate success look like in regard
to this achievement?

Next, glue down pictures of what you want. Include a
picture of yourself at the center. If you don't have a photo, write
your name. Let the glue dry.

Next, spray your perfume into the air and fan the board
through it. At this point, you can add a few optional strands of
your hair or drops of blood if you like.

After she was done, Mrs. Delacroix would laminate her
board. This step is also optional. If you choose to do this,
follow the instructions on the laminating pouch. It typically
requires an iron on warm, not high heat. Make sure it's fully
cool and complete before moving to the next step.

Place a few cups of graveyard dirt in your baking pan,
smoothing out the dirt until it covers the base. Place your board
on top of the dirt, then cover the board with more dirt. Make
sure it's fully covered.

That night, place the board outside under the full moon. The
moon opens a portal between the world of your intention and
your physical realm, allowing your spirit guides to clear a path
of success within your spiritual world. This path inadvertently
bleeds into the desires of your physical world in such a way
that you spiritually and physically begin to manifest your astral
intentions within the physical plane.

The next morning, hang the board inside your home as
an acknowledgment that the vision quest is within reach as
the spirit guides are working overtime to guide our steps to
abundance.

A Fool's Journey

Let's return to the idea that talent should be the main ingredient in your money spells. I didn't pull this concept out of my butt—you must bring a bona fide skill to the table if you want to increase your chances of seeing potent results.

I've met women whose idea of a money spell is having magick materialize a rich man who'll hand over his bank account to run through as they please. I'm here to tell you that no one wakes up with a superhero pussy, and even superhero pussy doesn't have the power to bleed a bank account dry. If your idea of putting work into getting what you want is for a man to keep his wallet open, there are jobs for you. I can think of two: prostitution or one of those social media models with paid links attached.

My point is, be prepared to work for what you want so that you can unequivocally respect the journey. Put your Ase on it, then you can let magick have the final say. If after that you still believe a man equals money, I won't judge you. I will ask that you first go pull out your tarot deck and head straight for the Fool card.

The Fool is often depicted as being oblivious to what comes next in life but willing to trust blindly anyway. The Fool is unphased by those who, out of jealousy or regret, say it's important to be realistic or to stay in stable situations even when they're unfulfilling. When self-assured, the Fool is on a quest toward freedom and liberation, whether from gender roles, status symbols, fake friends, or shallow trends.

Here's an example: imagine your girlfriend is boasting about a new man who buys her whatever she wants and treats her like a queen. He insists she doesn't have to work; she just needs to be beautiful for him 24/7. Listening to this, the self-hating Fool in you believes that if you could only reach an ideal state of beauty—whether by losing weight, buying a longer weave, investing in curlier lashes, bracing up your teeth, bleaching your skin, buying a bigger butt and boobs—you too could find a man who'd whisk you away from your 9 to 5. However, what your friend isn't telling you is that it's damned near impossible to play Barbie all day every day. Not only is she emotionally taxed, but physically, she just wants an oyster po'boy.

You can't spend your life on a Fool's journey where you're molded by somebody else's whims. What happens when your value to them runs its course? Forever Fools can also get stuck because they're convinced irrevocable mistakes are waiting for the moment they decide to take another path.

We've all played the Fool at some point, but the self-assured diva won't get sucked down that rabbit hole. She may have tried to play that game, but since it didn't work, she's now walking toward a new portal.

EXERCISE: THE SUPERHERO PUSSY REHAB RITUAL

Here's a working for pussies feeling overworked and disrespected. It's a rehab ritual to keep you from becoming forever the Fool. Not every person will need to perform this spell, and that's okay. You'll know without a shadow of a doubt if your looks or what lies between your legs has become your primary source of currency. If after introspection you answer yes, this spell has your name written all over it.

Needs:

* 2 paper plates
* 1 black marker
* 1 black candle in a glass container (banishes while healing)
* 1 white plate
* Black salt (heals by keeping out)
* 1 Joker playing card
* 1 piece of selenite (cleanses)
* 1 Fool tarot card
* 1 piece of black tourmaline (emits a force field of good energy)
* 1 handheld mirror
* 1 picture of you in your youth (between birth and your teenage years)

* 1 picture of you now
* 1 vase filled with water
* 1 brown paper bag
* 1 freestanding dildo
* 1 pocket pussy

Instructions:

Write *penis envy* on one plate and *pussy envy* on the other. Set aside.

Next, take the black candle and place it on the white plate. Make a circle of salt inside the plate. Then, using the black marker, write across the Joker card *Have your fun. You're about to be done.*

Place the Joker to the left of the candle and the Fool to the right. Put the selenite on top of the Joker card and the tourmaline on top of the Fool card. Next, prop your current picture against the candle's glass. Position the mirror so it faces your image as if your picture is staring into the mirror.

Next, place the vase with water next to the candle, close enough that their sides touch. Position the photo of you in your youth against the vase of water. Place your penis envy plate on the table and put the dildo on the plate, then put the pussy envy plate on the table with the pocket pussy on top.

Light the candle. Tell Penis or Pussy about your first sexual encounter—How did it make you feel? How did the encounter shape your sexual worldview. Tell them about your most painful experiences, and your most fulfilling. Discuss the ways you use sex as a weapon, a tool, proof that men or women cheat. Talk about how sex often becomes proof that sex isn't love and love isn't sex.

Next, mother them both by offering each candle three compliments. Place your hands on your sacred sex and offer it three compliments. Touch your heart space and promise yourself to

honor love and sex as pleasure, not as a tool to manipulate others through hate and jealousy.

Sit for fifteen minutes listening to music that inspires you. Try Nina Simone's "In the Dark," "Since I Fell for You," and "Turn Me On." Repeat this exercise once a week for nine weeks.

Hoe Cake Profits

My mother likes to tell the story of how her own mother introduced the term *hoe cake* into their family vernacular. According to my grandmother, after exhausting their goddess-given talents for the evening, Black prostitutes would earn extra cash by offering their customers a little heat from their kitchen. For a fee these gents and ladies could buy a deliciously round sweet cake from the hoe's kitchen, which was affectionately called a "hoe cake." These cakes, which were more like pancakes than layer cakes, were also sometimes called Johnny Cakes, no doubt in honor of the "johns" or purchasers of the sexual healing acts.

Now my grandmother said they came with hints of cinnamon or nutmeg or vanilla and were served draped in molasses or maple syrup alongside a cup of black coffee. Some women turned immense profits from baking hoe cakes, which oftentimes exceeded their earnings from sex work. These women eventually moved on to more legal enterprises and even became comfortable businesswomen.

In honor of the hardworking women who chose to sell their sex and weren't simply pimped into a life of prostitution, I share with you the following ritual to bring abundance into your life.

EXERCISE: WHO YOU CALLING A HOE? EAT MY CAKE! RITUAL

The ritual has two parts. First you'll make Hoe Cakes, which you'll use in the work. I encourage you to perform it after listening to Nina Simone's "Ain't Got No, I Got Life" or a similar song that inspires you. (*Note: Remember to use biodegradable paper plates and cups for offerings. A New Age witch always honors her environment.*)

Needs:

* To make the cakes:
  - 1 cup cornmeal
  - 1 cup all-purpose flour
  - 1 teaspoon baking powder
  - 1 tablespoon sugar
  - 2 eggs
  - ¼ teaspoon salt
  - ¾ cup buttermilk
  - ½ cup water
  - ¼ vegetable oil or melted butter
  - honey, molasses, or maple syrup to taste
  - Optional:1 teaspoon nutmeg, vanilla, or banana extract
* 1 paper plate
* 9 dimes washed in Hoyt's cologne (brings luck)
* 1 liquid offering such as milky coffee with loads of sugar, or if you're feeling generous, gin or whiskey
* 1 small paper cup

Instructions:

Before making the cakes, take a few minutes to ask yourself what you're willing to grind for. . This will be part of your ritual petition. Seriously think of an answer beforehand, and don't go crazy. You want to call forth what you deserve because you're actively working to tip the balance in your favor. Keep in mind you'll be petitioning the friends of the woods, not praying to them. This means you shouldn't beg for something you haven't already been working to put in motion. Often when folks pray, they have a bad habit of putting the onus on divine intervention with no desire to get up off their lazy asses to grind. When it's time, only ask for that which you're willing to grind for.

When you have your answer, it's time to make the cakes: Stir all the dry ingredients in a large bowl. Then, in a separate bowl, whisk together the wet ingredients. Combine the ingredients and mix thoroughly.

Grease a skillet with the oil and heat. When the griddle is warm, use a ladle or ½ cup measure to scoop the batter into the skillet. When bubbles form on top, flip. Cook on the other side for several minutes, until the bottom is golden brown. Put on a paper plate and lightly drizzle with molasses, honey, or maple syrup.

Now you will perform the ritual. Place the cakes at the base of a tree found within walking distance of a motel, casino, bar, or at a park. Walk around the tree clockwise while reciting the following invocation:

I call on the Guardians of the East and the Element of
Air—I welcome you to the base of this tree.
I call on the Guardians of the South and the Element of
Fire—I welcome you to the base of this tree.
I call on the Guardians of the West and the Element of
Water—I welcome you to the base of this tree.
I call on the Guardians of the North and the Element of
Earth—I welcome you to the base of this tree.
I call on all the Universal spirits to imbue these cakes
with love, peace, and divinity, and as the elemental

spirits of the woods partake, may the balance of fate's abundance swing in my favor and I be showered with fortune in the form of [what fortune looks like to you].

Remember, don't go crazy with your petitioning. Only call forth what you're willing to grind for.

Next speak to your washed dimes. Tell them about your financial difficulties. You can do this part before you get to your destination. I'm aware that prying eyes might make you uncomfortable. You might even find yourself reciting the invocation at top speed. I get it, baby, do you?

Next, place the paper cup with the offering near the base of the tree to offer your wooded friends a liquid libation. Finally, drop the dimes around the tree's base counterclockwise.

Leave it the same way you came, and don't dwell on the efficacy. Believe, and you shall receive.

Shekere Blessings

The next ritual will use a shekere, which is one of the earliest drums in Africa. A shekere is a gourd that's been hollowed out and covered in a net of beads or cowrie shells. It's commonly found in the regions of Nigeria, Togo, Ghana, Benin, Sierra Leone, and Côte d'Ivoire. When the musician taps the shekere against their palm or flings it in rhythmic patterns, the beads or shells on the skirt rattle, creating a seductive pattern of tones as they graze the gourd.

When playing the shekere, start by cradling it diagonal to your body, letting the gourd's weight rest on the heel of your hand. Next, lightly tap the gourd's bottom with your fingertips while flinging the weight of the gourd from the bottom, middle, and top of your hand. Move the weight in and out and left to right. Using your wrist, fling the gourd away from you in a circular pattern, then in and out, up, and down, and side to side.

There's no wrong way to play the shekere. Trust that the beaded skirt will work its magick and make you sound like a shekere aficionado. Don't be afraid to create your own rhythms. The key is to find the sound that opens you to Spirit. When you hear the song of your heart, you'll know.

EXERCISE: SHEKERE BLESSINGS

The following ritual is one that takes the money you have and doubles it. Some folks don't like that this work depends on how much money you begin with. They feel it's not swift enough, and it doesn't make their money multiply like a gremlin dunked in water. I'm here to tell you this work will bless you right on time.

Needs:

* 1 shekere
* all the money in your wallet
* 1–2 unscented dryer sheets
* 1 teaspoon Hoyt's cologne (showers with luck)
* 1 saucer

Instructions:

Lay the money on a towel. Cover it with an unscented dryer sheet, two if you need to. Sprinkle Hoyt's cologne onto the sheets.

Next, take the shekere into your hands. Hold the neck with your dominant hand and tap three times into the palm of your opposite hand. Then, shake away from your body, shaking three times with no tapping. Go back to the three-count palm tapping. Repeat this for three rounds.

With the shekere raised above your head, tap the palm three times then tap away from the body three times. Repeat the above-the-head tapping three times. Once complete, set the shekere aside. You have awoken the ancestors and opened the portal between worlds.

Repeat the following incantation: *Money, multiply to open the current flow to help me survive the bill collectors, help me survive any debts incurred preventing my desire to treat myself once in a while. Money, grow and travel to the hearts of folks who once stood in my way. They will now hear the song reverberating within your fibers. Bless the world fruitfully and in turn bless me.*

Return the money to your wallet. Fold the dryer sheet into a square and tuck it inside your wallet. Keep the sheet for a month, then discard it in the trash. As the money stretches from your hands, your abundance will grow. Repeat the incantation over your open wallet as often as needed.

Black-Eyed Peas and Rice

In my family, black-eyed peas and rice have always been a symbol of good luck. Under my parent's roof, they were a staple dish we ate to welcome in the New Year or anytime we needed monetary abundance.

The dish has a long history in Southern culture. By the end of the Civil War, Union soldiers had consumed so much Southern livestock that there was little nourishment left to sustain the war-torn Southern diet.[17] As the Northerners retreated from Southern territories, they left behind large quantities of black-eyed peas, which they considered a livestock or slave food and thus unfit for human consumption. Faced with malnutrition and starvation, Southerners turned to the black-eyed pea, which was the most plentiful legume at their disposal. By New Year's Day of 1866, the black-eyed pea was praised for its good luck in lifting the South from the depths of despair.

Black-eyed peas are native to North Africa and were first domesticated in Western Africa in 3000 BC.[18] Their journey to the West Indies and the Amer-

....

17. "The Legend of the Black Eyed Pea," Civil War Family, December 31, 2013, https://www
.civilwarfamily.us/2013/12/the-legend-of-the-black-eyed-pea.html.
18. Joseph E. Holloway, "African Crops and Slave Cuisine," Rice Diversity, September 19, 2009,
http://ricediversity.org/outreach/educatorscorner/documents/African-Crops-and-Slave
-Cuisine.doc.

icas came through the slave trade. In Africa, black-eyed peas are fried into fritters, pounded into moi moi, or served as the main ingredient in soups and stews with shrimp and occasionally red sauce. In African American homes, black-eyed peas are served on New Year's Day over rice and with ham hocks under the Gullah name of Hoppin' John.

This is the story I was told: A man named John, who was crippled, heard his wife calling him home for supper. When he caught the scent of the dish spilling into the streets, John threw down his walking stick and began hopping, rather swiftly, all the way home. The black-eyed peas were so delicious the resourceful John decided to sell portions of it on the street and hide a shiny dime inside the meal. My grandfather followed his example and also included a dime in the meal, but he placed it on top to avoid choking hazards. Whoever found the dime was said to be blessed with good luck for the next six months.

Hoppin' John leftovers from the night before are called Skippin' Jenny. Skippin' Jenny is considered an extremely lucky meal. It's believed that if you eat it you'll have good luck all year long, and no problem earning or saving money.

EXERCISE: BLACKEN YOUR EYES

You won't be making Hoppin' John for this exercise but instead using the magick of black-eyed peas and rice to help you both attract and save money.

Needs:

* 1–2 cups of your favorite dried rice (prosperity and luck)
* 3–6 drops green food coloring
* 3 tablespoons Hoyt's cologne (luck)
* ½ cup dried black-eyed peas (manifests the reality of abundance)
* 1 teaspoon pumpkin spice seasoning (financial security)
* 3 tablespoons green chili powder (protection of personal belongings)

* 1 dry bay leaf, crumbled (increases awareness)
* 1 dry cabbage leaf, chopped into tiny pieces (amplifies energy)
* 1 dollar bill, cut into tiny strips
* 1 large mason jar
* 2 dark-colored kitchen towels
* a selection of small mason jars and satchels

Instructions:

Combine the rice, food coloring, and Hoyt's cologne in a jar with enough water to cover the rice. Seal the jar tightly and shake the jar for five minutes. Let the jar rest outside for twenty-four hours (I put it in the center of my flowerbed).

In the morning, drain the water from the rice using a strainer and a dark kitchen towel. (Dark towels help you see every grain better than white towels.) Next, place the strained rice on the second dark towel and let it sit out to dry for two to four hours. After the rice has dried completely, put it in a bowl and mix in your pumpkin spice, green chili powder, crushed bay leaf, cabbage, and the dollar. When thoroughly mixed, add the dried black-eyed peas.

Pick up your shekere and play a rhythm that feels good to you. Keep this going for the next ten to fifteen minutes.

Put the mixture in jars or a satchel to use as needed. I put it in uncapped mason jars in the corner of my room. I also place the rice in satchels and put them in my van's glove compartment. I have a client who placed a satchel of the mixture in her safety deposit box at her local bank. You can also sprinkle some under your home's welcome mat or in your desk at work.

EXERCISE: RICELY YOURS

Rice opens the portal to prosperity and alleviates the mourning of not having enough or going without. My grandmother would sprinkle rice throughout each room of her home and say three times each: *Health, wealth, giggles. May we never hunger or waste a want.* She'd look at me and we'd laugh. Then she'd sweep up as much rice as she could find and toss it into the street.

In the corner of her home, my grandmother would also hide satchels of rice she gathered from weddings to keep the home's harmony and a forever flowing abundance of love. Did you know that if you place a satchel of rice in your bank's safety deposit box it will increase the flow of money that travels into your account?

The following is a similar rice ritual for abundance. While performing it, think about the prosperity your life could use right now. Don't be greedy, but it's always okay to be needy.

Needs:

* 1 cup rice (brings prosperity and abundance to finances)
* 3 tablespoons Florida water (protects earnings)
* 3 tablespoons of Kananga water (invites ancestors to aid in getting the money desired)
* 1 paper denomination of money of any amount

Instructions:

Place the money inside a large mason jar, then add the rice, Florida water, and Kananga water. Whisper to the uncovered jar the amount you inserted. Repeat nine times.

Seal the jar and place it near the front door. Don't think about it. The rice will do its work.

Replace the contents of the jar each year on New Year's Day. Take the old money out and purchase a toy for a child, or buy a meal for a homeless person. Depending on how much you placed inside, you actually might be able to do both.

Thrifting

In our contemporary era, many of us are finding that what we buy is more important than where we buy. A large percentage of us are thrifting more than ever, perhaps for the first time. Whether it's a guilty pleasure or a necessity, ain't nothing wrong with shopping secondhand, so don't look down on yourself or others for doing it. Plus, the money you'll save can go toward buying something priceless that won't depreciate as fast as last season's sequin cocktail dress. You can also unearth major couture finds in another person's castoffs while avoiding the depression that comes with breaking the bank.

When I was in high school, we thought all thrift stores were vintage goldmines. What I quickly learned is that all that glitters may not be gold. Years later, I heard stories of people who brought home angry or heartbroken spirits and needed to cleanse their home thoroughly before the atmosphere settled. Taking home somebody else's castoffs should come with a warning. These items carry the residual impressions of every individual who has ever handled them, whether with warm or malevolent intentions. This goes double for toys and children's clothing. These impressions can result from trauma—physical, emotional, and even death. I don't say this to spread fear but to emphasize that you should cleanse the item so its energy moves on and doesn't attach to you and cause anxiety, sickness, or accidents.

EXERCISE: GET YA THRIFT ON RITUAL

Here's a quick divination ritual to help you decide whether or not to take home a thrift find. It's imperative you listen to the divination's results as if your sanity depends on it.

Needs:

* 4 pennies
* 1 bar of black soap or ½–1 cup liquid black soap (provides spiritual release)
* ¼ cup Florida water (removes negative vibrations)
* 1 Palo Santo smudge stick (brings clarity)
* 2 tablespoons black salt
* 2 tablespoons red brick powder (offers protection)
* 2 tablespoons asafoetida powder (acts as a repellent)
* 1 large basin of water
* 1 piece of black tourmaline (grounding)
* 1 selenite wand (creates an unseen force field of warm energy)
* white tea light candles (enough for nine days)

Instructions

After finding a prize at the thrift store that you just can't live without, take out your four pennies. Cup them in your hands and whisper this incantation over them:

A penny for your thoughts.
A penny for your dreams.
A penny's not just a penny.
A penny has a voice of its own.
A penny's lesson will be shown.
Who goes with me?
Friend or foe?
Friend?

Yes, yes!

Foe?

Hell NO!

Clench the coins in your dominant hand, forming a fist. Tap that fist into your other hand three times, then let the coins spill into your nondominant hand. Study how they land:

* 4 faces up = Great. Wash the item with black soap and Florida water.
* 3 faces up = Good. Wash it with black soap and Florida water.
* 2 faces up = Workable Pain. Wash it with black soap and Florida water. Then, smoke cleanse the item with Palo Santo. Finally, sprinkle it with black salt and let stand for twenty-four hours. Dust or shake off the black salt and flush what falls down the toilet.
* 1 face up = Stagnant Instability. Wash with black soap and Florida water, cleanse with Palo Santo smoke, then sprinkle with black salt, red brick, and asafoetida. Let stand for twenty-four hours, then dust or shake off the salt, red brick, and asafoetida and flush what falls down the toilet.)
* No faces up = Trauma above Your Pay Grade. Leave that there! Unless you have a spiritualist on speed dial, I wouldn't load that shit in my ride for a gazillion bitcoins. The no faces are saying it's just too risky to bring said item into your personal space. It might even be dangerous.

What if you bought an item that can't be doused in water? Rub the black tourmaline and selenite wand over the item, then sprinkle on the red brick, asafetida, and black salt. Let sit for forty-eight hours before using the item.

EXERCISE: AIN'T GOT TIME TO GO BROKE RITUAL

Thrifting is a practical way to save money. Here's another quick ritual to help you stop spending and start saving.

Needs:

* 2–5 sticky notes of any color
* 1 plastic zip-top bag, quart size
* 1 bill of any denomination
* 1 teaspoon each:
  - cinnamon
  - nutmeg
  - anise oil

Instructions:

On the sticky notes, write the following mantra. It may take two or more sticky notes to write it all down, depending on your handwriting size.

Save, Save, Save
In my pocket, in a bank, in my wallet, in my purse
In the freezer
Each pay day for an entire year
Ancestor, teach me to save
For what comes after the fun has closed its eyes and
*   slipped away.*

Put the notes inside the bag along with the money. Sprinkle the spices and oil into the bag, then seal it shut and sleep with it under your pillow for at least one night. Place it in a freezer for an entire year, after which you should take the money out of the bag and place it in your savings account. Over the year and beyond, you should begin to think more carefully about spending transactions. Money will start to grow in your life, and your urge to spend will slowly dissipate.

Finding Abundance

Life has programmed us to view coins and coin purses differently than when we were growing up. They used to be like mini pocketbooks filled with leprechaun treasures. I couldn't wait until my grandmother caught wind of my stellar report card or my impeccably folded towels and earn a shiny silver dollar. I'd race off to buy a praline and a frozen cup. Nowadays we tend to think that if it ain't in dollars, it doesn't matter. You either got greenbacks or you get laughed at.

I have my grandmother's last coin purse, which she kept in her bra wrapped in a handkerchief. It's not a fancy purse, just one she bought from a corner store, but it's my lucky coin purse. I use it when I want to show generosity in a place where kindness feels scare, vibrationally speaking. For the following ritual you'll need a similar coin purse, either one you buy or one you received as a gift eons ago and tossed in a drawer. It's time to spread joy so even more joy (and financial reward!) boomerangs right back in your direction.

EXERCISE: LUCKY COIN PURSE

This next work is an offering to help others increase their belief in the power of finding abundance in the most unexpected places.

Needs:

* 1 coin purse
* coins of all denominations, enough to make the coin purse bulge without tearing
* 2 cups cold water
* 2 tablespoons each:
    – Florida water (promotes healing)
    – Hoyt's cologne (brings luck)
    – whiskey
* 3 tablespoons cinnamon (stimulates the blessings of money in life)
* 3 tablespoons anise oil (promotes youthful vigor)

Instructions:

Mix the waters, Hoyt's cologne, and whiskey. Wash the coins in this solution, then let them air dry.

Sprinkle cinnamon and anise inside the coin purse, then Place the dried coins inside. Close the purse and shake vigorously while repeating the following: *May these coins thrown, dropped, or slipped in another's path bring luck, abundance, and healing to their day. May they open the door to future wealth to all who hold them dear enough to name them found treasures. May the Universe bring them the sweetest satisfactions known to humankind, and may they continue to pay this love forward.*

Carry the purse with you daily, or choose a specific day to be your generosity day. Drop a coin or two or three in an area where the vibration feels stagnant and the spirits are begging for a generosity transfusion. You'll know when and where; don't agonize over it.

EXERCISE: MONEY TEA FOR THE SOUL

Another way to open your spirit to abundance and wealth is to have a good cup a tea. Tea can settle the stomach, ease anxiety, and get our minds off the size of our bank accounts in comparison to the chick on social media flexing on all our dreams as she rides a camel in Egypt. This tea will put you in a better mood to balance your books or to pique your interest in the art of financial investments. It will open your soul space in such a way that you'll become more fluent in your money-making ventures. This money tea is one of my favorite drinks when I need to get my creative juices flowing.

Needs:

* 1–2 cups water
* 1 tablespoon lemongrass (feeds the lust for money)

* 1 teaspoon shredded ginger root (attracts money)
* ¼ teaspoon pumpkin spice (fills your life with luck)
* Optional: 1 strainer or cheesecloth

Instructions:

Bring the water to a boil in a pot or kettle. Once it reaches boiling, remove from the heat, add the rest of the ingredients, and stir. Cover the tea and let steep for ten minutes. Pour it into a cup through a strainer to separate out the herbs. Drink slowly while envisioning yourself in a room filled with money.

Growing Your Wealth

Oftentimes folks add a side job to their current income to make ends meet and still find it near impossible to afford groceries and other essentials. They may be lost as to how they can afford to live in a society where sometimes even baby formula can be hard to find.

When we're free to watch our money grow, we aren't living in self-imposed oppression where we're slaves to the next paycheck. The following two rituals address these needs.

EXERCISE: MONEY TREE RITUAL

This first ritual was originally designed for a sistah in need. After a month of performing it, this woman watched her bank account grow until she was able to save for a new car and move out of her apartment and into a starter home.

This work uses an actual plant you'll watch grow. The idea of growing wealth while catering to a plant was hard for that sistah to comprehend at first. But as she watched the tree bloom, she witnessed the continual blooming of her finances.

Needs:

* * 1 Wheel of Fortune tarot card (symbolizes luck and the cyclical effect it plays in life)
* * 1 bonsai tree potted in soil (grounds your urges)
* * 5 cinnamon sticks (sweetens disposition)
* * 4 denominations of bills (*Note: If you don't feel comfortable using real money, you can substitute fake money.*)
* * 4 lodestones (attracts money and induces a grounded state to focus wealth in a purposeful way)
* * 1 piece of green aventurine (attracts money)

Instructions:

Place the Wheel of Fortune card under the plant. Push the cinnamon sticks into the soil about halfway, forming a circle around the plant. Fold the money as small as you can and bury it in the soil. Place the lodestones around the base of the plant and bury the green aventurine in the soil.

Next, speak gently to the plant, asking it to grow your wealth. Promise that you'll use a portion of each new earning opportunity to bless someone less fortunate.

From that moment on, care for your tree per its care and maintenance instructions. Sit with your bonsai for fifteen minutes daily. From time to time as you water the plant, meditate on the Wheel of Fortune card. Imagine what fortune would look like in your life.

While performing this ritual, I like to play Nina Simone's "I Wish I Knew How It Would Feel to Be Free." For me, I believe it promotes the theme.

EXERCISE: FIVE FINGER MONEY GRAB

This second ritual will help enliven your family's prosperity. Watch out, your luck is about to change!

Needs:

* ¼ teaspoon–1 tablespoon dried cinquefoil (enlivens the bank account or any cash app)
* 1 copy of a picture of you, no larger than 4 x 5 inches
* 1 envelope
* 1 marker

Instructions:

Place the cinquefoil on the photo, then fold the photo toward you three times. Next, fold the ends inward so none of the herb can escape. Place the folded photo inside the envelope and seal.

With the marker, write on the outside of the envelope, *Inside lies enough money to satisfy my wildest desires and then some!*

Carry the envelope inside your wallet daily. Recite the message on the outside of the envelope each morning. You'll begin to see money entering your life just when you need it most.

Juju on the Fly

The Jack of Diamonds is the card of money. It indicates your ability to make your money work for you. It's the card that screams, "Nobody can do that thing quite as masterfully as you." I bet if you invested at least thirty minutes to an hour daily doing whatever that masterful thing is, you could, with patience, turn it into a business, a book, a screenplay, a musical compilation, a restaurant, a brand of cosmetics, or a clothing line.

In this age of social media influencers gone wild, folks are learning to lean into their abilities and to use any and every skill at their disposal to be financially self-sustaining. Don't believe me? Scroll through any of the social media sites and in a matter of seconds you'll witness a play-by-play of how once mere mortals propelled themselves into the ranks of financial gods and goddesses, right before your very eyes.

Carrying the Jack of Diamonds in your satchel ensures you'll investigate financial enterprises that best suit your expertise. Remember what I said at the beginning of this chapter: financial success begins with talent. As you assess your skills and employ the rigors of trial and error, your findings will open up your third eye and heart space to lucrative opportunities. You won't go to work begrudgingly; you'll honor the sanctity of creation. This chosen work will become your playground. But first, you have to be willing to start from the ground level, shaping building, and reconfiguring ideas until they're fine-tuned. Then and only then are you ready to unleash your tale of swapping the mundane for the awe-inspiring on the world. Who knows, a TED talk may even be in your future.

As much as the Jack of Diamonds is about moving toward generational wealth, it's also about saving so you don't overzealously live from paycheck to paycheck. I don't want you to become like those entertainers with a mouth full of hundred-thousand-dollar grills dreading the day they're no longer a hot commodity. That's when they're often forced to sell those grills to pay back taxes, or realize their home is more valuable as a roof over their heads than a showroom for Italian marble columns and pimped-out rides.

I have my own spending habit to battle. We all do. I personally love spending on occult books, tarot cards, gemstones, incense, oils, and sex toys. I'm also a connoisseur of the finer things, and I have a problem with impulse purchases. But when I carry the Jack of Diamonds, I no longer feel the need to spend that small fortune burning a hole in my pocket. I hold myself to the promise that I'll indulge in spending expeditions every three months, but only after thoroughly considering how that purchase would benefit my manor of macabre. In between splurges, I save a five, a ten, or a twenty here and there. I keep that money in an envelope labeled Occult Manor.

When I hold that card in meditation, I ask that my financial situation balance itself out and to make saving seem like less of a chore. I ask for help in regarding money as a tool for traveling the steep ridges of life. I also tell myself that by saving, I'm not punishing myself. I'm ensuring that I never became a slave to the next paycheck and that I'm always in a financial position to be a lifesaver for my family.

EXERCISE: JACK OF DIAMONDS/RECONFIGURING MY STORY

With the following ritual, you'll become a money magnet, a guru of greenbacks, and a pro at saving. The Jack of Diamonds will increase your money flow and shower you with abundance beyond your wildest dreams, and teach you to maintain balance so it stays that way.

Needs:

* ¼–½ teaspoon Hoyt's cologne (brings luck and unknown fortune)
* 1 green satchel big enough to hold the card (ground needs)
* 1 Jack of Diamonds playing card
* 1 piece of pyrite (enchants the heart and mind to follow a life of chosen abundance)
* 1 tablespoon soil from the surroundings of a bank (increases wealth)
* 1 check or savings deposit slip (sets financial intentions in the physical realm)

Instructions:

First, commit to trying the three-month saving cycle I used: Save for three months, then splurge. Give your savings plan a name; I called mine Occult Manor.

The night before this work, pour the Hoyt's cologne into the satchel. Use just enough to leave a smell but still have a dry satchel come morning. Leave the satchel on a towel overnight to help it dry out.

The next morning, place your card and the pyrite inside the satchel. Add the soil, then set the satchel aside.

If you're using a deposit slip, add the date, your name, and your real account number. (If you aren't comfortable with that, use a fake set of numbers.) If you're using a check, fill in the date; your name and account are probably already on it. On the "Pay to the order of" and "Note" lines, write the name of your savings plan and what the money is for. For example, I wrote my check to Occult Manor and noted the money was for artifacts.

Next, write in an amount you think would suffice to make any purchase(s) that will bring you joy when it's time to splurge. Commit to saving that amount and make sure to do it.

Next, place the deposit slip or check inside the satchel and breathe into the bag while repeating the following: *Money comes, money goes, and all that remains should either be soul-sustaining or life-affirming. If the purchase doesn't make me emotionally richer, it shouldn't make my bank account sicker. I decide, not social media, which material gains hold a position of reverence in my life.*

Tie the satchel tightly and attach it to your bra strap, or place it in a purse near your wallet. Keep it nearby so you can breathe into the satchel and reinvigorate your work with the incantation whenever it's needed.

You can rework this ritual every six months. Keep your pyrite, satchel, and card. The check or deposit slip can be torn into small pieces and left at the base of a tree with the soil.

Chapter Six
Goofer Dust in Your Eye

There have been many discussions for and against the teaching of baneful magick, which I like to call Goofer Dust in Your Eye. In Hoodoo *goofer dust* is a term commonly used for hexing. Some spiritual practitioners believe baneful magick, which is harmful or destructive, should be left to professionals who can properly assess the consequences of such magick. They argue that baneful magick in the wrong hands can unleash a world of irrevocable chaos. Still others argue that it's a gateway to evil, causing the magician to become an agent of chaos forever.

I don't subscribe to these beliefs. For one, chaos exists in our world, whether we engage with it or not. At some point we'll all get pulled into a manufactured drama that threatens our right to life, liberty, and happiness. When that day comes, we'll have to choose how we respond. I choose not to pray about it but to be about it.

As for the argument that baneful magick is evil, there are many examples of true evil in the world: killing unarmed Black people, separating Mexican children from their parents, forcing LGBTQ+ people into conversion centers, calling a virus "the China flu." Shall I go on? I got lots of Amerika's greatest hits to share: White parents hosting sleepovers and making the Black kids drink urine, a White teacher cutting off the hair of a biracial child against their will, another teacher standing on the neck of a Black student and sending a photo to the parents in response to the George Floyd verdict. The point is that evil exists; I didn't make it and neither did you. Sometimes we reach a breaking point and say, "enough is enough." That's where baneful magick comes in.

Playing It Safe

There's a quote by occultist Anton Lavey that reads, "The Atheist complains about the wind. The Christian prays for it to change. The Satanist adjusts his sails."[19] In other words, liberation in its baneful state requires adjusting values, beliefs, and coping mechanisms, in addition to magick. Of course there are precautionary measures and careful considerations that need to be addressed before engagement. Baneful magick should never be taken lightly. These next spells and rituals should be hurled in the direction of people who are causing true physical, emotional, and spiritual trauma that can adversely affect our survival or the survival of those we love.

Many of us have found ourselves at a crossroads where we understand without a shadow of a doubt that we can't win as someone unleashes their colorless, odorless gas of destruction into a situation. These people act as if we aren't equipped to derail our own lives if need be. Sometimes they go so far as to cause us physical and emotional abuse to the point we feel obligated to suffer through it, hoping others, especially God, will witness our path to canonization.

Then, when we're finally clutching that last nerve and our patience is so thin it's now transparent, we realize we need help. It's at this moment when we're sick and tired of praying for these toxic individuals to leave us the hell alone that we realize our manic rage, depression, or even withdrawal from society requires ample amounts of therapy. This is also the moment to allow baneful magick to sweeten the scornfully sour aftertaste of hatred. This chapter will teach you not only how to settle the score, but how to bring back tranquility to your fast-paced life.

To be clear, I'm not telling you to invest time and energy in something I haven't found personally necessary. I've had to deal with racist people at work who have made me cry my eyes out to the point I believed I was going to have a nervous breakdown. I'm talking about individuals who wrote "black bitch" across my classroom board, put feces in my garbage can, broke my personal items, and used the N-word after learning of my hiring. I've endured sexual assaults and been drugged by my own boyfriend. During that incident, I called to the ancestors for help, and they answered. Afterward, when I was cleaning up and healing, I remembered the power of intention. I told myself

....

19. "65 Anton Lavey Quotes on Success in Life," Overall Motivation, last modified June 12, 2021, https://www.overallmotivation.com/quotes/anton-lavey-quotes/.

that this was my life and from now on, I would make the rules. From that day forward, all ends would justify the means.

Again, remember my warning: These spells aren't intended for folks who are only stage one bothersome. With these spells you can't wake up and decide you want to take it all back. That's not how these babies work. What will be done will be done: signed, sealed, and delivered. So think about it very carefully before you start.

Now, if you're ready, let's get wicked, you scoundrel you.

EXERCISE: PROTECTION AND SAFETY FIRST RITUAL

This ritual will ground and protect you from anyone trying to do you harm, deflecting all malice back to the sender. Note that it uses Van Van oil; the recipe follows the ritual.

Needs:

* 1 cup Florida water (protects)
* 2 tablespoons sea salt (fortifies your aura energy)
* ¼ cup liquid witch hazel (acts like barbwire protecting from psychic intruders)
* 2 incense sticks of any of the following blends (acts as a force field from boomerang effects):
  - cedar
  - frankincense
  - myrrh
  - sage
* 7 pieces of devil's shoestring (protects against backfiring spells)
* 1 red satchel
* 1 teaspoon each:
  - basil (prevents malevolent energy from residing in the body)
  - lavender (acts as a peacekeeper)

- osha (protects and heals the aura from psychic
    vampires)
- rosemary (ensures good sleep and physical grounding)
- thyme (promotes courage and energy)
* 1 tablespoon rosebuds (enhances psychic power)
* Van Van oil (destroys nasty errant energy)

Instructions:

First, play a song that inspires you. I suggest a song by Princess Nokia. The one I enjoy for this work is "Honey Iced Tea."

Next, bathe in a solution of the Florida water, salt, and witch hazel. When you're done, dry your body and cleanse it further by burning the incense. Whisk it around your entire body.

Next, place a piece of devil's shoestring at the four corners of your bed, then stash the other three pieces in the satchel. Add the herbs and rosebuds (make sure you put all the herbs inside the satchel at one time). As you place each item in your satchel, tell the mix to quickly send malice back to its owner and to leave you extremely successful in all your thoughts, reactions, and deeds.

When you're done, keep the satchel in your purse or tied to your bra for one week. Then, on the evening of the seventh day, take it to a cemetery and toss the contents in an unkempt area. (Keep the satchel to be repurposed.) When you return home, rub your hands with the Van Van oil.

In the coming weeks up until a month's time, you'll be the farthest thing from any hater's mind.

EXERCISE: "VAN VAN, THANK YOU MA'AM" OIL

Creating your own Van Van oil not only makes you feel invigoratingly witchy but it also keeps you from feeling spiritually icky. The name Van Van comes from the French word *verveine*, a plant known as verbena or vervain in English. Its strong lemony smell can repel insects as well as conjure luck, inviting the ancestors to purge malevolent energy from your life and open roads. It also has the potential to make you appear even more attractive than you feel.

Needs:

* 1–2 cups avocado oil (opens heart chakra)
* 1 tablespoon vetiver (breaks hexes)
* 1 tablespoon vervain (brings clarity and peace)
* 1 teaspoon cinnamon (increases a sense of spiritual calm)
* 1 tablespoon lemongrass oil (protects against electromagnetic energy)
* 1 tablespoon citronella oil (smart ass repellant)
* 1 tablespoon ginger grass oil (heightens your power)
* 1 tablespoon orange essence oil (lashes back against psychic emotional and attack)
* 1 tablespoon palmarosa oil (encourages self-love)
* 1 tablespoon vanilla oil (invites pleasure and excitement)
* 1 tablespoon patchouli oil (grounds)
* 1 each of the High Priestess and the Magician tarot cards (*Note: These cards can be used anytime you invoke these hexing works. The addition of these cards increases the oil's potency as a spiritual agent of protection as well as heightens your abilities as a Hoodoo.*)

Instructions:

Pour the avocado oil inside a large mason jar. Add the vetiver and vervain, stir. Slowly add the cinnamon, then add the oils.

Seal and shake vigorously for ten minutes, then stand the mixture on its head for four weeks in a cool dark area with the High Priestess on top of the jar and the Magician underneath. After four weeks, this will be a potent and power-filled addition to your work.

Inspiring Voices: Princess Nokia

Princess Nokia is the sistah I wish to Goddess I'd met in high school—we would've formed the most goth girl coven ever! Many have called her "a radical intersectional feminist,"[20] and she proves that when we unpack our fears of traditional spirituality, we realize those fears were woven by those seeking to annihilate our allegiance to a goddess who's sexy, smart-mouthed, and will kick your ass while maintaining her right to be very in your face spiritually. Princess Nokia speaks out fearlessly on topics like gentrification and societal male domination, and she encourages girls to take up space wherever space is being soaked up. Be seen, witches!

I was introduced to Princess Nokia's music by my eldest daughter, Nzingha, who sat me down and stuck her earbuds in my ear so I could properly absorb the song "Brujas." Child, I was not only devouring the hip-hop lyricism but also the video's imagery. What's not to like about Princess? She's an openly queer artist who gained viral fame on SoundCloud. Her 2017 hit "Brujas," which coincidentally means "witches" in Spanish, earned 6.3 million views on YouTube by 2021 and 6.5 million streams on Spotify.[21] The song and video both reconfigure the identity of the non-White witch, giving a postcolonized survival persona to the indigenous practices of deeply hued people. "Brujas" has Princess Nokia resonating feminine energy while stepping from the shadows and assuming her rightful role as a revolutionary bad bitch.

....

20. GirlTalkHQ, "Artist Princess Nokia Is the Intersectional Feminist & WOC Advocate the Music Industry Needs," GirlTalkHQ, November 23, 2017, https://www.girltalkhq.com/artist-princess-nokia-is-the-intersectional-feminist-woc-advocate-the-music-industry-needs/.

21. GirlTalkHQ, "Artist Princess Nokia."

Princess Nokia, whose birthname is Destiny Frasqueri, is a rapper who, like the bad boys of the genre, can easily transition through hegemonic tropes of gunplay, sexual jousting, fast cars, and stacks of money. However, she never lets you forget that women are more complex in their being than traditional Judeo-Christian lore would have us believe. In the "Brujas" video we have references to Yemaya, the Yoruba water deity of mothering and nurturing. Then we have an ode to 1996's cult witch classic *The Craft*, depicted with a cast of all-brown brujas. My Goddess I love that sistah, for truth.

Princess Nokia once said, "My ancestors had to keep their customs secret for fear of death or persecution, so it's common to be secretive and discreet about Regla de Ocha. But it's my family's spirituality, so I don't want to keep it secret. It's very important to keep these traditions alive and to speak about them openly."[22] Her defiance in the face of Christian ideology creates, in my opinion, insurrectionist music, and I'm totally on board for that. As I groove to the hip-hop rhythms of Princess Nokia, her sounds are a pleasant reminder that baneful magick doesn't have to be dreary or steeped in Hollywood-esque black mass motifs.

"I come from strong, resilient women," she said. "I don't like to lose sight of that. Because my people were oppressed, murdered, and their spirituality was taken away from them, I feel it's my duty to exhibit that in my art. As young people of color, we're seeing this is still a racist, archaic world, and we're aware of how strong our cultural identities make us. We want to celebrate everything about us that's been oppressed."[23]

Rappers are often portrayed as tough, hard legs who refuse to stand down and go through life soft. The best of their craft speak their minds in bars with such eloquence of wordplay and finesse with English that it would make even Noah Webster blush. However, few use the totality of their presence to rearrange how we view the genre and its signifiers. Even fewer acknowledge the Old World spirits as Princess Nokia does, without it being some type of

....

22. Shanice Davis, "Princess Nokia Talks Infusing Santería in Her Music," *Vibe*, December 14, 2016, https://www.vibe.com/features/viva/princess-nokia-talks-santeria-473957/#!.

23. Leah Mandel, "How 5 Women Use Religious Traditions to Navigate Modern Life," *The FADER*, November 9, 2017, https://www.thefader.com/2016/12/08/women-religion-fashion-faith.

fad. For her willingness to put herself out there both spiritually and musically, I adore Princess Nokia. She gets it and refuses to stand down or be denied.

Troll Me No More

Unless you live under a rock with no semblance of Wi-Fi, you've probably encountered at least one troll. Even if you're lucky enough to have avoided them, trust me, they're out there, just waiting for the right post to sink their fangs into. But what's the difference between trolling and cyberbullying? I bet you thought they were the same thing, like tomato and tomahto—not so, my darling. According to psychology experts, online trolling is defined as "malicious online behavior, characterized by aggressive and deliberate provocation of others. 'Trolls' seek to provoke, upset and harm others by way of inflammatory messages and posts."[24] Trolls target people they don't know personally, thus they don't fear any backlash—who gonna check them, boo? Cyberbullies, on the other hand, typically know their victims and use personal level information to harass and intimidate them. I'll address bullies later; right now, I'll focus on trolls.

The average age of trolls is twenty-five with 68 percent being female and 43 percent being male.[25] People often troll for comedic effect, poking fun at others to try to provoke a reaction. Once they've latched on to a target, they usually keep stalking this person and look for future opportunities to make others ROFL at their expense.

Trolling isn't harmless. It's been linked to disrupted sleep patterns, depression, self-injurious behavior, and even suicidal tendencies.[26] Unfortunately, there's no way to be online without running into trolls; these pit vipers are an inevitable part of our cyber travels. But we can make their interactions as unpleasant and unfulfilling as the venom they spew.

....

24. Evita March, "A Psychological Profile of Online Trolls Shows High Self Esteem and a Penchant for Sadism," *The National Interest* (The Center for the National Interest, September 17, 2020), https://nationalinterest.org/blog/reboot/psychological-profile-online-trolls-shows -high-self-esteem-and-penchant-sadism-169047.
25. Emily Lawrenson, "Online Trolls and Cyberbullies: What's the Difference?," Qustodio, November 23, 2021, https://www.qustodio.com/en/blog/difference-online-trolls-and -cyberbullies/.
26. March, "Psychological Profile of Online Trolls."

EXERCISE: TROLLS, YOU ARE DONE

This short working will halt those pesky workplace trolls, those people we don't really know but who strive to email us into submission with impossible demands. It can be adapted for internet trolls or others.

Needs:

* 1 piece of Little John (galangal) root, about 1 once, sliced (*Note: Little John root breaks the connection a troll makes to you, and it will help make others see them as the fool. If you have more than one troll, add more pieces.*)
* 1 snack size plastic zip-top bag

Instructions:

Chew a sliver of Little John root. As you chew, repeat the following: *Trolls live on social media, and at my job. Trolls are forever trying to steal my high. Not this time, fuckers, I am going to chew you up and spit you out. Won't give you the pleasure of keeping my name sashaying in your mouth. Bitch, you dead to me!*

Next spit a portion of the root in the four corners of your workspace. The Little John will prevent trolls with not enough work on their plates from dragging your reputation through the mud.

Spit the rest of the root into a plastic bag, then speak into the bag and into existence whatever unsavory outcome you would like to see happen to your troll.

Flush the bag's contents down a toilet and toss the bag into a dumpster far from your home (the smellier the better). Or you can simply toss the entire bag with the root into such a dumpster.

Halloween Skulls and Runes

On Halloween, my family often visited my maternal grandfather, the most fantastical keeper of oral history I knew. My grandfather's lineage spanned the US Low Country of South Carolina and Georgia, and he proudly identified as a born and bred Geechee man. The Geechee people were descendants of enslaved Afrikans from Senegambia and Sierra Leone who retained their West African roots, language, and culture through Gullah traditions, including top-notch skills in cultivating crops like rice, cotton, and indigo.

My grandfather had a story for every occasion, and Halloween was no exception. He always began with the same preamble: "Every action is riddled with consequences. Sometimes we concede and just accept, and other times we rewrite the story so that the next person who hears it hears a different version—a new set of consequences."

One Halloween he told me the following story: There once was a boy who was groomed at the foot of a magnolia tree where dead Black bodies taunted the wind with a scent that lingered in my grandfather's nostrils until the day he died. The boy grew into a man who eventually became a bigot, a rapist, and a fiend who preyed on Black people. He eventually owned a butcher shop and forced women to choose between sex or the starvation of their children. He would pretend to be a friend to Blacks only to lure them in with the promise of low prices: meat for meat.

One Halloween, three women hatched a plan to stop paying for their meat with their bodies. They told the butcher they were throwing a party and would pool their money to the necessary ribs, hamburger meat, and roast. They also told the bigot he could have all three of their bodies at once in exchange for the enormous order. The butcher agreed without thinking twice. Lust clouded his mind so much he couldn't see the spirits moving in the women's eyes. Something was conjured, something long dead awakened, and it was unspooling beneath their courage.

He closed his shop an hour early to meet the women in an abandoned icehouse. When he stepped past the heavy metal doors, he was met with a shovel to the head. As he lay on the cement floor the women stabbed him and severed his head, then buried him in an overgrown field behind the icehouse. A year later they dug up his body and used some of his bones to conjure his spirit and enslave it to do their bidding. They put these conjure bones in a cedar box, latched it with steel chains and a lock, and carved two figures into the wood, one on the outside and one on the side where the bones were nestled.

As he told the story, my grandfather drew the carvings on a torn piece of brown paper bag.

With some research, I eventually learned the image on the outside of the box was the Algiz rune, while the one on the inside was the Thurisaz rune of chaos. Grandfather said these women were smart enough to understand the best way to gain control of White folks was with their own magick.

He went on to say that these bones were passed down between female relatives of the three women for years. Whenever a Black person wound up dead, raped, or beat to a pulp, this enslaved spirit would be called up to cause all manner of calamities. His favorite was to strangle folks in their sleep. Grandfather said, "The bigot still moans for his freedom, but he'll never know peace. He'll never know release."

Now that I've told you this story, let me be very clear on one thing: I would never advise anyone to kill or hurt in vengeance. Yes, we live in a society that oftentimes behaves in an uncivilized manner. We may find it hard to believe the police or courts will make injustices right, and seek to relieve our pain by taking matters into our own hands. I understand pain, loss, and trauma. But I don't want to see us vindicated and living behind bars. Let baneful magick serve as your weapon. In time, we'll witness the beauty of what happens when our will frees our hands.

EXERCISE: RUNE OF PROTECTION WARDING RITUAL

The Algiz rune is a Nordic symbol of the god Heimdall. This god possessed the power to ward off evil and protect the gods and goddesses of Asgard, the realm of the gods in Norse mythology. I incorporated the Algiz into this work, which will aid you in confronting extreme workplace bigotry. It will keep the instigators out of your space, and they won't have the first clue why the fuck they can't get a rise out of you. This one is my favorite rituals because it's so in your face that it always goes overlooked.

Needs:

* 1 picture frame big enough to fit the drawing, no larger than 8 x 10 inches
* 1 drawing of the Algiz rune that you can trace (offers protection)
* 1 tablespoon hyacinth (relieves stress and tension and connects to the spirit realm of the ancestors)
* 1 red or black tube of lipstick or bottle of nail polish

Instructions:

Place the picture of the rune in the frame with the hyacinth resting on the back of the image. Seal the frame in place. Trace the rune on the glass with the lipstick or nail polish. As you hold the frame, say, *If you want people to recognize who you are, you got to show them where you've been!* Display the frame on your desk or back wall. Make sure the frame is facing the entrance to your space.

I always say this phrase when I perform hexing spells, because there are individuals in this world who wake up just to spit in your face; no amount of civility will change how they deal with you. That's facts, and I'm too grown to spend my waking days trying to figure out why the popular kids don't like me.

EXERCISE: I WELCOME THE THURISAZ CHAOS RITUAL

In Norse mythology, the Thurisaz rune is Thor's power symbol. It's heavy with warrior energy. If it gets a whiff of danger, it automatically creates a force field around you that shuts you off from physical or emotional injury. In turn, it sends chaos to the sender, whoever they are.

Drawing the rune with intention also awakens turmoil. While you work, try playing an inspiring song. I enjoy from Princess Nokia's "It's Not My Fault."

Needs:

* 1 paper plate
* 1 black marker
* 1 pen with a sharp tip
* 1 photo of your target, if possible (*Note: It's imperative to use a photo that has no other folks in it. If that's hard to find, cut the other folks out of the picture. You aren't trying to cause harm to anyone who doesn't deserve it. By keeping the images of those we aren't targeting, we run the risk of charging them for crimes they aren't guilty of, and that is so very unfair.*)
* 1 red candle
* 1 saucer
* 1 cast-iron cauldron or fireproof container
* Optional: 1 Moon tarot card (*Note: The Moon card symbolizes calling down the night energies of the spirits who travel under the blanket of darkness. If you're performing this spell in the waking hours, you can still call down the darkness by giving this card a prominent position on your table as an overseer.*)

Instructions:

Draw the Thurisaz rune in the center of the paper plate alongside the name of your target. Visualize the person causing you disarray. Pick up your candle and begin stroking it from top to bottom, then bottom to top. As you stroke, ask that all the pain, loss, and angst you feel be sent back to the perpetrator's domicile one hundred times squared. After noticing a definitive transfer of energy from your stroking, you can add some Get the Fuck Out My Way Oil (recipe follows this ritual), but it's not required.

If you have a picture of your target, draw the Thurisaz over their image too, then place the picture under the saucer. Light the candle and set it in the center of your saucer. Hold the paper plate and tell it you'll no longer tolerate the indignation wrought on you. Be specific when stating the pain you're feeling, and be firm in telling it to cease immediately.

Hold the plate and spit onto it, fold it over like a hotdog bun, then place it on the floor and stomp it. Keep stomping until you feel vindicated, then tear the plate into shreds. Toss it into the cauldron and set it ablaze. Sit for fifteen minutes, envisioning yourself free from the situation. Allow the candle to burn for another thirty minutes, then snuff it out. Remove the image from beneath the saucer and save it for when you have to take a shit. When you do, wrap the image in toilet paper. Wipe your ass with it, toss it into the toilet, and flush.

EXERCISE: GET THE FUCK OUT MY WAY OIL

I enjoy rubbing this oil onto my hands before workings because it removes jinxes. You can use it for different workings. In the warding ritual, try rubbing it on the picture frame's glass. Do it once a week to clean away any vibrations from enemies. You can also use it on spiritual tools for the same purpose.

Needs:

* 1–2 cups sweet almond oil
* 1 teaspoon asafoetida
* 3–6 mandrake chips (protects the oil's creator)
* 1 teaspoon each:
  - black thorn root (binds)
  - wormwood (contacts ancestral spirits to infuse work with potency).
  - stinging nettle (pricks the situation, causing it extreme pain)
* 13 drops patchouli oil (sends jinxes back to your enemy's front door)

Instructions:

Pour the almond oil into a large mason jar, then add the asafoetida and mandrake. Stir. Add the herbs one at a time and stir again. Add the patchouli oil, seal, and shake vigorously. Leave standing right side up for two weeks, then upside down for another two weeks. After four weeks, use the oil to anoint the candle in the Thurisaz ritual.

Spirit Dolls

While I try my best not to let my nerves get vexed to the nth power, some people just live to push you to your limit. For these extremely maniacal people, I go full poppet. Poppets serve as stand-ins for your target, and they're an easy tool to add to your baneful magick. Whatever terrible things you dream of sending your target's way, you can take out on the poppet instead, transmitting them to your tormentor. With just a photo, a tuft of hair, or a piece of clothing, you can rain down pain or sweeten the affect of a sworn enemy—it's up to you. Either way, I promise they'll never see it coming.

The poppets I use most are little muslin dolls. You can them online or at most arts and craft stores. Poppets can also be made out of clay, dough, cardstock, or cardboard. In a pinch I've used fashion dolls too.

I once held a seventeen-woman workshop dedicated to making poppets, also called spirit dolls. While most participants were interested in ancestral dolls, some wanted to create dolls specifically for baneful magick. Sometimes you get to a place where a person's energy has you deeply vexed, and the only way out is through the magick of a dollar-store doll. I'm not ashamed to say that poppets in all forms are a staple in my work.

EXERCISE: I'M ABOUT TO POPPET YOUR ASS

This spell uses a muslin doll. As I said earlier, you can buy them at most craft stores. When doing this work, I like to play Princess Nokia's song "Hands Up." Give it a listen, or find a tune that suits you. And be warned: things are about to get messy and funky!

Needs:

* 1 blank bendable muslin doll
* 1 photo of your target
* ¼ cup honey (sweetens the target so they don't sense what's coming)
* 1 cup manure (symbolizes the world of shit they're about to live in)
* 1–2 yards of parchment paper
* 30 stick pins (creates an ailing environment that moves from the physical to the soul space)
* Optional:
  – ¼ cup corn syrup
  – 1 pair of plastic gloves

Instructions:

Lay the parchment flat, then spread the honey onto the parchment with either your fingers or a spatula. Next, roll your muslin doll in the honey. Make sure the entire doll is covered,

adding more honey if necessary. (Sometimes I use corn syrup in addition to the honey. This is totally up to you.)

Place the doll at a different end of your parchment so you can begin spreading a layer of the manure. Roll the doll's entire body in the dung. As you roll, tell the doll, who now represents your target, everything you'd love to tell the physical target.

Once the doll is covered, place the printed image anywhere on the doll: its head, ass, stomach, groin, back, all are fair game. Make sure the stick pins hold the image securely in place. Use all thirty pins.

Next, tell the doll that being placed in the trash could be considered a reward, and it's not that deserving. Tell it that it deserves to live under a dumpster and rot. Then, spit on it. Take the doll to a dumpster at least nine blocks away. Throw it under the dumpster, or real close to it.

EXERCISE: ASSED OUT OF LUCK, FEEL ME IN YOUR GUT

Some people have a hard time not making your business their business. They pry their way into your life, trying to unravel your sanity. Making use of another muslin poppet, this work forces your target to maneuver through their own well-being as their health becomes a pressing issue. This work will channel your messy side. I like to play Princess Nokia's "Goth Girl" while I perform it. Give it a try, or pick another song that inspires you.

Needs:
* 1 4-ounce package of baking chocolate or 1 cup of semi-sweet chocolate chips (promotes sweet deception)
* 1 12-count package of 15mg chocolate laxatives
* 1 blank bendable muslin doll

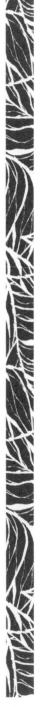

* 1 teaspoon knotweed (restricts movement in a direction that causes drama)
* 1 teaspoon black mustard seed (rids trauma)
* 1 yard of twine
* 4 tablespoons corn syrup

Instructions:

Melt the chocolate and the laxatives together in the microwave or on the stove over low heat. Once melted, remove from the heat and add the knotweed and black mustard seed. Stir.

Next, tie the poppet's arms and legs together with the twine. Place the poppet in a bowl and pour the melted chocolate mixture over it. Make sure the mixture saturates the poppet from top to bottom. Repeat the following:

Every time you say my name
From this day forth
Or think unsavory thoughts of me
Taking my kindness for weakness
Your ass will leak
Your guts will bubble
For all the toil
And all the trouble
Keep my life out your mouth
Weak bowels
Weak stomach
Swim, child, in a chocolate river of
What you full of
Shit
Shit
Shit

Remove the poppet from the mixture and bury it in your yard, or leave it by a train track.

Vengeance Is Mine

Sexual crimes are a major concern for many of my clients. For example, they might wonder how to get back at an individual who sexually assaulted them. It's often a loved one, and perhaps the assault was never reported to authorities. The victims can see their assailant on social media and find themselves reliving the victimization all over again.

I know because I've been there. No amount of blocking the person changes the fact that, even at your strongest points in healing, an image of your assailant can come across your screen and cause you pain. This work is aimed at healing by virtue of getting back at your assailant for the pain that never left, even after therapy, a career, children, and friendships. It's time to go to war.

EXERCISE: SEXUAL WARFARE, BITCHES

With this work the target will find arousal difficult and, if aroused at all, an orgasm most assuredly won't manifest. I find when helping sexual assault clients who are the victims of serial assailants that using anatomically correct candles aids in protecting future victims as well. These candles should be red or black—red heightens the magick and sends the intention into the cosmos quickly, while black aids in healing and protection of anyone in the assailant's immediate line of fire. When doing this work I like to play Princess Nokia's "G.O.A.T." Try it, or play another song that inspires you.

Needs:

* 1 red or black penis candle or vagina candle, depending on the gender of your target
* 60 stick pins
* 2–3 tablespoons Get the Fuck Out My Way Oil (see page 149)
* 1 tablespoon black salt (see page 84; sends all target's energy to torment their dream and waking spaces)

* 2 charcoal discs
* 1 teaspoon each:
  - ague weed (helps you regain strength)
  - balmony (weakens the target)
  - poke root (invites destruction into target's life)
  - vetiver (disrupts target's sex life)
* 1 cast-iron cauldron or fireproof container

Instructions:

Carve the person's name onto the candle with a pin. Next, use the oil to rub the wax portion of the candle. Rub vigorously upwards and backwards nine times both ways. Let the candle sit for twenty-four hours inside your refrigerator.

On the next day, stick the pins all over the candle while reciting the wrongs this person has wrought on your life. Next, place the candle in the middle of a saucer and place both in the cauldron. Sprinkle a ring of black salt around the candle, then place the charcoal discs inside the cauldron.

Light the candle and both charcoal discs. Begin placing pinches of the herbs onto the discs. (This work sends an exuberant amount of energy toward your transgressor, which is why it calls for two discs.) Let the candle burn as long as the discs are still usable. You may need to relight both for safety. After three days of relighting, I discard all the remnants in a trash bin that's at least nine miles away from my home.

The Story of Four Thieves

Four Thieves vinegar is a staple in protection magick, and it has its own story that goes something like this: In the year 1413 the bubonic plague swept through Europe. As people died, their homes were raided by thieves who, over time, amassed a mountain of stolen goods. When they were caught, the king asked the thieves how they could go into infected areas and not contract the disease, especially since they were also robbing graves and stealing from highly contagious bodies. The thieves claimed to be protected because they drank a special herbal vinegar. They also washed their bodies and dipped all of their clothing in the liquid. As much as the thieves reeked, they didn't show any signs of possessing the plague, and the concoction came to be known as Four Thieves vinegar.

EXERCISE: FOUR THIEVES VINEGAR AND THE MOFO ON A ROPE

This ritual uses Four Thieves vinegar to protect you against a specific person. You can also use the vinegar for other work, such as spritzing up an area that's seen its share of arguments and other unwelcome misfortunes. I like to play "Samurai" by Princess Nokia when I'm mixing up this formula.

Needs:

* For the vinegar:
    - 1 tablespoon black peppercorns (crosses up a target and gives them hell)
    - 1 teaspoon each:
        › angelica root (protects from enemies anywhere around the globe)
        › bloodroot (binds those who loved to their truth)
        › coriander (protects from the evil eye)
        › rosemary (eliminates evil intentions)
        › sage (sees through people's bull)
        › thyme (makes the creator's health improve)
        › wormwood (prevents accidents)
    - 1 tablespoon crushed garlic (wards off conniving people)
    - 9 teaspoons lavender (makes the creator more loving and loveable)
    - 3 cups apple cider vinegar (encourages healing)
    - ¼ cup gin

* For the ritual:
  - 1 blank bendable muslin doll
  - 1 marker
  - 1 yard of twine
  - 1 teaspoon cayenne pepper

Instructions:

To make the vinegar, pour the apple cider vinegar into a large mason jar. Slowly add the herbs, mixing after each addition, then add the gin. Seal and shake vigorously. Put the jar in a cool, dark space upside down for two to four weeks.

Next, write the name of your target all over the poppet. Tell that poppet every ill-meaning verse you ever thought in your head. Be bold, and don't cut corners. Set that MOFO aside.

Tie the poppet's hands and feet with the twine, then place it near the jar. Once a day for two weeks, spank and curse the poppet. After two weeks pour a cup of the vinegar into a pot big enough to accommodate the poppet and let it soak for one hour. (You're using the Four Thieves vinegar to drown the poppet, which serves to silence the target by filling their head with migraines, confusion, loss of concentration, and constant meaningless daydreams.) Pour the cayenne pepper onto the poppet's head as it soaks.

Afterward, hang the poppet upside down from a tree and leave it there. Pour any vinegar left in the pot at the base of a tree.

Juju on the Fly

The Ten of Clubs card is all about effective communication. With this card, folks will come to see you in all of your glory. Why? Because they'll hear your words and understand your boundaries as you overcome obstacles and steer yourself toward success. If you're not being challenged right now, it could be because you're, dimming your light either to keep the peace or because you don't believe you're worthy of success. Either way, you aren't living up to your true genius and being the creatress you were born to be. It's time to get recognized for the talents you've been giving away for free.

Times like these call for us to burst out of our introverted shells and engage head-on with like-minded influencers. Let's rewrite the rules of the game and embrace the alter ego of big clit energy—self-promotion! Remember, closed mouths don't get fed, closed legs don't get juicy orgasms, and artists without conviction and purpose don't get paid. Nothing will haunt you more in life than the time you didn't use.

I remember pitching the manuscript for this book to agents, editors, and publishers. They all questioned why my voice was needed when there were White authors who had already written about Hoodoo. I remember being asked if I really believed my target audience—people of color—bought books more than they pirated them. One agent said that if I were a sexy blond, a quirky goth chick, or even a gay White man he would lead the charge in agents breaking down my front door. As much as he believed I had talent, he equally believed Black witches and occultists were too few and far between for him to even consider championing my story. According to him, there was no moneys to be made in turning my words into a book. If I let it, this type of illogical thinking could've silenced my voice before I even started.

The Ten of Clubs is about channeling your venom and frustration into making a positive change. Use baneful magick to reset your life's course. This card helps folks realize what they truly want on a deep, subconscious level, as opposed to what they *think* they want. Believe in the Ten of Clubs and watch as your fire is realized without compromise. That's Hoodoo, baby.

I worked the Ten of Clubs into my life by wearing it every day for a month, and then for another week into the following month. Suddenly I got an email asking to see my full manuscript. Within two weeks I had several offers from folks vying to publish my manuscript—even the guy who said it couldn't turn a profit!

EXERCISE: FEAR DON'T LIVE HERE, NOT WITH TEN OF CLUBS

This is the ritual I used. Ancestors will step aside in honor of your return so you can be a badass. Go get your; don't worry about the hows or whys. Just keep saying, "It's my season."

Needs:

* 1 Ten of Clubs playing card
* 1 green satchel big enough to hold the card (keeps you grounded)
* 1 teaspoon cayenne pepper (spices up movement so you don't give up)
* 3 tonka beans (invites abundance)
* ¼–½ teaspoon Hoyt's cologne (brings luck and prosperity)

Instructions:

The night before this work, pour the Hoyt's cologne into your satchel. Use just enough to leave a smell but still have a dry satchel come morning. Leave the satchel on a towel overnight to help it dry out.

In the morning, take the Ten of Clubs into your hands and rub the card between your palms vigorously for three minutes. Feel the heat transfer from your palms to the card. As you rub, repeat: *It's time to shake up the world. I have a divine purpose because I'm part of someone's divine plan. You don't know it yet, but it's about to get wicked. You think you know, but you're in for a rude awakening. Ancestors, let's do the thing.*

Place the card inside the satchel and tie the satchel, by its cord, to your bra strap. You can also place the satchel in your pocket or purse. Your life is about to get really crowded with abundance.

Chapter Seven
Mother Earth Sustains Me

Grounding, also known as earthing, is all about the way we connect our bodies to Earth's electromagnetic receptors. Grounding requires we be fully present within our bodies. When we fall out of alignment, we run the risk of opening ourselves up to stress, which can lead to a host of health-related maladies. According to author Shannon Kaiser, "Grounding's benefits include reduced inflammation, supports organ functions, reduces organ pain, jet lag, symptoms associated with menstrual hormonal fluctuations, improves sleep, energy, blood pressure and normalized body functions."[27]

The earliest humans didn't have shoes. We connected to the earth through our bare feet. As civilization progressed and we began to cover the soles of our feet, we threw our physical and emotional balance out of whack. For me, grounding is a way to release tension and refocus intentions after a long day of work. Daily grounding with brown noise helped my students with autism, ADD, and ADHD focus more and perform tasks more accurately. Meditation, gemstones like black obsidian, smoky quartz, and jasper, and even literal tree-hugging get you into a grounding mindset. Walking barefoot in the grass or along a beach or even using an earthing or acupressure mat can also jumpstart your sacred calm.

Getting Connected

At work, I ground by taking off my shoes and socks and standing with bare feet on the floor or a mat. Then I tune in to some online solfeggio frequencies or tap my tuning forks with their mallet. I do this three times near each ear, or until I feel peace travel from my crown to the soles of my feet. By taking time to ground, you'll tap into a deep personal serenity every time your heels kiss the earth.

....
27. Shannon Kaiser, "What Is Grounding?," Spirituality+Health, April 11, 2020, https://www .spiritualityhealth.com/articles/2020/04/10/what-is-grounding.

EXERCISE: TURF WALKING RITUAL

There are many ways to ground. Here's an easy technique for you to try.

Needs:

* 9 drops eucalyptus oil (cleanses and purifies)
* 3 tablespoons liquid black soap (spiritually cleanses psychic doodoo)
* ½ cup water
* 1 small spray bottle
* 1 pair of earthing sandals with faux grass or turf inside
* a 1-hour recording of the 963 Hz solfeggio frequency (awakens your crown spirit)
* 1 timer or watch set for one hour

Instructions:

Combine the oil, soap, and water in the spray bottle and set aside. Step into the earthing sandals. Start the recording and your timer, then go about your regular routine—if it's work around the house or a walk around the neighborhood, go for it. (Don't forget to bring the recording with you.)

As your hour winds down to five minutes, be fully present. Engage in slow, rhythmic breathing that allows you to take in the generosity of the Universe and release the toxins of all things sour and depressing.

After the hour, remove your sandals and spray them with the oil solution. Turn them face down to dry on a towel.

Inspiring Voices: Sade

Sade Adu, born Helen Folasade Adu, is a Nigerian-born British singer, song-writer, and actress. She's also the muse extraordinaire for this section of "grounding" rituals. Born on January 16, 1959, Sade is considered one of the most successful British female artists in history. Her music blends soul, funk, jazz, and Afro-Cuban rhythms. What I love about Sade is her Emperor stance. My use of Emperor instead of Empress isn't an oversight—when you see Sade, you're watching a woman who owns the room, fully in control of her destiny in that moment and the moments thereafter. We're talking about a woman who rarely gives interviews, having ghosted the media way back when it wasn't a vogue stunt bent on gaining empathy from a diminishing fan base. As Sade says, "You can only grow as an artist as long as you allow yourself the time to grow as a person."[28]

Sade Adu has won 4 Grammy awards, in 1985, 1993, 2001, and 2010. At the age of seventeen she studied fashion at Central St. Martin College of Art and Design in London. Upon graduation she modeled and designed mens-wear. Her musical career began when she filled in for the lead singer of the funk band Arriva. Later, she would sing with a different funk band, Pride, eventually breaking off to form what would later become her own band. In 1984 Sade Adu won a Grammy for Best New Artist for her album *Diamond Life*, which featured hits such as "Smooth Operator" and "Your Love in King."

Choosing Sade as my symbolic representation of grounding was easy. The woman performs shoeless! You can't get any Earth-ier than that. I always read her shoes-off approach as her way of channeling stability within the Universe by pulling up through her feet the indigenous dormant energies that continuously bring clarity, sustenance, and reasoning to a region. It's almost as if she's saying (and this isn't a quote), *I am here to make my presence known with a peace sourced from the combining of my chakras and the peace I offer to you through my melodious serenade.* At least that's what I envision her saying.

What also resonates with me is how she consistently sets boundaries between herself and record executives, industry moguls, advertising agencies,

....
28. "Sade," Marshall Arts Ltd, accessed April 17, 2023, https://marshall-arts.com/sade/.

and fans. In 1992, her single "No Ordinary Love" won a Grammy. After a world tour she disappeared from the limelight to become a mother. She would later return to music in 2000 to create the most critically acclaimed album of her career, *Lover's Rock*. In 2010 she returned from another hiatus to pen the Grammy-winning single "Soldier of Love." Then, in 2018, after another soul retreat away from music, Sade contributed to the soundtrack for the movie *A Wrinkle in Time*. *Hiatus* is the key word. The fact that Sade Adu can freely release her attachments to notoriety is an extremely remarkable feat, especially in a world where being seen is often synonymous with being alive.

Defined by Our Followers

Let's face it, we live in an age where social media feeds our inherent desire to become instafamous. Our followers nourish us, and as our numbers climb, we become prone to bouts of narcissism and cyberaddiction. This creates a society of people who go to great lengths to imitate the lives of their idols, with every waking moment consumed by the need to have more heart emojis than the next person.

According to a study by Media X, people spend more time surfing and posting on the internet than they spend eating, drinking, and making face-to-face connections.[29] On average, people spend two hours a day on social media, the equivalent of five years and four months in a lifetime. In one minute people publish 3.3 million Facebook posts, 448,800 tweets, 65,972 Instagram photos, and 500 hours on YouTube.[30] Social media platforms provide an instant mechanism for updating our followers about what we eat, what we wear, who we date, and where we find extracurricular release.

This brings me to the Like button and how this teeny tiny symbol drives our offline activities. We do crazy-ass shit for the sake of feeding our tribe with lifestyles that are nowhere near rich or famous. The problem is that all

....

29. Sara Atske, "The Internet and the Pandemic," Pew Research Center: Internet, Science & Tech, April 28, 2022, https://www.pewresearch.org/internet/2021/09/01/the-internet-and-the-pandemic/.
30. Dave Chaffey, "What Happens Online in 60 Seconds in 2021?," Smart Insights, June 28, 2021, https://www.smartinsights.com/internet-marketing-statistics/happens-online-60-seconds/.

of these antics contribute negatively to our mental health. Justin Rosenstein, one of the creators of the Like button, put it this way: "The main intention I had was to make positivity the path of least resistance, and I think it succeeded in its goals, but it also created large unintended negative side effects. In a way it was too successful."[31]

We humans spend 80 percent of our social media posts in conversations about ourselves while measuring our choices against the loftier scenes we see typed out or photoshopped before our eyes by family, friends, and most important, strangers.[32] Social media is one of the main reasons we feel less grounded spiritually, emotionally, and physically. This ever-present feeling of insecurity in our own skin leaves us longing for the skins of our neighbors. It must stop.

EXERCISE: POPPY FREE RITUAL

For some, grounding may feel more potent when they take the herbs internally. With that in mind, here's a ritual smoking technique using a crystal pipe. I use an obsidian pipe I ordered online. This smoking technique allows you to call forth grounding energies that bring not only balance but a calmer temperament and added focus. You'll be doing this work shoeless. If the thought of standing on the earth grosses you out, use a straw or yoga mat.

Needs:

* 1 teaspoon each:
  - raspberry leaf (induces love)
  - spearmint (increases sensual dreams)

....

31. Reece, "6 Signs You Are Addicted to Social Media," Anti-Dose, July 30, 2020, https://addictioncounsellors.co.nz/6-signs-addicted-to-social-media.

32. Alice G. Walton, "Social Media Taps into Our Most Primal Urge: Talking about Ourselves," *Forbes Magazine*, June 30, 2012, https://www.forbes.com/sites/alicegwalton/2012/06/29/facebooks-share-button-taps-into-the-wiring-of-our-brain/.

- mugwort (promotes astral projection)
- California poppy or *Eschscholzia californica* (attracts wealthy lovers)
* 1 plastic zip-top bag, small
* 1 gemstone pipe
* 1 lighter or matches
* 1 red satchel, small and satin
* 1 piece of osha root, about 13 inches (keeps losers out of our messaging apps and real life)

Instructions:

Place the osha in the satchel and tie it, by its cord, to your bra strap. If you're wearing an exercise bra, place it inside the bra in the space between your breasts. You can also use twine to tie it around your neck or loop it with ribbon.

Gather your supplies and ingredients and move outside to a safe place where you can perform this ritual. Once outside, lay out your mat, if using one, and take your shoes off.

Mix all the ingredients in a bowl with your fingers. Place a small pinch or two of the mixture into your crystal pipe. (You don't have to smoke all of the mixture in one sitting. Store the rest in a cool dark place in the plastic bag.) Light the herbs; as you smoke, recite this mantra:

> I am releasing my attachments to my past lives, past spiritual undernourishings. I am grounding my life so that I am present in the here and now.
> I shall fight for the freedom and liberation of my voice and my sistah's voice.
> I shall fight for the voices of all marginalized sistahs mishandled because of race, spirituality, sexual orientation, and economic choices.

*I love this body, and I welcome the enlightenment this
grounding will bring. Welcome Mothers! Welcome
Maidens! Welcome Crones!*
Welcome!
Welcome!
Welcome!
So mote it be!
As above, so below!
Ase!
Ase!
Ase!

Now smoke your pipe and feel yourself connecting to the
earth.

EXERCISE: PENDULUM, CLEAN MY SOUL

This ritual uses smoke as well as several crystals to call to the
ancestors for help. Remember, when you call to your ancestors,
omit people who sabotaged their own lives. Those individuals
can't offer you aid. When called on, they'll only give you what
they know best: unwarranted chaos, jealousy, or envy. It's their
type of energy we want to avoid.

Needs:

* 1 charcoal disc
* 1 teaspoon ground cinnamon (sweetens your success)
* 1 selenite wand (signals to spiritual warriors)
* 1 orgonite crystal, pyramid shaped (promotes healing
  that stretches back to earlier generations)
* 1 quartz pendulum (brings communication guidance
  and rebirth)
* 1 house plant, any variety
* 1 teaspoon ground ginger (invites love)

* 1 cast-iron cauldron or any fireproof container
* a mirror

Instructions:

Light the charcoal disc, then place it in the cauldron. Place a pinch of the ginger on the disc. As the aroma expands into the air, speak out firmly, asking for your sacred and emotionally secure ancestors to comfort and guide you. Ask them to plant your ideas and footsteps on solid, forgiving soil. Call these ancestors by name.

Next, place the selenite wand in one hand and the orgonite in the other. Pass them simultaneously over the pendulum to cleanse it and to awaken its healing properties. This should be done over the span of five minutes, turning the pendulum as you go.

With your right hand, pick up your pendulum and hold it above your head. Stand near a mirror to watch as the pendulum moves. (If your arm or wrist gets tired, change hands.) Lightly swing the pendulum clockwise for one minute, then counter for one minute. Repeat for six minutes. At the close of the six minutes, recleanse your pendulum as you did at the start, then put it away. Allow the disc to burn out.

You should feel supported and grounded. Drink a tall room-temperature glass of water and go immediately to bed, or head out to conquer the world!

EXERCISE: NEW LIFE SOAK RITUAL

This next ritual uses a soothing bath to help you reset your energy while cleansing you, freeing your mind, body, and spirit of the world's pressures and expectations. You'll be creating an abracadabra sigil. This word literally means "I will create as I speak."

Needs:

* 9 drops each:
  - tea tree oil
  - lemon oil (promotes longevity in friendships)
  - lime oil (removes thoughts of inadequacy)
* 9 teaspoons baking soda
* 1 tablespoon sea salt
* 1 brown candle, encased in glass
* 1 brown paper bag, cut to approximately 8½ x 11 inches
* 1 black marker

Instructions:

Begin by writing the word *Abracadabra* on the paper to invoke the power of creating when you speak. Write it in this manner:

Abracadabra
Abracadabr
Abracadab
Abracada
Abracad
Abraca
Abrac
Abra
Abr
Ab
A

When done, run a bath (make sure the temperature is comfortable as you'll be spending a bit of time inside). In the bathroom, take the sigil and put it under the candle. Light the candle.

When the bath is ready, add the oils, salt, and baking soda to the water. Step in and sit. While there, ask the waters to bring calm into your life. Ask the waters to release anxiety, depression, jealousy, and even social media–driven expectations from your psyche. Repeat these power phrases:

I am whole. I am enough!
I am not in competition with what is known and unknown.
I am becoming a new me each day that I open my eyes.
I sing my truth.
My truth is authentic, and it resonates a beauty only I can impart.
The world needs me in all my splendor!
I am enough for me, for this world.

Allow your spirit to release as you sit for thirty minutes, then wash as you normally would. When you get out, spend time gazing at the sigil. Study the flow of the fallen letters. While gazing, try playing Sade's "Your Love Is King." The moment you feel a shift in your mood, proceed about your day as normal.

Emotional Grounding

What does it mean to be grounded? How can grounding help to increase our emotional security? Simply put, grounding is the act of being present in your body as you connect to the earth and all its inhabitants. When grounded you interact sensibly and reasonably while making decisions in life that enhance your spirit through balancing your soul space. A properly grounded person is free from excessive worry, low self-esteem, and self-pity. They exhibit a reliable moral compass and a drive to improve themselves daily, standing up for the rights of others as well as their own. They're nonconformists who live by the code of living individual lives with individual expectations, not to be determined by dogma or patriarchal rule. We aren't carbon copies of those before us who were too afraid to live organically.

Grounded people realize that an opportunity for one marginalized person is success for all marginalized people. When grounded, you don't have time to be consumed by jealousy, inadequacy, or anger over other folks' abundance. You don't have time to tote around anxiety caused by inadequate, self-deprecating thoughts. Nobody has time for that.

I'm not saying that being grounded will make your problems immediately disappear or that it's easy to maintain. However, it creates a more focused mind space where you can creatively process solutions to daily concerns. Grounding sharpens your awareness, and self-care becomes as easy as the food you eat and the water you drink. Through this practice of earthing, we call forth the best version of ourselves while decreasing the need to tailor our lifestyle to those around us. The grounding spells in this chapter have led me personally to the most sacred space of being good with me and the story of my truth, something that's constantly unfolding before my very eyes.

EXERCISE: TWINKLE TOES DANCE CIRCLE

The next work is powerful and fun. It will help you feel reinvigorated and comfortable in your skin.

Needs:

* 3 tablespoons each:
    - angelica root (enhances healing visions)
    - calamus root (promotes mastery over troublesome situations)
    - cascarilla (opens the crossroads)
    - jezebel root (allows woman's intuition to thrive)
    - licorice root (promotes lust)

- – peppermint (removes anxiety and disillusionment)
- – rosemary (promotes healing during sleep)
* 1–2 feet of thin pink decorating ribbon or yarn, cut into two pieces (*Note: You need enough ribbon to wrap securely around your ankles.*)
* 10 small bells
* a recording of an inspiring song such as Sade's "Sweetest Taboo"

Instructions:

Slip the ribbon or yarn through the loop at the top of each bell. Put five bells on each strand. (You may need to knot the spaces between each so they don't clump together in one spot when tied around your ankle.) Fasten the yarn around each ankle.

Start your recording and mix the herbs in a bowl with your hands. As you do, hold an image in your mind of what it means to be grounded. Once you have that image vibrating in your mind's eye, stop mixing.

Gather your bowl of herbs and your music. Go to a safe spot, preferably outdoors (in a pinch, indoors is fine too). Sprinkle the herbs in a circle big enough for you to get your groove on. When done, step inside the circle and blast your music.

Recall your image of groundedness and invite it to dance with you. Play your song three times while in the circle, then step out. If you're outdoors, leave the herbs to scatter on their own. If you're indoors, sweep the herbs outside. You're now reinvigorated.

EXERCISE: SWEET LIFE RITUAL

This ritual promotes grounding and connection. It also helps you learn to love yourself as you are, and to promote a connection to your spirit.

Needs:

* 1 teaspoon sweetgrass (calls one's spirit back)
* 1 teaspoon cedar chips (purifies the body)
* 1 charcoal disc
* 1 cast-iron cauldron or fireproof container
* 1 large bell or singing bowl (welcomes the soul home)
* Optional: 1 rose quartz stone (promotes self-love)

Instructions:

Gather your supplies and remove your shoes. Sit in a chair or yoga mat and position the cauldron directly in front of you.

Next, light the charcoal disc and place it inside the cauldron. Add a pinch of sweetgrass and cedar to the top of the disc. Close your eyes and begin ringing your bell in sets of three, then pause and repeat nine times. Pay close attention to your breathing—hold each inhalation for a count of four, then exhale through the mouth for a count of four. Repeat four times.

When your bell session ends, lie on your bed, sofa, or floor. Play music that inspires calm in you; I typically play Sade's "By Your Side." As the charcoal disc burns and then fizzles out, imagine your heart's eye opening to loving yourself.

To help promote self-love, you can place a rose quartz on your third eye or heart space when you're lying down. You can even slip it inside your bra.

EXERCISE: PINK MIST SMOKE

This is a calming and spiritually soothing smoking blend that focuses on emotional grounding. It helps to bring out the intentions centered around your heart space.

Needs:

* 1 teaspoon each:
  - pink lotus stamens (promotes devotion)
  - wild dagga (attracts a lover who travels to the ends of the earth for you)
  - *Calea zacatechichi* (invigorates dreams; *Note: Calea zacatechichi can have hallucinogenic affects and should be used with caution.*)
* 1 wooden or crystal pipe

Instructions:

Mix all the ingredients thoroughly with your fingers before placing half to one teaspoon inside your pipe and smoking it.

Spiritual Body Care

My own spiritual journey includes the care of my entire body, both inside and out. The following selection of workings have aided me in finding peace as I worked through my own trauma and guided others through theirs. But first, I must tell you a story involving a local building that was used as a schoolhouse around the 1930s. The town was predominately White at the time, and from what I've been told, the few Black inhabitants that did live in the area were lynched and thrown in the nearby Red River if they got out of line. To add insult to injury, a few weren't even lynched before the tossing. They were just weighed down with sacks of heavy metal.

This particular building, which was aptly dubbed White Hall, has since become a paranormal mind pluck. The first time I stepped through the door, I felt my entire body freeze and spin into a vortex pulling me back in time.

I could smell the magnolias in the hair of the blond teenagers racing to and fro. Then came the whispers of the father who caught himself a prize: a nigger hidden in a shed on the wrong side of town. The plot was to burn their catch alive before feeding what was left to the river: a baptism by fire and plunge.

When I exited, the trip back was equally mind altering. My throat felt like it was closing in, and my eyes burned as if I had stepped out of a bonfire with its flames still dancing beneath my flesh. I was dizzy and disoriented. It was as if I was traveling astrally. It took more than ten minutes to shake sanity back into my spirit. I went home and immediately began this next series of workings, which were created to ease the grounding of my spirit back into a productive and safe space.

For years I couldn't avoid this place. I was even forced to tutor in the building. That was when I knew I needed to make peace with the residual haints frolicking through the place. I needed to ground myself to combat the flesh and the wood pilings of White Hall. I corralled my ancestors, the Orisa, and my Hoodoo guides, and I rooted myself in the land of the Indigenous folk. I summoned those who presided there long before sandstone bloodied the river and long before the trees wore gruesome ornaments of flesh. I taught every class barefoot, my feet caressing the pine floors. With each step I could feel my resolve strengthening and the malevolence peeling from my flesh, dead skin seeping through the crevices into the earth below. The motion came with a deafening silence. I could breathe again.

Today, only weeds grow beneath the floorboards of White Hall. I'm thankful that a situation as spiritually oppressive as this building is no longer a physical challenge for me. To be clear, I didn't remove the energies from the building. That wasn't my purpose, and they're still there. What I did do was create a space where grounding techniques keep the entities in a time out corner when they feel my presence. This wasn't a one-time action, either. I still have to get my warrior work on every time I venture inside White Hall. These works are ones you too will find yourself returning to as you experience the satisfaction of these profound techniques. Use them as you see fit.

EXERCISE: MINTY FRESH MEDITATION RITUAL

The following grounding ritual helps strengthen and calm you by warming your body with a soothing herbal tea paired with a short meditation.

Needs:

* kava root tea, either a prepared tea bag or fresh herbs
* 9 drops each:
    - winter mint oil (increases luck)
    - spearmint oil (increases conscious thought)
    - eucalyptus oil (promotes good health)
* 3 teaspoons bluing (acts as a stand-in for an ocean bath)
* a glass or vase filled with water
* 1 charcoal disc
* 1 cast-iron cauldron or fireproof container
* 1 pinch ground ginger
* 1 pinch ashwagandha powder (increases self-love)
* 1 green candle
* Optional: 1 strainer or cheesecloth if using fresh herbs
* Optional: honey or agave syrup to taste

Instructions:

Prepare your kava root tea according to the package directions. If you're using fresh herbs, pour one to two cups of boiling water over the herbs in a mug. Cover with a saucer and let steep for seven minutes.

While your tea is steeping, place the drops of oil and bluing in the vase and stir it with your finger or a spoon. Next, place the cauldron with the lit disc next to the vase. Add a pinch of ginger and ashwagandha to the disc, then place the green candle directly behind the vase and light it.

If you're using a tea bag, remove the bag from the mug. If you're using loose herbs, pour the tea into a different cup through the strainer to separate them out. Add honey or agave syrup to sweeten, if you prefer.

When your tea is ready, stare into the vase's water as you prepare to sip your tea. At a comfortable stopping point, recite the following:

> *I am whole. I am enough!*
> *I am not in competition with what is known and unknown.*
> *I am becoming a new me each day that I open my eyes.*
> *I sing my truth.*
> *My truth is authentic, and it resonates a beauty that only I can impart.*
> *The world needs me in all my splendor! I am enough for me, for this world.*

Stare into the vase for fifteen minutes more before dousing the flame. You can use this same vase water for up to a week, but keep it refrigerated. Once you're done with the water, flush it down the toilet.

EXERCISE: FOCUS AND FANCY FEET OIL

Use this oil on the soles of your feet at bedtime to ensure that you approach the next day grounded.

Needs:

* 1 teaspoon each:
  - pink lotus stamens (invites enlightenment)
  - spearmint (improves mental clarity)
  - red raspberry leaf (promotes compassion)
  - wild dagga (increases spiritual allyship)
* 1–2 cups avocado oil, dried (promotes the acceptance of one's unique beauty)

Instructions:

Place the herbs inside a large mason jar and mix. Add the oil, seal tightly, then leave upside down in a cool, dark place for a week. Turn right side up and leave for three to five weeks more before using on your feet.

This oil can also be used in candle work in association with that same mantra used in the Poppy Free Ritual on page 165. If using the oil to anoint your candle, use a green or brown candle, preferably.

EXERCISE: SOOTHING FOOT BALM

Moisturizing and calming, this foot balm is another way to promote a sense of peace.

Needs:

* 1 cup raw shea butter (promotes prosperity and the good life)
* 1 cup cocoa butter (brings wisdom)
* ¼ cup shredded coconut (cools a restless spirit)
* 1 lidded plastic container, quart size
* Optional: 13 drops tea tree oil (helps to overcome psychic infection)

Instructions:

In a small pot, heat the shea butter and cocoa butter on low. When the butters have melted, add the coconut and stir. When well mixed, remove from the heat and let cool until you can safely move to the plastic container. (You can add the optional tea tree oil during this cooling phase.)

This is now your foot balm. Massage it into your soles when you want to feel an even stronger sense of calm.

EXERCISE: HEMP HAIR RINSE WITH HONEY ALL OVER ME CONDITIONER

As I've already said, baths and body cleaning are great ways to rid yourself of daily stress help you ground and handle trauma. Here's a rinse and conditioner that does more than clean your hair. Use it whenever you need to ground and cleanse the spirit.

Needs:

* For the rinse:
    - 1 cup liquid castile soap (cleanses the soul so even the spirits recognize it as refreshed)
    - 12 drops hemp oil (promotes luck and advantage over others)
    - 12 drops peppermint oil (purifies the soul space)
* For the conditioner:
    - ½–1 cup raw honey (sweetens one's deepest desires)
    - 1 tablespoon apple cider vinegar (aura cleanser)

Instructions:

To make the rinse, simply add the soap and oil to a large mason jar and shake vigorously for five minutes. Try listening to inspiring music as you shake. I like Sade's "No Ordinary Love" (be prepared for replay). Use the rinse to cleanse the soul and bring you calm.

To make the conditioner, mix the honey and vinegar. Put the mixture on your hair, let sit for fifteen minutes, then rinse. Again, try listening to music as you wait (no surprise, I listen to "No Ordinary Love" again). This rinse will help promote sweetness in your life.

Juju on the Fly

The Nine of Hearts card beckons us toward healing both soul and spirit. It calls forth our spirit and marks the requirement of a Soul Retrieval, a Limpia, or a Rogacion. *Limpia* is the Spanish word for a cleansing that removes stagnant energies, malevolent entities, and physical illness. Another Spanish term, *Rogacion*, deals with the spiritual cleansing of one's physical and spiritual head to align one with their present destiny.

The Nine of Hearts also reminds us that we can't unknow what we know. We must do the tough work to heal. This card says that our emotional presence as well as our spiritual presence have been depleted of Universal love. It calls us to therapy, meditation, reiki, acupuncture, divination, and grounding. This card warns of the emotional peril we face when we refuse to set clear boundaries or when we tear down our boundaries too soon.

When I pull the Nine of Hearts, I'm reminded that relationships end or go on hiatus for reasons outside my control and comprehension. Sometimes I'm left with disappointment, other times relief at finally having the personal space to question my earthly desires. With this card we have the chance to heal through conventional and unconventional modalities. It's not a card that you stick in a flannel and go about your day. This card is a pact and a promise that says you have nine Mondays to find the nearest diviner, spa, reiki, acupuncturist, or even a sauna and give yourself over to it. Go find your peace.

Every New Year's Eve my family participates in a cleansing, which can sometimes be intense. At the close of some years the spirits want a bath brewed with alcohol, herbs, and oils, while other years they want an elaborate Olokun ritual with fish and water from specified rivers or oceans. Some years they want divinations and Rogacions. The cleanse ends with a specific message for everyone, a prescription for what the new year will bring their way. It details the obstacles they will face and the consequences of given paths. The Nine of Hearts oversees whatever work is needed, reminding us this cleanse doesn't mean we'll never get dirty again. It demands we learn how to prioritize our satisfaction.

EXERCISE: BOUNDARY HUNTERS RITUAL

Needs:

* * 1 rose quartz (helps reacquaint one with self-love)
* * 1 Nine of Hearts playing card
* * 1 pink satchel
* * Optional for variation: 1 photo of a loved one

Instructions:

Touch the rose quartz to the top of your head, the center point of your forehead, and finally your heart. Place it inside the satchel. Next, rub the card vigorously between your hands, repeating the following: *You can't unknow what you know. I accept the power to heal. I have life, I have compassion for those I've wronged, but most important, for myself. I opened my eyes. I am breathing. I can think. I can laugh. I can cry. I can heal, and I can ask for forgiveness. I can bandage my wounds with time, patience, and therapy. I will better manage the rough patches and still love the longing parts of my bruised soul.*

Place the card in the satchel and carry it with you for nine weeks. As you carry this card, know it will protect you from fixating on emotionally self-injurious behaviors.

Variation: If you feel someone else is experiencing issues surrounding the letting go of painful situations, people, or ideas, you can carry this card on their behalf. Place a photo of them inside the satchel along with the card. Open the mantra with *This work is for (the person's name),* then continue with the rest of the earlier incantation.

Chapter Eight
Just for the Men

In 2013, Black Lives Matter (BLM) was formed after the fatal shooting of Trayvon Martin, an unarmed Sanford, Florida, teenager whose murderer was acquitted under Florida's "Stand Your Ground" law. BLM was formed after the failure to not only lock Trayvon's killer behind bars but also the failure to prevent police assault on communities of color. The movement fights against violence aimed at Black and Brown people—a violence that has also led many people of color to conclude that saving ourselves from Amerika requires the old-time mysticism of Hoodoo.

Just hearing or seeing the letters BLM sends some White folks seething with rage, either because they don't understand or refuse to understand the outcry of its proponents. Instead, they politicize BLM, linking racism, race, and power to an underhanded plot aimed at dismantling the morality, beliefs, and value systems of the White race. What BLM hopes to achieve is a global understanding across all communities that the humanity of Black people—their lives, their liberty, and their pursuit of happiness—is just as important as the humanity of White folks.

Racism has a significant impact on the health of Black men, including leading to higher levels of death from suicide, disease, and homicide. Racism has also led to poor physical conditioning and mental health. About 60 percent of Blacks report high levels of day-to-day discrimination leading to depression, anxiety, substance abuse, and suicide. The life expectancy at birth of Black men is 71.9 years, yet for White men, it's 78.5.[33] This reality and these statistics should concern us all.

We are losing our Black men. Black men are at higher risks for death by cancer, stroke, HIV, and homicide. For young Black males, homicide is the number

....

33. "This Is the Toll That Everyday Racism Takes on Black Men in America," World Economic Forum, July 2, 2020, https://www.weforum.org/agenda/2020/07/george-floyd-racism-opportunities-life-expectancy/.

one cause of death.[34] We're losing this battle, and yet we're constantly at war with each other, angry for not being able to flaunt our stuff through this world like the White people we idolize on television and in the real world.

I've listened to both male and female clients squawk about this more times than I have fingers and toes. It's been especially topical over the past five years, which have been more stressful than usual. I had husbands spending college tuition, retirement, and life savings on virtual peep shows. They were buying cars, houses, and wardrobes for their fantasy lovers. One male client said, "Every time I drop a few dollars on OnlyFans I get called honey, baby, daddy, and I'm always heard and never ignored or fussed at. What brother don't want that?"

I'm not saying we need to spend our days and nights trying to best virtual vixens. (Trust, you will not win that game.) What I am saying is that some men—the ones we love and who treat us more right than wrong—need us to see and hear us. Their mental stability hangs on our solidarity. As Hoodoo superstars, we can reach for our brothers, fathers, and sons, and we can wash their wounds in Hoodoo waters.

With that in mind, the following workings are for the males we love, the males we want to be around so they can see many more days of success. Performing these workings won't make you less of a woman. Count your blessings that you can love a man who loves you back, insecurities and all. New avenues of communication might open for the both of you, along with new modalities of channeling peace. Sometimes you'll find the relationship is solid, other times you might find you're both wasting time. That's okay. These workings will help each of you find your truth and fight for individual healing and relationship liberation, if needed.

Now I never want to come across as some bougie know-it-all spiritual diva with a cowrie-shelled besom broom stuck up her saditty ass. I too battle with insecurities. My relationship with my own husband is no different than

34. USAFacts, "Men Are Likelier to Die Each Year than Women. Black Men Have the Highest Mortality Rates," USAFacts, July 1, 2021, https://usafacts.org/articles/men-die-more-often-than-women-black-men-are-the-hardest-hit/.

others. In fact, I put up with the OnlyFans sistahs too. I even recently for the first time in my life bought a subscription to a sex site known as BlK Touch.

Yet I'm a proud mother who loves her two intelligent activist male sons and the Baba who aided in their conception. I couldn't walk away from creating this guide without devoting a smidgen of sacred space to the survival of men of color—my brothers, my confidants, and my tribe. These workings are for them. It will show our men, cisgendered, gay, or transgendered, the love and respect the world has denied them since birth.

Before You Do the Thing

Keep in mind that the following rituals can be performed with same-sex couples. My suggestion is that the individual with a more masculine energy is the recipient, while the individual with the more feminine energy is the provider. But that's just a suggestion. You and your lover can and should always do whatever feels good for your union.

In addition, with any of these male-energizing rituals, you can create your own incantations to whisper into your preparations while you work. You don't have to use mine. When you create your own, keep in mind the areas of the individual's life that need improvement and guidance. An incantation that I often use goes as follows: *I call on the spirits of (name of the person)'s past lives. I call on the energies that lived, died, and returned to continue the journey. Make it so that what was does not conflict with what will be, what must be. May truth always prevail, and may (name of the person) evolve into a better version of self-surviving, thriving for themselves, and for their people, many lives and across many waters to come.*

EXERCISE: WE REAL BLACK AND SATISFIED

Here's a beard or face freshening ritual to get you started in this work. Find music to play that inspires confidence in your man while relaxing his spirit so he isn't besieged by past life trauma. This simple cleaning ritual is an excellent protective measure particularly when he's facing racism in the workplace.

Needs:

* 13 drops nag champa oil (promotes relaxation and
  protection)
* 6 teaspoons sweet almond oil or coconut oil (strengthens
  confidence)
* 1 charcoal disc
* 1 teaspoon dried snapdragon (prevents deception and
  underhandedness brought on by racism)
* 1 teaspoon dried peppermint (purifies your heart so
  you're receptive to love)
* a recording of an inspiring song (*Note: I've performed
  this work while listening to an album titled* Roberta Flack
  and Donny Hathaway.)
* 1 bar of black soap, unscented (leaves objects and
  people blessed and spiritually sound)
* 3 sticks of nag champa incense (aids in relaxation and
  the search for find meaning in life)
* Optional: 1 small-toothed comb

Instructions:

At least a week before this work, make a nag champa oil
blend: In a small mason jar, dilute the nag champa in the
almond or coconut oil. Let sit in a dark place for one week.

Begin the work by lighting your charcoal and placing the
snapdragon and peppermint onto the burning coal. Turn on
your music and light the nag champa sticks.

Run the water in a sink or basin, then lather your hands with
wet soap. Distribute the lather onto your lover's face. Massage
the entire face, including his beard, if he has one. Make sure
your lover has their eyes closed.

Next, wet your towel, wring it out, and wipe the soap from
his face. Repeat the lather three times and wipe away. Dry his

face completely, then place a quarter-size dollop of your nag champa oil blend into your hand. Rub your hands together and massage his entire face. Drizzle a bit of the oil blend onto the comb and gently comb through the beard, if he has one.

When done, allow the face to dry for five minutes before encouraging your lover to carry on with their day or night.

Slavery and the Fake Marriage Bed

Where does the disconnect between Black men and women stem from? How did this vitriol begin? When I ask my male clients their opinion, some bring up slavery, which treated their relationships and marriages with Black women as slapstick absurdity. If the White man wanted to have sex with your wife, he could. Enslaved women were forced to submit to their masters' sexual advances no matter their age or marital status.[35] The Black man was forced to step aside and deal with it, and if the woman objected, she would be beaten.

If a man got out of line, he too could be raped, which was called buck breaking. It took place in front of the entire plantation.[36] If he wasn't raped, his sons were raped in front of him. Many Black men, after having suffered buck breaking, ran away from the plantation in humiliation.

Essentially, the enslaved man was expected to not let his *fake marriage* get in the way of his job. A marriage was simply a consolation prize bestowed on slaves to calm their desires for freedom. Give a man a wife and children, and suddenly he will believe that fleeing the plantation is much more trouble than his family's life is worth. He will feel, plantation owners believed, almost equal to the White man—minus the shackles. Enslaved men learned quickly that it's best to get your happy however you can acquire it for as long as life will allow. One brother said to me, "It's in our DNA not to want to be played. You expect it, but you're never ready for it. You just pretend when it happens that what was lost you didn't want to begin with."

....

35. Jae Jones, "Antebellum South: Sexual Abuse against Enslaved Women on the Plantation," Black Then, February 12, 2020, https://blackthen.com/antebellum-south-sexual-abuse-against-enslaved-women-on-the-plantation/.

36. USAFacts, "Men Are Likelier to Die."

During that time, enslaved men and women were forced into an agreement with their master concerning intimacy and marriage. The plantation owner decided when and how often the couple could be in proximity to each other, including their living quarters and working relationships. He decided when conception was to take place and how many children were considered enough. Married or not, slaves could still be sold, as well as the children born from their union.

How much value or stock would anybody take in a marriage that was treated as a minstrel show to amuse a master? If men were believed to be the "strong arm," what happens to a woman's faith in her man when he can't protect her, his children, or his own humanity? What happens to a man's own ability to reason? What happens to his self-worth when he's forced to breed and use his brawn from sunup to sundown? The couple couldn't take their resentment and anguish out on the master, so they lashed out at each other. No doubt, relationships suffered.

EXERCISE: BEARD SPRITZ RITUAL

This spritz forces individuals to see our men as equals, and it blocks society's desire to treat anyone wielding the title of man/male like a child. Your ideas won't fall on deaf ears but rather go straight to the heart of the intended receiver. This ritual spritz can be used over the entire body.

Needs:

* 2 cups tap water
* 1 cup fresh rose petals (increases the potential to create loving bonds)
* 1 tablespoon each:
    – bergamot oil (strengthens and protects the aura)
    – nag champa oil (promotes relaxation and protection)
    – vodka (fire water adds strength and courage)
* 1 plastic spritz bottle

Instructions:

In a medium pot, bring the water to a boil on high, then add the petals. Turn the heat to low, cover, and allow to simmer for twenty to thirty minutes. Watch for the moment the petals lose their color or turn pink. When they do, remove the pot from the heat and let sit, covered, for thirty minutes.

Next, add the oils and vodka. Stir, then pour into a mason jar and place in a dark place for safekeeping. When you're ready to use it, pour some into a small spritz bottle and spritz away. (You can strain out the petals if you don't want them floating in your spritzer.) It will ensure you're emotionally safe as you go about your day.

Do Something. Anything.

In a scene from the 2002 movie *John Q*, Denzel Washington's character, John, is urged by his wife to "do something" to ensure his son gets a lifesaving heart transplant. John takes drastic action, wielding a gun and holding an entire hospital hostage. Despite going to jail in the end, John's son survives thanks to the availability of a heart made possible by a motorist who dies at the beginning of the film.

I'm not suggesting that violence is the answer every time we feel denied an inalienable right. But it is true that Black and Brown people experience a maze of helplessness similar to the one in the movie. We're born already holding the short stick and start playing the game of life from behind. Catching up means we're sometimes forced to make choices that go against our core beliefs simply to keep food on our tables, a roof over our heads, and clothes on our backs.

For many of my female clients today the "do something" rule is a constant burden in their relations with men. Many of these women feel as if it's the Black man's refusal to "do something" that makes them complicit in the violence done to their brethren like James Byrd Jr., Amadou Diallo, Oscar Grant, Trayvon Martin, Tamir Rice, Elijah McClain, Ahmaud Abery, and

George Floyd. One sistah told me, "If they'd just step up, for themselves and for us, I'd be willing to date them again." Black women are also victimized, as seen in the murders of Sandra Bland, Breonna Taylor, Ma'khia Bryant, Tamla Horsford, Atatiana Jefferson, Pamela Turner, Miriam Carey, Rekia Boyd, and many others.

Historian Orlando Patterson argues that the belief in the Black father's inability to protect his family from White dominance is the root of the "uterine society" principle.[37] Slave owners reinforced this idea by separating more sons than daughters from their parents. In the 1850s for every 1,000 enslaved men there were 857 females ranging in ages from twenty to twenty-nine years old. After slavery ended, the lack of available men to choose from forced many women to scramble after, as my grandmother would so eloquently put it, "a piece of man, because a piece of man was better than no man at all." In other words, as much as Hoodoo became a defense against the violence of slavery, through insurrections or by running away, Hoodoo also became a key way for many women to solve the dilemma of how to keep a man you borrowed, stole, or received.

EXERCISE: YOU LUCKY SO RITUAL

I know we ladies love our gemstones tucked in our bras or adorning our waist beads, and men can get in on the fun too. I love seeing a man in a hematite or black tourmaline bracelet or necklace. And one secret they might know is that many women love men who are into aligning their chakras with gemstones. That right there is full-throttle sexy.

In the following ritual, you'll birth a satchel that will create a potent force—one to be reckoned with. You can create the satchel as a gift for your man. In this case, your own love and care will serve as an anointing for this work. Your man may

37. Liz Mineo, "Orlando Patterson Explains Why America Can't Escape Its Racist Roots," *Harvard Gazette*, June 4, 2020, https://news.harvard.edu/gazette/story/2020/06/orlando -patterson-exp.

choose to create his own satchel. In this case, the work allows him to directly align his physical state with his spiritual need for balance. Either way works.

Regardless of who makes the satchel, it will become your man's go-to as it connects him to his higher self while redistributing a belief in the genius and talents that are his rightful inheritance. This work can also be done for your sons, male friends, or other male-bodied people in your life.

Needs:

* 1 red satchel big enough to hold the stones (heightens the power of whatever gemstone is placed inside)
* 1 piece each of
  - hematite (grounds)
  - turquoise (calms creativity)
  - lodestone (increases fidelity)
* 1 teaspoon Hoyt's cologne (increases luck, as well as physical and mental prosperity)

Instructions:

Place the gemstones into the satchel, then pour in the Hoyt's cologne. Next, hold the satchel in your hands and clearly state what grounding looks like to you, what calm creativity looks like, and what fidelity looks like.

Some men like to carry the satchel in their pocket or wear it on a piece of twine around their neck. The decision is up to you. Be flexible in how you acclimate gemstones into your spiritual healing, and above all have fun experimenting.

Sharecropping, Babies and Beyond

The issues facing Black men and their families didn't end with slavery. During the sharecropping era, Black men were allowed to work land owned by Whites in exchange for a share of the crops and profits. One major asset for sharecropping families was the labor of their offspring. The more children working the land, the bigger the harvest crops, which meant a larger profit for the landowner. At the same time, sharecropping kept the Black family employed. In his journal, my grandfather wrote, "You had children out of necessity. A new baby was another pair of hands, fuller sacks, fuller plates. You were most times too afraid not to make babies."

A 1900 census report shows the average rural family had at least eight children, not out of love but out of a need to make enough profit to keep them fed, clothed, and housed.[38] "During sharecropping, there wasn't time to fall in love," my grandfather wrote. "There wasn't time to even love the children you had. Men and women had uneasy alliances. You were grateful for the right number of fingers and toes the baby had, but you couldn't make a fuss about a new baby coming into the world. Boy or girl, neither mattered."

Hoodoo was still an important part of many people's lives during this time. It was used to protect the family's overall health so all members were physically able to work the land. "I think in the backs of most people's minds they always thought, what if they shackle us up again? We'd better make and keep making more of us and worry about falling in love when the time is right—in other words, when we have enough borrowed time stored on layaway," my grandfather wrote. Our survival was a form of "underhanded getting over," but it came at a price. "The world was a cold place; we didn't make it that way. We, men or women, didn't know how to trust. We just lived like machines. Many of us couldn't remember a time when we weren't somebody's mule. We forgot how to be human, I reckon that's right to say."

The struggles continued well into the twentieth century. In the 1960s, Southern states such as Louisiana, Mississippi, Alabama, and Arkansas forced a disproportionate number of Black males into the conflict in Vietnam. Forty-five percent of the 100,000 troops who enlisted in the Army and Marines were Black men. For them, combat was inevitable. Black men between the ages of eighteen and twenty-five made up much of the United States casualty

....
38. Jeff Hoyt, "1800–1990: Changes in Urban/Rural U.S. Population," Senior Living, May 20, 2022, https://www.seniorliving.org/history/1800-1990-changes-urbanrural-us-population/.

count.[39] Wallace Terry, author of *Bloods: An Oral History of the Vietnam War by Black Veterans*, wrote, "Over 60 percent of the men on the front lines dubbed 'Soulville' were black, and they accounted for more than 23 percent of American fatalities even though only 10 percent of America's overall population."[40]

The men who survived Vietnam's physical toll suffered ongoing mental traumas, which led many to resort to drug use in hopes of numbing the pain. Black men returned from war impoverished, addicted to drugs, and infected with sexually transmitted diseases. They had no job, no prospects, no nothing except an urge to survive America's "catch back" in the best way they could, with sex and drugs topping the list. This combination led to a rise in drug-related violence, gangs, dealers, and skyrocketing unemployment.

EXERCISE: LIBERATION LOVE BATH

This working will get our men ready to release their day and invite a calming sleep rhythm into their astral space. This bath is a call to the astral realm; it serves as a protective force field against the woes of Western life.

While deciding whether to include this work, I spoke to some fellas who said they don't take baths, they shower. While men can use this same working in the shower, I would implore these sworn shower devotees to consider a good old-fashioned bath.

Needs:

* ¼ cup Epsom salt (peels back layers of past life trauma)
* ¼ cup baking soda (allows the heart space to be penetrated by love)

39. Andrew R. Chow and Josiah Bates, "Black Vietnam Veterans on Injustices They Faced: Da 5 Bloods," *Time*, June 12, 2020, https://time.com/5852476/da-5-bloods-black-vietnam-veterans/.

40. Earl Smith and Angela Hattery, "Black Men, Vietnam, Drugs & Prison," Smith & Hattery, February 14, 2016, https://smithandhattery.com/black-men-vietnam-drugs-prison/.

* 13 drops nag champa oil (contacts those ancestors beyond the veil)
* 13 drops peppermint oil (keeps out unwanted entities from our dream space)

Instructions:

Place all the items inside a large mason jar, seal, and shake vigorously for ten minutes. Store the love bath upside down in a cool, dark place.

When your man is ready, have him draw a bath and add the preferred amount of Liberation Love Bath to the water. He should stir the mixture evenly around the entire tub with his hands, then bathe as usual.

When he's bathing, he should cup his hands together, allowing water to fall onto his head. It's important that every inch of his body is included in this spiritual bath, allowing the healing to manifest throughout his mind, body, and spirit. When he gets out and dries off, he might want a moisturizer to soften his skin.

You can use this Love Liberation Bath Ritual for yourself as well.

Reality Love versus Real Love

In contemporary America, we have new problems, such as trying to foster relationships under the influence of reality television. I love you, sistahs, but we aren't absolved. When we watch female influencers, we often see ourselves portrayed as undesirable castoffs under the guise of society's standards of Western beauty. We're forced to choose between femininity and self-sufficiency. We're forced to live up to the stereotype of a chocolate Barbie: a mouthy spitfire, money hungry, oversexed, and ready for a fight. The message being that few Black men want dark-hued women, women with natural hair, women who choose not to wear makeup, women who are intelligent, and women who are hardworking go-getters.

Pastor Calvin Roberson of Lifetime's *Married at First Sight* told *Madame Noire,* "One of the biggest problems we have on the show when trying to match is finding Black men who want Black women."[41] I had a male client who agreed, "I've dated Black women and White women. The thing with White women is they don't overextend. They give you enough rope to live. They don't kill dreams just for the sake of having something to say." It's worth noting though There are plenty of Black men who value Black women as partners. I've divined for many of them! In fact, 75 percent of Black men in the United States marry Black women.[42]

For those wanting to know when the Black couple revolution is going to happen, it's already here! I've had clients come in for bone throwing or Lenormand divination, and their love, finances, and health are in alignment. These couples refuse to let fake media shows run or ruin their relationships. They work within the parameters of their union by viewing each other as a human with their own set of core values, beliefs, and deal breakers. They develop economic, health, emotional, and spiritual plans that keep them communicating their needs, wants, and desires to each other as partners, never as adversaries. Dead is the notion that a Black woman is just a stepping-stone on the way toward a White woman. Gone is the assumption that Black men don't make sound partners because they don't make enough money to be good providers, or that they're only loyal until the next big booty drops it like it's hot in their face.

It's time to convince our men to stop letting the failures of enslavement, Jim Crow, Vietnam, and personal traumas haunt their DNA. We must challenge them to be better than they were yesterday. Let's stop lying to each other about what is and isn't acceptable behavior in a loving coupling. If you love men, keep loving them. Hold their asses accountable and praise them when they make what was impossible, possible.

....

41. Victoria Uwumarogie, "Pastor Cal Says Black Men Auditioning for MAFS Might Prefer White Women, but 'White Women Don't Prefer You,'" *Madame Noire,* July 18, 2018, https://madamenoire.com/1033090/pastor-cal-mafs/.

42. The Root Staff, "Myth-Busting the Black Marriage 'Crisis,'" *The Root,* August 18, 2011, https://www.theroot.com/myth-busting-the-black-marriage-crisis-1790865391.

EXERCISE: BALDIE HAIR RITUAL

For the men who are going bald, I'm not leaving you out of the mix. This next working protects you from overbearing bosses and jealous coworkers, and helps you hold your tongue when faced with people who wake up only to try your last nerve. It can also be used on men with a full head of hair.

Needs:

* 1 cup almond oil (promotes success in business ventures and when engaging an overbearing boss)
* 1 teaspoon meadowsweet (aids in keeping the peace when others try to start confrontations)
* 1 teaspoon plus 1 pinch lavender, divided (protects against the evil eye)
* 1 tablespoon frankincense oil (uplifts your spirit)
* 1 charcoal disc

Instructions:

Pour the almond oil into a large jar, then add the herbs and frankincense oil. Stir the mixture slowly to distribute the herbs evenly throughout the oils. Seal the jar tightly, turn upside down, and let stand for two to four weeks in a cool, dark place.

When the mixture is ready, light the charcoal and put a pinch of lavender on it. Apply the oil to your man's head or hair, making sure to massage gently but lovingly.

Bonus work: Add nine drops of peppermint or lavender oil to one to two cups of liquid castile soap. Wash his hair with this mixture weekly. The lavender will help reduce his stress and decrease restless leg syndrome. The peppermint will clear his head while stimulating the unconscious to act on life's pleasures.

Hardly Working in New Shoes

My father used to say, "A man who doesn't own at least one pair of run-down shoes ain't working hard, instead he hardly working." Shoe workings in Hoodoo are nothing new. Some are performed to keep a flighty lover grounded to one boudoir. Others, like this next one, are for protection.

Remember, energy is everywhere. It attaches to us whether we're cognizant or not. The best defense is preparing before the energy turns malicious. Make sure to keep all the man-spa items within an arm's reach. That includes all the ingredients listed in any of the rituals in this chapter. In my own home the spa is always open, because getting pissed off can happen any day of the week. Don't believe me? ask the next brother you encounter.

EXERCISE: LIBERATION WALK OR HERBS IN MY SHOE

After you perform this work, you or your man will find that as you cross the threshold to and from work, the successes or pitfalls you've encountered won't scar your life together.

This working has two parts. First, you'll make a soothing after-bath moisturizer, then you or your man will make a foot bath.

Needs:

* For the moisturizer:
  - 1 cup olive oil (increases sexual potency and alleviates stress and anxiety headaches)
  - 1 teaspoon each:
    › rosemary (ensures peaceful sleep)
    › myrrh oil (ensures that one comes and goes as a bringer of peace)
    › rosemary oil (ensures negative vibrations remain outside the home)
    › sloe blackthorn flower (banishes unwanted spiritual residue)

* For the ritual:
  - 1 basin or plastic bucket big enough for two feet
  - 1 tablespoon each:
    › rosemary (ensures negative vibrations remain outside the home)
    › myrrh, finely ground (ensures that one comes and goes as a bringer of peace)
    › sloe blackthorn flower (banishes unwanted spiritual residue)
  - ½ cup castile soap (spiritually alleviates the energy of psychic vampires)
  - 1 loofah
  - 1 bay leaf (promotes liberation and a refusal to go against the family dynamic)

Instructions:

Pour all the moisturizer ingredients into a large mason jar. Stir. Make sure the herbs are swirling in the mixture and are evenly moistened. Seal tightly, turn upside down, and let sit for two four weeks. (You can use it immediately if you prefer.)

When the moisturizer is ready, bring a large stock pot of water to boil, then remove from the heat. Add the herbs, cover, and let sit for fifteen minutes.

Next, add the castile soap to the basin or bucket. Pour in the herb mixture. Check the water's temperature before placing your feet in. Once the water is at a comfortable temperature, place one foot in at a time to ensure no overflow, then relax for thirty minutes.

Use the loofah to scrub the feet, ankles, and lower legs. Start with slow and smooth strokes, then become more vigorous. Do this for fifteen minutes. When done, dry the feet and legs, then massage the moisturizer into the skin for five to seven minutes using vigorous strokes.

You or your man are now prepared to walk in peace and strength. Top off this ritual by placing the bay leaf inside his left shoe at the heel area. Pick up the shoe to charge the bay leaf by whispering, *You are nobody's fool, nobody's buck, nobody's slave. Bless the world with your brilliance, and always come home wearing abundant love and abundant peace.*

Juju on the Fly

The King of Hearts card invokes power through the use of emotional charm. This is the card I use before embarking on crossing work. The King of Hearts makes it so others see you as a charmer, a compassionate being who's emotionally connected to others of your own volition. This is the card I call the "throw a stone and hide your hand" card. It allows you to keep the object of your disdain under wraps while your secret weapon brews.

We all get pissed, and sometimes keeping it real isn't the wisest choice. So we step back, reassess, and conclude the long con is the better option for the situation at hand. This card reminds us that it's more fun to plot the course of events methodically than it is to deliver quick blows.

I had a client whose boss decided the entire staff would take the company Christmas picture in MAGA hats. My client was the only Black person on the staff. She felt insulted and humiliated. She viewed this as an assault on her Blackness. She was ready to make her boss pay, but after consultation and after days of deliberation, she decided she would let the King of Hearts work it out.

We turned the tide in her favor by asking for the slow demise of the boss's professional career. Within a week, the boss was denied a promotion. Within six months, she was placed on leave while being investigated for mismanagement of the company's budget. By the Christmas photoshoot, the boss had been transferred and a report to human resources revealed the MAGA hat idea, which was canceled immediately.

Magick can help us use the trespasser's own insistence on living the life of a scoundrel against them. When we use baneful magick to reposition our target in the right place at the right time, we can relax, sit back, and wait for the eventually unscrupulous rampage to unfold.

EXERCISE: YOUR BORROWED TIME IS UP

Take a deep breath and let the King of Hearts work a situation out for you.

Needs:

* 1 King of Hearts playing card
* 1 black satchel big enough to hold the card and photo
* 1 photo of your enemy
* 9 peppercorns (fires up the ritual)
* 1 marker

Instructions:

Take the King of Hearts in your hands and rub vigorously. Repeat the following:

Emotionally, I am pissed off, but for now
I must behave as if all is right with the world. I am in
*   charge of my emotions. I determine what deserves my*
*   wrath.*
I determine what deserves my pity.
Through clear thoughts and quiet clarity, I will pursue
*   revenge as a means of protecting my present sense of*
*   self-worth.*

Place the card inside the satchel with the peppercorns. Next, take the photo and write the following words on it: *suffer, lose, pain, sickness.* Put it in the satchel.

Wear the satchel or carry it daily for nine days, then place it in a jar of first morning urine. Leave in a bushel nine blocks from your home. Return and don't look back.

Chapter Nine
Goddess Bless the Child

When I talk to clients who care for little people, nightmares and bullying are a major concern. Some of these women are biological mothers, while others perform mothering duties at various stages throughout children's lives. Without fail, spiritual assistance in preventing nightmare or terrors and stopping class bullies from intruding into one's home via the internet rank high among their ritual requests. These situations are more than pressing—they demand mandatory spiritual healing and, in serious cases, counseling and school or even police intervention.

Before turning to the work, I highly recommend seeking counseling for children whose nightmares are causing them to lose sleep. The same goes for any form of bullying; I always suggest involving the school and the proper authorities. Levels of cruelty can escalate quickly, and an adult caregiver may not always be aware of the toll it takes on a child, especially if that adult is old school and insists the child should just ignore the problem. That's never a good idea. It's almost as bad as saying, "Just fight the bully and get it over with." One form of violence can quickly escalate into other forms of violence, often resulting in loss of life. In some cases, a child may be so afraid of their bully they would rather take their own life than live in constant fear or ridicule. Always seek professional help.

Here's another piece of advice: When performing magickal workings for your school-age children, it's important to discuss magick in terms they can understand so you can ask for their consent. Never perform work on your children's behalf without first having their definitive okay. Performing a working without consent sets a bad precedence and can color how children view magick from here on out. You can ask, "Is it okay for me to use magick to clear a new path for you?" Then explain what that new path might look like.

You also need to explain any changes or consequences the working may cause over time. Be sure to discuss the positives and the negatives, and allow the child at least twenty-four hours to contemplate. This waiting period gives the child a chance to figure out their own path to accepting or rejecting magickal assistance with their hardships.

For workings with children, I typically don't include music, for three reasons: First, I want them to take their role as a magickal apprentice seriously and with extreme focus to detail, and music can interfere with that. Second, these workings usually require that we go to a quiet place of introspection, and I want the focus to be on the intention. Finally, these works have a way of proving heavy on the soul. After completion, you or your child will need to take a sea salt bath and sleep in all white from head to toe, including white socks.

Stress of Bullied Humiliation

Let's begin by examining bullying, specifically cyberbullying. Research has shown that 32 percent of kids who experience cyberbullying also experience high levels of stress.[43] Many children blame themselves for the acts, feeling embarrassed, hurt, socially destroyed, humiliated, and isolated. They often feel powerless to stop their bullies and may believe their lives are ruined beyond repair.

First, if your child has experienced bullying or trauma that has led to thoughts of suicide, the National Suicide Prevention Lifeline (1-800-273-8255 can help. Their trained counselors understand the trauma associated with cyber misconduct and can help them sort through feelings of hopelessness. In extreme cases, cyberbullying can manifest in children acting out with drug use, skipping school, gun violence, ulcers, nausea, eating disorders, insomnia, and nightmares.

Cyberbullying can happen through texts, emails, online gaming, and social media sites, either public or school based. It's not enough to tell children to log off. We live in a technological age: School closures, whether due

---

43. Ivana Vojinovic, "Heart-Breaking Cyberbullying Statistics for 2023," Dataprot, last modified April 7, 2023, https://dataprot.net/statistics/cyberbullying-statistics/.

to weather or health concerns, can require a switch to online schooling. Screens are replacing schoolbooks and changing the way kids learn. This opens the door to a cyber highway riddled with trolls, bullies, and criminals of every race, creed, and gender.

The following workings are designed to help your children confront bullying in general—cyber or otherwise. Those geared specifically to cyberbullies can be adapted to address real-world bullies as well. However, it's important to remember that magick should only be one part of your work. Always seek professional help first.

Note also that all workings for children should be presided over by an adult. In cases where the child is too young to assist, a capable and discerning adult can perform the steps with the child's blessing.

EXERCISE: WE AIN'T GOT TIME FOR CYBER ENEMIES

This first ritual uses baneful magick. As an adult, you may now be familiar with the warnings about doing this work and understand the circumstances that justify it. At times, we act out of anger and later find ourselves consumed with regret. Before any baneful work, stop and listen to your inner voice. Ask first, can I live with what I'll unleash into the world?

Your child, even your teenager, may not understand this or think it through. Your job is to guide them wisely in this work. When asked what they want to manifest, guide them in selecting a reasonable result. Apply this process to all the baneful workings in this chapter.

Needs:

* 1 section of squill, dried and finely sliced (protects the heart from shame)
* 9 silver dimes
* 1 photo of the cyber bully, or their name written on a piece of paper

* 1 cast-iron cauldron or fireproof container
* 1 green satchel
* 1–2 charcoal discs
* 1 teaspoon wintergreen (heals and breaks painful cycles)
* 1 teaspoon toadflax (encourages self-confidence and inner strength)
* a small bowl of water

Instructions:

Place the squill and nine dimes in the satchel in an inconspicuous section of the child's backpack. Then, place the photo under the cauldron. Light and place the charcoal inside and add the herbs to the charcoal.

Have the child repeat the name of the bully three times and tell the charcoal and herbs exactly what they want to manifest, what they envision happening to the bully and where they want the bully to go. For example: *Aisha Davis, Aisha Davis, Aisha Davis, I want your computer to get so many viruses it malfunctions, and I want you to get kicked out of school for being a bully.*

Let the charcoal burn out. The work is done.

EXERCISE: GOODBYE BULLIES RITUAL

This is a protective working that uses a potato as a poppet to heal emotional pain. It also helps your child sleep more soundly if the trouble online or at school is causing nightmares or terrors.

Needs:

* 1 large potato
* 9 strips of brown paper bag, 1 x 3 inches
* 1 black permanent marker

* 9 thumb tacks
* 1 teaspoon asafoetida powder (ensures protection)
* 1 teaspoon cayenne pepper (purifies one's life and promotes sleep without anxiety)
* 1 teaspoon hot sauce, plus more for feeding (absorbs pain and sends it to the bully)
* 1 clay plant pot big enough to conceal the potato
* 2–3 cups soil, enough to cover the potato halfway

Instructions:

Help your child wash the potato with dish soap and water while thinking of all the mean and terrible decisions their bully has made. Allow the potato to dry overnight.

The next day, write the full name of the bully on each strip of paper. Take a tack and place each strip around the potato as if the potato is wearing a hula skirt. Draw eyes, and a mouth on the potato, then set aside.

Next, take the planter and have your child write words or phrases to end your bullying. For example, the child may write *suspension, move to a new city or state, kicked off the bus, sent to a school for troubled children.* (As with the last ritual, use wisdom when choosing what to write and advise your child accordingly.)

Place the asafoetida, cayenne, and hot sauce inside a medium pot. Place the potato inside and on its head so the face is at the bottom of the pot. Use the potato to gently stir the mixture.

Next, hold the potato in place while you sprinkle the soil around the inside of the pot planter until the soil's height reaches the potato's midpoint. When you're done, have the child scream at the potato. It should know exactly how the child feels. Have the child tell it everything they have dreamed of telling the bully. When the child is done, place the potted

potato in a sunny area of the yard or at the base of a tree. Once a week, feed the potato one tablespoon of hot sauce.

In time the bully will lose interest in your child and become consumed by his or her own troubles, which are heating up even as we speak.

EXERCISE: I BURY MY ENEMY BENEATH MY FEET

Bullying isn't just a problem for young kids. I've had college students come to me for advice on the subject. In these cases, the bully may be another student, a predatory professor, or a fellow sorority or fraternity member who's overstepping their bounds into harassment. The victim might be an athlete enduring severe hazing because they feel their family's legacy hinges on whether or not they join the team. Eventually the student feels there's no other way out without risking alienation, embarrassment, and anxiety.

The following working is one I offer students before beginning any divination. This work allows the student to begin to regain control of their lives while devising a plan to end their cycle of pain once and for all. It calls on the Black Annis, a blue-faced bogeywoman found in English folklore. According to her mythology, she has a taste for human flesh. She goes looking for angry-hearted children, whose disdain is her delicacy. It's said she rests on the branches of oak trees.

Note: This ritual is for adult use only.

Needs:

* 1 permanent marker
* 1 potato
* 1 sticky note
* 1 photo or drawing of the Black Annis
* 1 photo of the bully or an index card with their name

* 1 roll of duct tape
* 1 plastic zip-top gag big enough to fit the potato
* 3 tablespoons black salt
* 13 tablespoons Himalayan sea salt
* 1 bar of black soap
* Florida water in a spritz bottle

Instructions:

Using the marker, write the bully's name on the potato, nine times up one side and nine times down the opposite side. Prick the potato all over with a fork. As you do, recite the following: *Potato, I send you to cause confusion and nightmares. I send you far away from me. I sentence (the bully's name) to an abandoned place where your name and your face will become food for Black Annis. She will haunt your dreams, and the fear you send to others shall asphyxiate even your daily life.* Repeat 3 times.

On a sticky note write, *Black Annis, haunt this ugly-hearted bully and make their soul quake with fear.* Affix, the two pictures and the sticky note to the potato with duct tape. As you do, this repeat the phrase: *Scare them at night and during the day, make it so they hear your laughter in classrooms, bathrooms, libraries, hallways, the gym, and the auditorium.*

Place the potato inside the plastic bag and toss in the black salt. Shake vigorously for five minutes, then take the potato to an abandoned place, an overgrown area, or a cemetery and toss as far as you can. You can also toss your potato at the foot of a tree. Leave and go home. Don't look back.

When you get back, draw a bath. Add the Himalayan sea salt to the water, then bathe with the black soap. Afterward spritz your body with the Florida water and sleep in all white from head to toe.

After the ritual is done, the bully will have nightmares and be so confused from a lack of sleep they won't be able to even think about you. When the problem is solved, toss the potato into a wooded or wild area. Do not toss the bag—we don't want to litter.

Online Assignment

It's easy to say, "If you're being bullied, just get off the internet." But sometimes that simply isn't possible. Perhaps your child's teacher encourages internet research and doesn't care about cyber harassment. Maybe school is closed and classes have moved to e-learning, or maybe you need to take a special class that's only offered online. In these cases, it may not be possible to avoid a bully.

You don't have to put up with a class clown who only wants to attract attention by using the internet to chew you up and spit you out. Let's get to work on that situation.

EXERCISE: LEAVES ME BE RITUAL

This is a quick protection ritual that will send a strong spiritual message to your bully: "Leave me be."

Needs:

* 1 handful lime leaves (opens the heart to healing love)
* 1 bowl of water
* 1 photo of the bully or an index card with the bully's name

Instructions:

Place the lime leaves in a bowl of water in the room where your computer is. Soak the photo in the bowl. As you sit to work at your computer, stir the water with the index finger of your dominant hand. Say the bully's name three times and keep stirring, then repeat:

I drown your desire to make me hate myself.
I drown your desire to cause me harm.
I drown your desire to make me cry.
I drown your desire to make my life a painful chore.
I love me, and I know how to fight you.
Your words no longer define me.
I can block you and anyone who tries to welcome you
*   into my life.*
Be Gone, Enemy! Be Gone! Be Gone!

Dry your finger, and get on with the business of cruising the cyber highway.

EXERCISE: SOCIAL MEDIA SLOW YOUR ROLL RITUAL

This ritual is all about grounding your computer screen and stopping the bully in their tracks.

Needs:

* 7 tonka beans (creates the courage to live on without feelings of ridicule)
* 1 shallot, finely sliced (purifies the spirit so that hatred no longer resides there)
* 1 teaspoon slippery elm (gives back the child's voice and sense of agency in the world)
* 1 teaspoon wintergreen (heals what was broken)
* 1 white satchel, small
* 1 sock
* 1 pencil pouch big enough to hold the sock

Instructions:

Have the child take the tonka beans in their hands and tell them exactly what they want to manifest, what they envision happening to the bully, and where they want the bully to go.

(Remember to proceed with caution and wisdom when making the request.)

Next place the tonka beans, shallot, slippery elm, and wintergreen in the satchel and then place the satchel in the sock. Put the sock in the pencil pouch, then have the child carry the pouch to school until the bullying stops.

Friends of Our Dreams

A key component to staving off bullies is a strong group of friends with high self-esteem. The bigger your friend group and the more empowered and supportive your allies, the less likely you are to become the target of any attention-seeking bully. I've included two rituals to help you attract positive, life-affirming friendships.

EXERCISE: WHY CAN'T WE BE FRIENDS, NOT FRENEMIES

This ritual will help your child be more vocal as they become active participants in potential friendships. They'll discard the desperate lackey persona that make them punching bags for narcissists, and see themselves as the true prize. They'll begin to take pride in their outer and inner presentation and feel as though it's the world that should catch up. *Warning: Do not aim this ritual at a specific person.*

Needs:

- * 1 slip of paper
- * 1–2 charcoal discs
- * 1 teaspoon each:
  - – spiderwort (attracts love and genuine friendship)
  - – prickly ash (attracts honesty and goodness)
  - – ladies' mantle (makes others see one as extremely likeable)

Instructions:

On the slip of paper, write the following:

> *Send me friends who respect themselves, their family, and*
> *the rights of others to be whoever they want to be.*
> *Send me friends who embrace the differences in others.*
> *Send me friends who will help me embrace all of me, and*
> *I will do the same for them.*
> *Send me a multicultural world of lovers of laughter, and*
> *we will change the world.*

Tear the paper into tiny pieces and place it into the cauldron. Light the charcoal and place atop the shredded paper, then add the herbs on top of the charcoal. Repeat:

> *We will be friends. We will be friends. We will be friends.*
> *I am a great friend, you will see. Soon you will know.*
> *I am the friend you've always wanted.*
> *I am the friend you've been searching for.*
> *Give us a chance, we can be friends.*

Let the charcoal burn out. Within a month, the child will begin to experience a newfound confidence.

EXERCISE: A POTATO NAMED FRIEND RITUAL

Needs:

* 1 large Irish potato (acts as a poppet)
* 1 black permanent marker
* ¼ cup honey (enhances the powers of persuasion)
* 1 plastic zip-top bag, gallon size
* 1 tablespoon black salt (helps to ask the ancestors for assistance in alleviating mistrust and disloyalty from entering the friendship)

Instructions:

Using the marker, write fun activities you would like to do with your friend on the potato. Use single words or short phrases such as *ice skating, ComiCon, ParaCon, skateboarding, movies, football, basketball, concerts,* or *dances.* You get the idea.

Next smear the potato with the honey. As you do this, ask that these types of events manifest into your life along with a friend group to rival the die-harders from *Stranger Things.* In closing, repeat: *Friends forever, enemies never. Friends forever, enemies never. Friends forever, enemies never.*

Place the potato in the plastic bag and add the black salt. Seal and shake so the salt sticks to the potato all over.

Next, take the bag to a nearby tree. Allow the potato to spill from the bag at the foot of the tree. Whatever insect or animal that makes their way to the potato to feast will eat away the fake friendships you may still have or the ones that are trying to find their way into your life, leaving space for new growth, adventures, and friends.

Trash the plastic bag in the garbage (your own is fine). In a month you'll find yourself evaluating who your bestie is, but you'll have options and ideas about how you want to spend your time and with whom.

Midnight Monster Mash

Children's nightmares can cause morning drowsiness: theirs and ours. I've lived through it. If you haven't, believe me, it's not a pretty picture. The Cleveland Clinic reports that an estimated 10–50 percent of children ages three to six experience nightmares that often seem terrifyingly real.[44] Nightmares involve fear and anxiety, and can be induced by traumatic events. Some

----

44. "The Vicious Cycle of Exhaustion and Nightmares," Cleveland Clinic, December 14, 2022, https://my.clevelandclinic.org/health/articles/14297-nightmares-in-children.

children cope with nightmares by skipping bedtime altogether. I can relate—as a child I would sometimes sneak a few sips of chicory coffee to avoid the night monsters.

Studies show that after the age of ten, nightmares decrease in both girls and boys. After age twelve, girls usually have more nightmares than boys.[45] While nightmares in young children are typically caused by things like separation anxiety or a fear of monsters, older kids' nightmares are often caused by experiences such as watching too many horror movies, being the unpopular kid in school, or being made a "joke"—bullying.

Stick with It

When he was about three, my eldest son would pretend he had to use the toilet at night. He'd turn on his lights and shuffle to the bathroom with a bag of action figures, then make a palette on the floor—all to avoid the darkness of his room and the shrubbery tickling the windowpane. His objective was to stay up until the light in our room at the other end of the hall came on. He knew my husband and I made a habit of getting up to hit the treadmill, Tae Bo, or yoga at 3:00 a.m. every morning. After that he'd flush the toilet, lug his haul back to his room, climb into bed, and drift off to dreamland.

At some point, I started researching our family history and various herbal remedies, looking for anything that would work for my son and eventually his siblings. I have five children, and I found one thing remains key: every child is an individual, so go slow and note what's working.

I started by drawing pentagram sigils on the backs of my kids' doors using a dragon's blood resin incense stick. The stick wasn't lit, and you couldn't actually see the pentagram, but the motion of inscribing it made it a reality. Then I lit the resin and proceeded with the rest of the ritual work. In my working, I called out the names of a deceased relative they knew and loved, after which I placed a bowl of lavender water under their bed. For some of my children, that worked.

....
45. Cleveland Clinic, "Exhaustion and Nightmares."

Others needed a different approach. I took their favorite toy and put it on their bed, then I gave them a gemstone anklet, either hematite for power or tiger's eye for strength. They wore it while they were tucked in at night. During the day, it was tucked inside the toy. I always told my children the properties of the stones, and that, in the event a nightmare, the gemstones would awaken their toy to fight on their behalf giving them enough time to escape to a cozy dream space free from fear.

Did it always work? Some combination of different measures did. That's just the way it goes with children. You'll find yourself working through a lot of trial and error, but if you stick with it, the nightmares will cease.

EXERCISE: HERBAL TEA REMEDIES

Herbs to help quell nightmares include chamomile, lavender, juniper, bay laurel, and thyme. All of these herbs or any combination can be made into a drinkable tea that improves your young one's quality of sleep and softens their dream space.

Always test the taste of any blended mixture before you give it to a child. My kids loved lavender and juniper with a hint of bay laurel or thyme. Chamomile mixed with anything, however, was a no-go for them.

Needs:

* 1 cup water
* 1 teaspoon of your chosen herb
* 1 strainer or cheesecloth

Instructions:

Bring the water to a boil in a pot or kettle, then pour over the herb in a cup. Cover with a saucer and let steep for seven minutes. (*Note: If you're using more than one herb, don't blend yet! Instead, pour one cup of boiling water over each additional teaspoon of herb in separate cups.*)

Pour the tea into a new cup through the strainer to separate out the herbs. If using several herbs, this is where you blend, adding as much or as little of each infusion as you want. Add honey, agave syrup, or plain sugar to taste, then let sit until cool enough for the child to drink.

Beyond Tea

While my kids wouldn't drink chamomile tea, putting an oil infusion in a diffuser worked wonders. Here are some other herbal hints and tricks to try:

- Place three drops of any of the previously mentioned herb's oil onto a dryer sheet, then place the sheet inside the child's pillowcase.
- Soak the child's washed garments in a basin of water that contains nine drops of lavender or nine drops of chamomile oil, then wring out the garment and line or air dry it in the dryer. The scent will help the child experience a sound, nightmare-free sleep.
- Drop nine drops of thyme and lavender onto a plush toy or fabric ball and allow the child to sleep with it. I've been successful using this technique on a doll's hair and clothing. As the girls held their dollies close, the scent helped them gain control and to self-soothe their dream space.
- Place a bowl of rosemary under the child's bed. It will attract and trap negative energy so it doesn't inhabit the child's dream space.
- Place nine drops of rosemary oil on the child's socks and have them wear those socks to bed. This will help them sleep soundly and feel superhuman in their dreams.

EXERCISE: OSHA SPIRIT (RITUAL)

My great-nephew was experiencing wayward spirits crossing into his dream space. He struggled to get a good night's sleep, which affected his social life and academic performance. After a few nights of with osha root, he slept peacefully.

Needs:

* 1 osha root, about 1–3 inches
* 1 brown satchel
* 1 sheet of paper
* 1 pencil
* 1 glass of water
* a recording of thunder and rain

Instructions:

First, have the child create a story of how the root will become the superhero ending their nightmares. They can use words (written or verbal) or pictures to tell the story. Make this story part of their bedtime ritual to provide assurance that the root is always there to defeat those hardheaded monsters. Osha is the defender of dreams.

Have your child give the root a name and tell it how it wishes for it to handle their nightmares. (*Note: Talking to the root before placing it inside the satchel is imperative.*) Ask the root to please intervene and prevent the spirits from haunting the child's dreams. Tell the root that for this assistance, you'll be kind to it by keeping a glass of water near the satchel at all times.

Place a glass of water on the bedside table and turn on the thunder and rain recording. Keep the sounds playing throughout the night. The root will appreciate that you're making provisions to help it rekindle a sense of connectedness its home environment.

Put the root inside the satchel and place the satchel near the water on a bedside table, dresser, or chair, whichever is near the child's head. Keep it there as long as the nightmares persist. Remember to keep the glass filled with water.

Juju on the Fly

The Five of Clubs ushers in new friendships, or in some instances new lovers, who ease into our lives like a calm, steady breeze. These lovers of troubled souls teach us the value of triumph over sadness. This card invokes the spirit of knowing the difference between love and abuse, and connects us to people who bring out the sunshine in our eyes. These are the happy go-getters, the folks forever striving to be greater today than the day before. The Five of Clubs drowns out the noise from bullies and jealous peers and reprograms us to love the blessings stewing within our own bodies, and the blessings bestowed on us by the highest of our ancestors.

When I taught high school, I knew a girl so starved for notoriety that she gravitated toward the wrong friend group. She was a straight-A student who didn't find the type of popularity she thought would make her happy with her book smarts, so she became a five-dollar prostitute performing sex acts under the stairwell at school. She became popular, but for all the wrong reasons. In the end, her newfound fame soiled her reputation and that of her mother, a twenty-three-year veteran teacher at the school.

I ran into her years later at a coffee shop. I was reading Toni Cade Bambara's *The Salt Eaters* while waiting in line for a cup of green tea. The moment our eyes locked, her face begged me to notice how time had hardened and softened her all at the same time. She was different now, her face said, and she needed me to know just how far removed she was from that infamous stairwell. I found out that after two years of junior college she was now a freshman at a four-year university.

I reached into my purse for the deck of playing cards I carry just for occasions like this. I pulled out the Five of Clubs and wrote her name on the back along with "May the friends you welcome from this day hence be worthy of you forever and always." I gave it to her and told her to keep it as a reminder that our choices are what make the world a place of joy or suffering. With our every movement we invite others to join our sacred dance of renewal or not.

She smiled, pressed the card to her heart, and gave me a hug. The dance she was doing at that point in her life was so powerful even the trees waved in the wind, beside themselves with happiness. Before saying good-bye we promised that even if we never saw each other again, we understood no life is fully lived until we can lay our faults to rest by honoring our triumph over sadness.

EXERCISE: HONORING OUR NEW GROWTH

This Juju on the Fly is for high schoolers or college-age students struggling with stepping away from toxic peer groups.

Needs:

* 1 Five of Clubs playing card
* 1 marker
* 1–2 feet of yarn or a pretty ribbon, any color
* 1 hole punch

Instructions:

Take the card in your hands and write the following on it: *I'm grateful for the friends I welcome into my sacred circle. Thank you for second chances.*

Press the card next to your heart space, then punch a hole in a corner. Thread the yarn through, knot the ends, and hang it somewhere you'll see it and be able to read the words out loud, like your dorm or car. In time you'll experience renewal in your thoughts, actions, and reactions. This is one of those workings you can use as long as the card has life.

Chapter Ten
Crossing Over

In the United States, mourning is often a personal affair. We're usually attended to by our immediate family and given a set amount of time to grieve. We're told to seek comfort in the knowledge that the living world is crap compared to where the dead person has gone—in other words, don't be sad, be happy they made it out.

A procession of people tell us, "If you need anything, I'm here for you"—maybe twenty, thirty, forty, or sometimes a hundred folks. It's hard to hear this over and over and over. Needing something—anything—incurs a debt most are unwilling to pay. Still, folks repeat this line because we hope our words will ease the pain of not being able to bring the deceased back to life. So we say the words, we kiss and hug, and then we go back to work, to school, and to our lives. We try to redirect attention from the deceased to the survivors. We hope that those who still mourn heal quickly and shed their grief so they too can get back to the business of living.

Not everyone is just regurgitating the line, though. Some people genuinely want to help their loved ones, and even want a connection that lasts beyond death. But in many cases their religious leaders warn them that there's no such thing as ancestral veneration. They teach that communing with the dead is a sin against God and the natural order of life.

I call BS on that.

Death Rituals and Celebrations

Death rituals are a cultural phenomenon and are handled differently from society to society. I'll briefly share a few interesting death rituals from around the world. Many of these rituals help participants maintain a connection to their dying relatives as they cross the threshold into the afterlife.

In Indonesia, the Torajans believe the body stays with the family after death. They care for and talk to their loved one up until the final funeral rites are delivered. They view death as a form of sickness and believe the Rambu Solo ritual must occur for the spirit to move on. After the funeral, the person's soul is thought to finally reach the afterlife. Every three years afterward, the body is exhumed, cleaned, and redressed in a ritual called Ma'nene. [46]

The Japanese custom of kotsuage allows the family to be part of the process of revering their deceased ancestors. After the ash from cremation has cooled, family members pass the bones to each other, placing them inside the urn that will remain at the family shrine from thirty to sixty days before it's taken to a graveyard.[47]

In Accra, Ghana, ancestors' coffins could easily be mistaken for works of art on their way to a museum. The Ga people believe that, since the soul continues its journey in the afterlife, the coffins should be reminders of favorite pastimes in the physical realm. The beautiful coffins are part of elaborate funeral rites with strong parallels to New Orleans jazz funerals, which last all day.[48]

In the Hindu religion, people visit deceased family members' homes for twelve days after death. During this period, the family chants the soul toward the next world. On the thirteenth day, the family performs the rite of Kriya to show the deceased their appreciation.[49]

Members of the Sioux Nation believe the dead aren't considered passed away. They're still moving on their journey toward their next life. It takes four days for the spirit to journey to its next soul destination. Mourning in Sioux culture is expressed in wailing, singing, and ceremonial hair and body cutting.[50]

In Mexico, during the annual Dià de los Muertos, people decorate altars with candles, sugar skulls, flowers, pan de muerto (sweet bread), photographs, and other delicacies favored by the dead. The altars are an homage

....

46. Carolanne Allardyce, "Rituals and Ceremonies in Death and Dying," Awaken, January 1, 2021, https://awaken.com/2021/01/rituals-and-ceremonies-in-death-and-dying/.
47. Funeral Guide, "Death Rituals around the World: Different Funeral Traditions," Funeral Guide, May 24, 2018, https://www.funeralguide.com/blog/death-rituals-around-the-world.
48. Funeral Guide, "Death Rituals around the World."
49. Funeral Guide, "Death Rituals around the World."
50. Tracey Wallace, "Death Rituals and Traditions around the World," Eterneva, February 21, 2023, https://www.eterneva.com/resources/death-rituals.

to their ancestors and a space to house offerings to those who've crossed over from this world into the next. The tradition is a blend of Aztec and Catholic customs, with the altar being a meeting point of heaven, earth, and the underworld.[51]

Buddhists believe after a person dies, they're reborn and reincarnated. These actions expressed in life will determine how the person returns—a god, ghost, or creature.[52]

In the United States, there has been a growing movement around natural deaths, green burials, and home burials. These rites allow the deceased the freedom to liberate from their body in a spiritual manner that more closely involves those who loved them best.[53]

For example, in the Colorado town of Crestone, people of any religious denomination can be cremated, wrapped in cloth, placed on a wooden bed, covered in juniper berries, and cremated under the sky. Crestone is home to the only outdoor cremation facility in the country. Family members can even touch the torch to the bed, serving as their loved one's gatekeeper to the afterlife. This is just one example. US Funerals Online has a listing of green burial sites, and the Order of the Good Death (a death acceptance organization) is an excellent resource for planning home funerals and other alternative options for death rituals.

Mourners are also finding eternal connectedness in opting for death mementos. These are items like gemstones, jewelry, or memorial beads crafted from the cremated body of the deceased or from locs of their hair.

Laissez les bons temps rouler

In New Orleans, where I'm from, we have second-line or jazz funerals. There's a wake where a brass band trails the body to the church. The music is at first solemn and mournful, then the rhythms get the Holy Ghost and

51. Wallace, "Death Rituals and Traditions."

52. Amy Newman, "Buddhist Death Rituals and End of Life Traditions," LoveToKnow, February 24, 2022, https://dying.lovetoknow.com/burial-cremation/buddhist-death-rituals.

53. Kate Torgovnick May, "Death Is Not the End: Fascinating Funeral Traditions from around the Globe," Ideas.ted.com, October 1, 2013, https://ideas.ted.com/11-fascinating-funeral-traditions-from-around-the-globe/.

vibrate a possessed synergy of happiness and celebration. It's a jovial reunion where music rips the veil in every direction, allowing us to witness the last dance shared by the dead and the living in this earthly realm.

After the funeral, the band joins the family and attendees as they strut to the burial site. Again, the movements begin somber, then transform into high-spirited sashays. Libations are poured as family members lead the casket through the deceased's favorite stomping grounds. Some attendees even dance on top of the casket in a frenzied state, gyrating and chanting. This call-and-response session ends when the casket reaches its final resting place.

In a final rite of passage, the attendants share their fondest and most salacious remembrances of the deceased. The storytelling begins at the ceremony and follows the attendants to the house, where they enjoy a true feast. Gumbo, jambalaya, red beans and rice, collards, mustards, turnips, fried chicken, po'boys, étouffée or coubion, and the darkest of liquors fill the hearts, bellies, and the ancestral palate until the morning.

Honor and Healing

No matter how you handle grief or what you believe, one purpose of death rituals is to honor those we love and will continue to love. Funeral rites are the living's ways of keeping those we care about close. These rites not only provide a sense of control over difficult and oftentimes traumatizing events, they also create cathartic and healing avenues that allow many to celebrate their personal connection to life beyond this realm.

EXERCISE: RITUAL TO HELP THE DYING CROSS OVER

Begin this ritual right after you learn the person has died. I keep all the needed items on hand so I don't have to make a last-minute run to purchase anything.

Needs:

* 1–2 charcoal discs
* 1 tablespoon vanilla extract (restores energy)

* 1 bowl of water
* 1 white candle
* 1 teaspoon dried gardenia (calls on the spirits of the ancestors to come forward)
* 1 cast-iron cauldron or fireproof container
* 1 teaspoon dried myrrh powder (exorcises the Spirit of all misgivings in this bodily form)
* 1 teaspoon dried frankincense powder (consecrates the body)
* 1 brown paper bag

Instructions:

Place the vanilla extract in the bowl of water and stir it with your finger. Place the white candle inside the bowl and light it.

Next, light one of the charcoal discs and put it inside the cauldron. Place each herb onto the charcoal.

Sit and ask that your loved one finds peace and direction in the comforts of all who have traveled this path before them. Thank them for the gifts they've imparted to you. Remind them it's time to move forward on their journey of becoming an ancestor. After that period, in a year and two weeks, they will be able to help the living find understanding and solace in the physical world. It's this tutelage you'll wait for. Remind them.

After thirty minutes, snuff out the candle.

Do this ritual for nine nights. At the close of the ninth night, put all the items used in the ritual into a brown paper bag. Take the bag to a graveyard and leave it.

EXERCISE: ONE YEAR LATER

One year after you perform the previous ritual, honor the deceased again as they bring closure to their journey.

Needs:

* 1 white tablecloth
* 1 picture of the deceased
* 9 pennies
* 1 bowl of soil
* 1 glass of water
* 1 bowl of fruit or a bit of your meal as an offering
* 1 piece of obsidian
* 1 piece of citrine

Instructions

A year after your loved one has crossed over, cover a small table with the white tablecloth. Place their picture on the table.

Place the pennies in the bowl of soil. Make sure they're buried. This represents the Orisha Oya as well as your loved one's the transformation into an ancestor.

Place the bowl next to the photo, along with a glass of water and a bowl of fruit or sampling of your meal. Add the obsidian (representing the afterlife) and the citrine (representing change) to the setting.

Make sure to change the food daily for nine nights. After the final night, add the new ancestor to your ancestral shrine.

Between Worlds

Death rituals also help us, the living, release our attachments to the physical life of our loved one. If we're caring for a beloved elder in a hospice situation, we can expand our spiritual connectedness by making the most of whatever time we have left.

Some ways to do this:

- Play their favorite songs.
- Dress them in their finest clothes.
- Let them partake of their favorite meals plus a sweet treat, if they can stomach it.
- Talk about happier times shared with your loved one.
- Don't be afraid to cry and laugh as loud and as wide as your heart can stand.

Remember, death is the agreement we make when we accept the challenge of life inside this shell we call our body. At some point during our current incarnation, we'll all have to settle the score and cross into the vastness of remembrance. That's very much okay. Death isn't to be feared, but to simply be seen as our reward. It's the cashing in of our chips, taking our almost-final bow while the veil thickens between worlds until we're elevated as an ancestor.

EXERCISE: TRANSFORMATION DEATH OIL

This oil helps keep you calm as you proceed to a wake or funeral service. It helps settle your spirit as you return from a gravesite—an experience that can be emotionally excruciating.

Needs:

- 1–2 cups sweet almond oil (promotes prosperity and blessings for the living)
- 1 teaspoon each:
  - sandalwood oil (heals the heart space)
  - eucalyptus herb (relieves anxiety and emotional turmoil that leads to physical sickness)
  - narcissus (promotes self-love and confidence)

Instructions:

Pour the sweet almond oil inside a large mason jar. Add the sandalwood oil and the herbs. Stir. Allow the jar to rest upside down in a cool, dark place for two weeks before using.

Place this oil on your third eye, on your hands, and on the soles of your feet. It helps you stay emotionally grounded and center your soul space as you prepare to cut the cords that bind you to the dead.

EXERCISE: BYE-BYE, BABY—SOUL CORD-CUTTING RITUAL

Needs:

* 1 charcoal disc
* 1 teaspoon each:
    - jasmine (attracts loving Spirit guides)
    - cinnamon (raise the vibrations in the home)
    - powdered frankincense (promotes powerful meditative vibrations that cleanse the atmosphere)
* 1 length of thin biodegradable cord or twine, 12 inches
* 1 pair of scissors
* 1 small paper envelope
* 1 cast-iron cauldron or fireproof container
* 1 garden shovel

Instructions:

Light the charcoal disc in the cauldron and place the herbs on the disc.

Next, tie the twine into nine knots. As you tie, think of nine lessons the deceased person taught you in life. Speak to them out loud as you knot. If you can't think of nine lessons, repeat what you can remember nine times.

Next, cut the first knot, right on top of it. As you cut, repeat:

It is done, what you brought to my life.
It's done—the memories we've made together.
We are parting ways on this day.
I thank you and will continue to love you, but now is my
*   time to liberate us both.*

Continue cutting all the knots and repeat the phrase for each cut. When finished, place the cut twine in the envelope.

When the herbs are burned and the charcoal is cool enough, put the ashes in the envelope with the twine. Seal it and bury it in your yard in a beautiful area. (You can also burn the cut pieces.)

Sick and Shut In

When my maternal grandfather refused to spend a single night in a physical rehabilitation hospital after a diagnosis of stomach cancer, the entire family banded together to provide around-the-clock care for him. A major part of his care involved soothing his soul with spiritual healing. Many days he could sit up and write the stories of his life, paint beautiful landscapes, or tell me about his upbringing as a Geechee. We listened to Billie Holiday and Sarah Vaughn. We eventually performed a ritual to ease his walk between the worlds.

EXERCISE: EASING THE WALK BETWEEN WORLDS RITUAL

This is a ritual to help the infirm find peace as they prepare to cross over. This isn't a ritual to stave off death. If you're performing this ritual for a loved one, rub yourself with the transformation death oil before starting. This act will help you find peace in knowing the loved one's journey will continue, just not in this physical body.

One important note: While this ritual is soothing for the soul of the terminally ill, it should only be performed in the home. Due to the use of burning incense, this ritual would most likely not be permitted in a hospital or senior care facility.

Needs:

* 12 mothballs (absorbs disease and the energy of sickness, thoughts of depression, and fear of death)
* 1 cast-iron cauldron or fireproof container
* 1–2 charcoal discs
* 1 teaspoon rose geranium herb (protects the living from hauntings)
* 1 bowl of water
* 1 teaspoon patchouli oil (prepares the spirit for the afterlife journey)
* 1 teaspoon cedar oil (purifies the astral realm so that cord cutting isn't a hindrance)
* 1 raw egg washed in 1 teaspoon Florida water (absorbs residual energy of guilt left by the dying and prevents it from merging with the pain of the living)
* 1 tablespoon asafoetida
* 1 cup water

Instructions:

Prior to the ritual, gather a list of your ancestors. If the dying person isn't a family relation, try to gather a list of their recently transitioned relatives. (It's okay to have the names written on a list. There's no need to memorize anything.) Bring that list to the ritual. (*Note: if you can't find the names of the person's ancestors. That's okay too.*)

When you're ready to start the ritual, place three mothballs in each corner of the dying person's room. If it's hard to reach the corners due to furniture, place the mothballs as close to the actual corners as possible.

Next, place the charcoal disc in the cauldron and light it, then place the geranium herb on top. Once the smell begins to bless the air, walk around the room again and again, stepping in places that aren't cluttered. Keep moving as much as the room's inanimate objects allow. The goal is to not stand in one place.

Next, call to your ancestors and those of the dying. Keep in mind the goal is to use the aroma to call forth the ancestors and to help the spirit of the ailing person find peace as they begin their great journey. If you don't have the names of the person's ancestors, simply state: *To the ancestors and the recently transitioned loving spirits of (the person's name), we ask that you prepare the way for your kin, that when the time is ripe (he/she/they) will know peace. We thank you, I thank you, and your love is welcomed here.*

Once you feel spiritually satisfied that you've opened the portal to the ancestors, place the cauldron in front of the door leading into the room.

Add the patchouli and cedar oil to the bowl of water and stir the mixture with the index finger of your dominant hand. As you stir, ask the water to release the person from pain and cool their fears. Next, place the bowl under the person's bed. If beneath the bed is cluttered or it otherwise seems impossible to place the bowl underneath, put it on a nightstand near the person's head.

Next, pick up your egg. Hold it near your third eye and breathe in and out three times, then place it near your heart and repeat the breathing. Cup the egg in your hands and thank it for agreeing to be the one chosen for such an auspicious occasion.

Next, grasp the egg with the fingers of your dominant hand and move it over the ill person's entire body. (You can touch it to the person's clothed body or hover it a few inches above.) Begin at the head and roam over all areas in between and down to the feet. If you can, try turning the person onto their sides to hover over their back.

Once finished, touch the egg to their third eye area and the middle section of each foot for five minutes each. Then take the egg, crack it into an empty bowl, and pour it into a glass. Add the asafoetida and water. Leave the glass outside, in front of the person's home, overnight. The egg, water, and asafoetida pulls out any negative attachments that are still lurking. It also absorbs any feelings of anger, desperation, and the desire to cause mischief for mischief's sake after transitioning.

In the morning, tie the glass up inside a paper bag with the contents still inside, then drop the bag into a dumpster.

Keep the water near the bedside until the person passes, changing it once daily. Flush the old water down the toilet.

Spirit Boards

There are ways to stay in touch with the dead after they've passed. Spirit boards are one of them. According to witch and author Raymond Buckland, talking boards or spirit boards are "an ancient form of communicating with spirits of the dead used in China and Greece from as early as 600 BCE."[54] The spirit board you're most likely familiar with is the Ouija board, created by William Fuld in 1892. Parker Brothers still heavily markets the board today as a spooky paranormal game. As you can imagine, sales spike during the Halloween season.

The boards have developed a bad reputation over time. You've probably seen movies in which Ouija-conjured spirits send séance participants to early graves. Hollywood at times can be all about making money and not making

....

54. Raymond Buckland, *Buckland's Book of Spirit Communications*, 2nd rev and expanded ed. (Woodbury, MN: Llewellyn, 2008).

sense. Consider also that some folks use talking boards, as they're also called, during moments of mischief, at parties, or on ghost tours. During these events, inebriated individuals can be insensitive and downright disrespectful to the spirits. Would you call your grandparents to a room and flash your boobs, penis, or bare buttocks for amusement? Probably not. Yet I've actually heard of this foolishness being done while engaging the Ouija.

Dos and Don'ts

First, it's important to remember that spirit communication isn't a joke, game, or parlor trick. Any spirit board, including Ouija boards, has the potential to connect you with ancestors and other wayward spirits.

The typical spirit board is rectangular and contains letters and numbers forming a curved shape. The words *yes, no,* and *good-bye* are also printed on the board. As the users pose questions, the planchette (a triangular tool with a clear viewing hole in the center) moves along the board to indicate various letters, numbers, or words. These form messages from Spirit realm. When engaging with the board, all individuals rest their fingers on the planchette. Each participant must be careful to place their fingertips lightly, ensuring the viewing hole isn't covered.

Here are some basic dos and don'ts when using a board:

- Avoid using the board in cemeteries. Why? Because you're inviting all comers to your party. Without a spiritual cleaner on speed dial, your hocus-pocus fantasies could disturb the spirits' travels. As retaliation these angry spirits might follow you home, causing you many, many days and nights of unwanted disturbances.
- Construct your own spirit board. This infuses your energy, conscious and unconscious, into the process. It also helps you establish a direct line to your own ancestors. Mass-produced boards have too many mortal hands involved in their rituals of production, manufacturing, and distribution. These rituals will greatly hinder your direct line of communication with your ancestor.

- Contact well-intentioned Ancestors only. This ancestor should be a guide of good character, someone who had your best interest in mind while alive. It goes without saying, if they comforted you in life, you'll get more of the same in death. Don't waste candle-light on the awful because their motives are still apparent in death. Death doesn't automatically transform a person's character from maniacal to saintly.

- The type of spirit you call will dictate the type of help you receive.

- Before starting, ground your physical body and protect your environment. When you aren't grounded properly, your ancestors may find you incapable of interpreting their energy as guidance. You may even view their intervention as a hostile takeover of your life.

- Always start with a greeting, and always close with a thank you and good-bye. Do this even if you believe no contact between worlds occurred.

- Invite others to the party. Spirit boards are intended for use by two or more people. Folks who've gone one-on-one with a board report feeling as if their energy was zapped. They achieve communication with Spirit but can't pull themselves away. Some say it felt as if an assembly line of spirits kept manifesting. Although the users didn't feel as though they were in physical or psychic danger, they said another set of hands wielding the planchette alongside would've helped.

- Don't go spirit boarding when you're sick. If you don't have the physical energy to communicate with Spirit and you go boarding anyway, there's a greater chance you'll experience a weakened signal. Your ancestor won't hear you clearly, or they might think you're in distress. They may interpret this distress as your wanting them to manifest as a full-body apparition or orb so they're better equipped to see you through your mess. You may not be ready for that type of connection.

Try to approach using a spirit board the same way you would throwing a house party. First, you narrow your guest lists to blood relatives and your spectacular superfriend group—the most loyal and loving people in your world. As guests arrive you sit, talk, and laugh, sharing drinks and appetizers. Once the gang's all present, make sure the front door is locked—you wouldn't allow random stragglers to pop a squat in your physical home, right? Then serve dinner and, when it's all over, say a polite farewell.

Don't be afraid of your spirit board. The purpose of this work is to contact our spirit guides so they can help us achieve successful transformations. Take baby steps while mastering it, and you'll develop your intuitive powers and understanding of how not to fear Spirit, but to make Spirit your ally.

Igba Iwa

In Yoruba tradition, *Igba Iwa* is the term for the Calabash of Destiny. It also means "good character attracts blessings." In times of crisis, we can use the spirit board to call on the elevated—an ancestor of good character—to assist. Now, such an ancestor is not a saint. We've all done dirt; some are proud of that dirt, while others want to sweep that dirt under a rug and never look back. What I mean by good character is someone who loved every inch of your being and would go out of their way to see you protected, successful, and happy. When we select these ancestors with Iwa Pele, we're afforded the proper guidance to get our lives under control. We're that much closer to spiritual elevation.

In Ifa, we're taught that whatever we imitate in our youth will persist till old age. Our character and our destiny are one. If we can't live harmoniously in our bodies and lives in this realm, where will we gain the knowledge to encourage others once we become ancestors? The tragedies, traumas, and scar tissue in our family tree are direct roadmaps to deciding who should and shouldn't be called on during our spirit board sessions.

In the following exercise, you'll use the same methods I've taught many clients, none of whom have ever recorded unruly energies presenting themselves in any way, shape, or form. However, crazy stuff does happen, even when we're well prepared and even for seasoned spiritualists. That said, the stuff that happens to novices is usually the result of disobeying one of the basic rules. Someone was sick, didn't ground, or forgot pictures or items owned by the deceased. In other cases the invited guest was problematic, such as someone who wasn't of good character, someone who was a murder or accident victim, or someone who spent their life playing the fool and loving it.

Be very careful when making your list of guests. Also note that use of the spirit board isn't a Yoruba practice. I'm using it here because it requires no initiation, just attention to detail.

EXERCISE: DIY SPIRIT BOARD/PENDULUM RITUAL

The board you're going to construct in this work can be used alone. I've simplified the questioning technique for ease. This technique allows you the flexibility to sit with your board between five and fifteen minutes, or more if you choose. Instead of a planchette we'll use a pendulum, and our board will consist of a circle, a vertical line, and the words *yes* and *no*.

You'll be grounding to the rhythm of a shekere. The shekere calms misgivings and eases any confusion associated with Spirit communication. The photos and items your ancestor once owned are necessary to ensure the individual spirit we're talking to hears us loud and clear.

Needs:

* 1 pyrite pendulum (transforms misfortune to fortune)
* 1 silver candle (promotes spiritual reflection)
* 1 photo of an ancestor or item they once owned
* 1 piece of cardstock, 11 x 17 inches or 12 x 18 inches
* 1 silver marker
* 1 shekere

Instructions:

Before beginning, write out your questions to avoid wasting Spirit's time and to aid in a comfortable flow of divination.

When ready, begin by tapping out a tune on your shekere. Feel the spirit consume you. Once this is achieved, set the shekere aside.

Take the cardstock and draw a large circle in the center, then draw a vertical line directly down the center of the circle. Around the entire circle write the word *yes* in large letters. Along the vertical line write the word *no* in large letters.

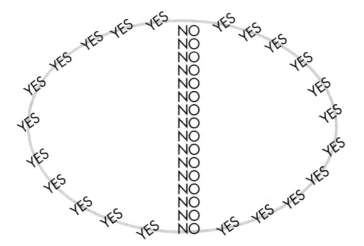

Hold your pendulum clasped inside your palms and breathe onto it. As you breathe, envision your ancestor breathing healing breaths onto the pendulum with you. Once you have given the pendulum three cleansing breaths, set it aside.

Next, take the photo of your ancestor and place it to the left of your board. Place the silver candle to the right and light it. Pick up your pendulum again and whisper your ancestor's name three times.

Holding the pendulum by its chain end (not the gemstone end), allow the pendulum to hover above your board directly in the center. Tell the pendulum yes answers will be conveyed by the pendulum swinging in a circular motion over the board, and no confirmations will follow a vertical line pattern.

You're now ready to ask for confirmations of yes or no questions. I like to start by asking if the ancestor is willing to serve as my spirit guide. If you get a no choose another spirit, or wait nine days and ask again. If you get a no again, choose another ancestor.

If you get a yes, spend time with the ancestor. Ask questions and listen to the answers. When you're done, offer a respectful good-bye: *As all meetings must come to an end, I ask that as you follow the path back to your seat of elevation, may nothing enter into my world that doesn't already possess the code of permission. Even then only the resurrected saints among you have my blessing to visit my dreams, to speak through déjà vu or to whisper through the ramblings of strangers near, far, and virtual. Until we meet again, go in peace and love. Ase, Ase, Ase.*

When the spirit has gone, ground yourself and store your board and pendulum until it's time for the next dinner party.

Juju on the Fly

The Ace of Spades represents a life-altering spiritual experience. It marks the end of any longstanding situation that has reached crisis mode and needs to die a clear death. The Ace of Spades explores your secret desire for knowledge as you prepare to launch a new you, a new career, a new occupation, or to take more control over your decisions. This card heralds an ending that spawns a new beginning filled with adventures.

You carry this card when you need to ease into a transformation with style and grace. The Ace of Spades wants you to be happy for any new opportunities for change without the need to go around town tooting your behind at what's now in the rearview. Always remember that the folks you meet on your way up could be the same people workings to mastermind your downfall. Don't give anyone a reason to root against you.

Transformations can be difficult and traumatic, especially with the world trying to reset after a global crisis. Carrying the Ace of Spades keeps anxiety and uncertainty at bay. It also helps you be gentle with yourself.

I had a sistah friend who worked hard to release a childhood lover in prison for an assault he swore he didn't commit. According to her, he was everything she ever wanted in a man—handsome, fine, the works. He could be her trophy man, the guy who'd make other women wish they were in her shoes.

She came to me for readings every month for an entire year. Every one said no to questions concerning his readiness to love her. Eventually she decided she wanted a second opinion. When she received the same answer, she decided to pay a fortune to have a diviner magickally free the man from jail so he could be her husband. About a month later, she phoned me for a reading about his release date. I giggled and told her in three months, she'd have much more than she bargained for.

After his release, they were married by a justice of the peace and she made him a partner in her lucrative business. They had been married for only seven months when she found out he had become romantically involved with a woman and a man. When she confronted him, he quickly said something about continuing to have as much cake as he could grab even if it was more than his fair share.

Neighbors and friends joked about how much time she had wasted getting him out of jail only for him to play her like a washboard in a zydeco band. She felt so embarrassed that she didn't get out of bed for a week except to drink wine and use the toilet.

In my consultation, I told her she was dying to make way for a rebirth of consciousness, awareness, and an acceptance that she was enough. This rebirth would serve her well in her future searches for love. After their divorce, she was eventually ready for that transition.

EXERCISE: THE SMELL OF DEATH AWAKENS MY REBIRTH

The Ace of Spades is about dying, whether through traumatic events or not, and coming back to life. It's also about valuing the lessons of what lies beyond the veil of common sense. Transformations can burn through our flesh, leaving scars that sting every time we even think about traveling back down a dead-end road. Those are the lessons that cut deep through our bones.

Needs:

* 1 green satchel big enough to hold the card
* ¼–½ teaspoon Hoyt's cologne (adds luck and unknown fortune)
* 1 Ace of Spades playing card
* 1 teaspoon chamomile (soothes luck back into a sour life with shattered possibilities)
* 1 teaspoon grains of paradise (sends luck to newly set intentions)
* 3 cloves (attracts what your life is lacking)
* 1 teaspoon cinnamon (draws down enough money to keep one moving in a positive direction)
* 1 green satchel big enough to hold the card

Instructions:

The night before this work, pour the Hoyt's cologne into your satchel. Use just enough to leave a smell but still have a dry satchel come morning. Leave the satchel on a towel overnight to help it dry out.

In the morning, place your Ace of Spade card into the satchel and add the chamomile, grains of paradise, cloves, and cinnamon. Repeat the following:

Today I offer myself up to change soft and radical.

*I will expose moments of discontent and be brave enough
to say enough is enough.*

*I know the exact moment the terrain changed from down
feathers to sand, to gravel.*

*I recognize the moment I died, the second I left my body
and traded my self-worth for an acceptance that was
never coming.*

Today my luck is changing; my fortunes are being written.

*Today's change is the beginning of me honoring my
destiny.*

*The hardest lessons are born out of fire and blood and
slice through bone.*

I give light and praise to a new me.

Tie the satchel, by its cord, to your bra strap. Carry it for
fourteen days and let the Ace of Spades help you in your
transformation.

Chapter Eleven
Lagniappe

The word *lagniappe* denotes a small token or gift given to a customer as a show of appreciation for being a loyal patron. Though small, the treat is usually of high quality and given with sincerity. Such a random and unexpected trinket no doubt keeps customers coming back for more.

What you'll find in this chapter is just that: a small gift. These passages and workings are important parts of magick in general but had no definitive place in the previous chapters. They will teach you more about the practice of Hoodoo and also help you understand how learning a little something extra can enhance the efficacy of your spirit workings. Consider this a token of appreciation, a literal baker's dozen housing deliciously sweetened morsels. Go slowly—you'll want to savor each magick-filled bite.

Psalms

Throughout the Americas and beyond, the Bible has played a pivotal role in the enslavement of Afrikan minds, just as the whip enslaved their physical bodies. Over generations of brainwashing, Afrikan thought was infused with Biblical ideas and iconography, including the Psalms. To survive within that developing Christian worldview, our ancestors created a new belief system that incorporated Biblical elements but shielded indigenous beliefs such as ancestral reverence, rootwork, and the praising of spiritual essences. Because of that merger, these practices survive today, deeply embedded with Hoodoo.

Those people, who were once forbidden to read and write, transformed the object of their subjugation into a language of freedom. They turned their captors' words and beliefs inside out, breaking both the rules and their former chains. These descendants of Afrikans learned how to enslave the Bible to the will of their ancient ancestors. Its words were now and forever at the mercy of Afrikan interpretations.

Today, the Psalms are used frequently in Hoodoo to remember how the once-enslaved Afrikan mastered and enslaved the White man's language. Some argue that there's no Hoodoo without the Psalms—they reminder us how far we've traveled. Other say that since Hoodoo was born from the horror of enslavement, the White man's tongue should never be used to invoke the practice. This is the belief I was brought up on. However, as I stated earlier, I always want Spirit to be the one who says no or ignores petitions; I don't know what Spirit has in store for anyone. So just call out and see for yourself who opens the door, or who spits in your face for having the audacity to knock in the first place.

Since Hoodoo is the language of retribution, it makes sense that it would champion those with the spirit of survival, rebellion, and liberation. Hoodoo revivals often spike when people have grown fed up with longstanding racism, sexism, or any other phobia or ism.

Working with Psalms

Use the Psalms with any of the workings in the book. I added them here to give you an extra brand of seasoning to flavor your craft. Recite them on their own or before, during, or after your workings, always in groups of three. Before you do, I recommend placing a teaspoon of honey on your tongue to sweeten your words. You can also chew Atare peppers seeds and then spit the mush into the earth to clear your aura of negative energies and influences. Please note, this list doesn't include the actual psalm—you'll need a Bible (King James version) for that.

- Psalm 3—heals body aches from head to toe.
- Psalm 7—transports the hex or crossing back to the sender.
- Psalm 9—brings ease to a sick child or ends the child's night terrors.
- Psalm 10—protects from automobile accidents or any travel hazards.
- Psalm 14—banishes an unworthy person.
- Psalm 20—helps win a court case.
- Psalm 36—reveals lurking liars, haters, and trolls.

- Psalm 42—helps balance the attitudes of family or friends by sweetening their disposition toward each other.
- Psalm 43—sends ancestors to one's astral space to aid in prompt decision making.
- Psalm 48—squashes any attempts at success an enemy has; ensures one is deserving of bringing on another's failure and isn't acting out of jealousy; ensures the enemy hasn't been moving toward repentance, which would cause the psalm to backfire.
- Psalm 49—brings about a successful surgery.
- Psalm 53—protects from drama and emotional terrorism, whether from known or unknown enemies.
- Psalm 57—reverses fortune.
- Psalm 62—attracts any blessings when in a rush; brings about success.
- Psalm 65—clears all blockages, bringing success closer.
- Psalm 68—removes unruly energy from your home; also a good Psalm to use before moving into a new domicile.
- Psalm 72—attracts power so nothing upsets one's movements or motivations.
- Psalm 73—protects a person from scrutiny while traveling abroad.
- Psalm 79—seals the fate of a murderer, rapist, or abuser.
- Psalm 89—encourages the legal system to release someone from jail.
- Psalm 92—increases wealth and success in business ventures.
- Psalm 98—ends family and tit-for-tat arguments.
- Psalm 104—cleanses the home, workspace, or car from negative energy sparked by a disgruntled lover.
- Psalms 106, 107—help dementia and Alzheimer's patients feel more at ease.
- Psalm 109—curses anyone who has viciously maimed or killed a loved one.
- Psalms 116, 121, 125—invoke protection from burglary, carjacking, rape, or death, especially under cover of darkness.

- Psalm 118—stops a thieving relative, friend, or social media troll from draining one's bank account.
- Psalm 127—protects a baby in its first year from crib death.
- Psalm 128—ensures a sexual liaison leads to pregnancy.
- Psalm 139—calls forth a lover who will marry the speaker within three years.
- Psalm 147—helps heal broken limbs.

No Time for Work

Usually when I'm moving through life quickly, there's no time to go into full-blown "witchy mode." That transformation is a waltz, one so mesmerizing it takes my breath away. But the time isn't always there, and life can easily dictate the limits of my focus. That's why I keep a stash of quickie herbs to burn away the blues and help me prioritize how events play out in my life. If you don't have a cast-iron cauldron, you can use a cast-iron skillet. It works just as effectively, and many of our grandmothers have them stashed in their pot.

Quick Herbs to Burn in a Pinch

Here are the herbs and supplies I like to keep on hand for quick work. Look for them in the spice aisle at the dollar store before heading to your local high-end metaphysical or online herb shop.

- *Asafoetida*: Burned in powder form. Aids in exorcism and protection. Use it to banish negative energy after work or after going to a crowded venue where you're uncertain of everyone's spiritual intent. Warning: asafoetida has a very pungent odor.
- *Anise*: Buried in dried leaf form. Drives away anger, jealousy, or evil deeds. The leaves are also sometimes placed in a bowl on a dresser or under a bed for this same purpose.
- *Calendula Flowers*: Burned to bring luck to the day. The aroma removes any hint of the evil eye or jealous intent folks try to send toward you.

- *Basil*: Brings protection from restless spirits when sprinkled around the corners of an infant's room. Burn it to ease temper tantrums, especially if you have teenagers. Keep a few sprigs in your wallet to attract money. Keep a few sprigs in your mailbox to ensure you always pay your bills on time.

- *Bay Laurel Leaves*: Encourage a sick person's body to heal itself when placed in the corners of an ill loved one's room (whisper a prayer or healing affirmations into the leaves before placing them). Write a power word such as *Fight, Strong, Win, Beauty, or Fierce* on a leaf and place it in a shoe at the heel—this will strengthen one's stride and protect from psychic vampires. Make a wish on a bay leaf, then burn it to watch desires manifest.

- *Chicory*: Burned in its dry form, it prevents a person from over-spending. Use it before shopping, even cyber shopping, and run your money or credit/debit cards through the smoke. It's also good for purifying any object. Just run the object through the smoke.

- *Magnolia Flowers*: Placed in a bowl of water under the bed, keep relationships intact. Place the leaves under a mattress to increase passionate lovemaking and explosive orgasms.

- *Nutmeg*: Promotes spiritual rejuvenation and helps you focus and retain pertinent information.

- *Osha Root*: Wards off malevolent spiritual attacks when carried in a black or red satin satchel. Place a picture of a loving, strong-willed ancestor inside.

- *Onions*: Stick an onion with thirty or more stick pins, then place on any windowsill of the house to prevent home invasions and absorb unsettling energy. As you stick the pins, speak loudly or yell, by name, exactly what you want to keep out. Place sliced onion halves around the outside perimeter or corners of the home for the same purpose. Use pins to attach a note to each onion slice detailing what you want to keep out of the home.

- *Pokeberry Leaves*: Carry in a white satin satchel to promote courage.

- *Potatoes*: Used as poppets. Use a marker to write the person's name all over the potato, or draw their features. Prick the potato with a fork, then state your discontent. Stick it with as many stick pins as your spud will allow before burying it outside in a planter full of soil and manure.

- *Patchouli*: Brings prosperity and abundance when the oil is sprinkled on money, a checkbook, student loan papers, income tax documents, or on clothes. Rub it on your wallet or even your hands before doing your work or craft.

- *Pomegranate*: Attracts sweetness. Cut it open, speak your wish into one half, and leave it at the base of a tree. Bury the other half in a plant pot along with a picture of your children, lover, or anyone. You can even do this for yourself. Sweetness will follow them for a month.

- *Parsley*: Soothes and calms when burned on charcoal. Make a regular practice of dabbing your child's school supplies with parsley oil to encourage concentration in class.

- *Pine*: Sprinkle pinecones with lemon verbena oil and place them in a hanging basket to welcome visitors. Carries away negativity or self-loathing from guests as they enter the home. If you can't hang it near your front door, place the basket on a table or floor near the front door. If you have a fireplace, burn pine needles before company comes, especially if there's a known mess maker in the bunch. After they leave, repeat to rid your space of drama.

- *Pumpkin Spice*: Sprinkle on top of a green candle to help grow your money. Sprinkle it inside your wallet to attract money. Sprinkle a little in your shoes on your way to work. Made of a combination of cinnamon, cloves, ginger, nutmeg, and allspice, this spice blend will help your employer recognize your worth, positioning you in line for a promotion or a long overdue vacation.

- *Rose Petals*: Made into a body spreadh, honey and rose petals promote sensuality. Rinse two to three pesticide-free rose petals under a trickle of water and place in a large mason jar. Cover the petals with raw honey. Seal the jar tightly and leave upside down for two weeks in a dark cupboard. Try writing a petition on edible icing sheets with edible ink markers, then drop it inside the jar.

- *Rosemary*: When burned, the herb alters a space's vibration. Place a blue or pink satin satchel filled with dried rosemary under your pillow to improve memory.

- *Red Brick Dust*: A useful tool for protection. Mix white vinegar, urine, cayenne, and honey in a bucket with water. Dip a broom into the mixture, then use it to sweep the steps leading to your home or the walkway in front of your home. This will keep out errant energy and ensure that everyone living inside reaches their destiny.

- *Sage*: Curtails both an inflated ego and jealousy. Burn sage or wear it in a locket. Sprinkle dried sage in your shoe. It's exceptional for young people because at their age, jealousy tends to runs rampant in their social circles. Because white sage is facing extinction, I burn dried cooking sage to achieve the same results.

- *Thyme*: Burn when feeling weak or just dead tired. It's an energy drink for your spirit. Burning it will also remove grief by helping you repurpose your happiness.

- *Turmeric*: Purifies your home and makes it a sacred abode. Sprinkle it on the floor and let it sit for fifteen minutes while solfeggio frequencies emanate throughout, then sweep it up and toss it out the front door!

- *Tonka Beans*: Carried for courage and insight into business or financial ventures. Sleep with the beans wrapped in cloth or in a brown satin satchel tucked inside your pillowcase. Add two strips of paper labeled *yes* and *no*. In the morning follow the advice of the slip of paper you first pull from the satchel. When carried in a coin purse, brings abundance into your life. Take one out and make a wish on it. Then, for added luck, toss it into a body of water or down a dark alley.

Quick Energy Release Ritual

If you're short on time, here's how to do a quick ritual using herbs.

First, light a charcoal disc and place it inside a cast-iron cauldron. Add the needed herbs, which will alter the energy of your surroundings and the mood that has attached itself to your aura. Close your eyes and chant—one chant I use for a quick energy shift: "Release me, I am not yours, and you are not mine."

Breathe in and out to a count of four between chants. Repeat the phrase as often as you feel necessary to adjust your spiritual attunement. I typically do this until the herb burns out.

Makeup Bags

You may need to carry some of these herbs for use on the road or while you're out. Toting your witchy supplies should involve just as much couture and cunning as deciding what to wear to class, work, or play. I bet you know where this is going: Go to the dollar store and buy a travel makeup bag. These bags are reasonably priced, durable, cute, and discreet.

I suggest keeping a few of the herbs listed in the Quickie section in your bag. You can store dry herbs in plastic zip-top bags or in small bottles. Use duct tape or blue painter's tape and a permanent marker to create labels noting the name and use of each herb. Try writing the herb's usage in a quick incantation form, such as, "Anise, Anise, Drive Away Fear."

Spiritual Cleansing and Protection

Spiritual cleansings are our way of purifying and rejuvenating our soul space. As we constantly engage with the natural world, there's no surefire way to avoid psychic poop. No matter how psychically charged you are before setting out to meet each day, we all manage to get dirty in the metaphysical sense. We intentionally and unintentionally open ourselves to toxic frequencies instead of nourishing vibrations.

In a less than perfect world, we can't block or unfollow annoying people or situations out of our lives. It's impossible to argue with certain family, friends, colleagues, and even that hated boss and walk away totally unscathed. That's why, when we get the funk that just refuses to unhand us, it's time to deliver a cleaning that reaches way past flesh and bone. We need the kind of cleaning agents that jumpstart our soul.

Spiritual Cleanse Must Haves

The following is a list of items I always have on hand to help cleanse, purify, and protect in a pinch.:

- *Black or Castille Soap*: Use both to cleanse yourself and wash any clothes that were worn during confrontations with annoying people or energy vampires. I sometimes add a tablespoon of Florida water to the mixture when handling items gifted from a deceased person's treasures.
- *Garlic*: Hang fresh garlic braids in your kitchen or at your front door to keep troublesome people from entering. Garlic provides protection and healing and strengthens your physical resolve. Leave whole dried bulbs in the four corners of a room or at your workstation. It will rid your space of drama quicker than slamming the door, locking it, and throwing away the key. I also love cooking with it when I have confrontational guests, such as after funerals, during family reunions, or at work potlucks. You get it.
- *Ginger Root*: Sprinkle this at work to keep your space drama free. Sprinkle the powdered root on doorways, windowsills, or any other kind of threshold. I once used it to stop a messy coworker from unpacking their racism in my direction. Afterward, when that coworker entered my office, she was a different animal. Her attitude was so loving, it was like we were long-lost friends.
- *High John the Conqueror Root*: I carry one to two of these scrotum-looking roots in my satchel with my lodestones. They help me conquer all situations known and unknown.
- *Lodestone*: Carry two pieces of lodestone (one with female energy, the other with male) in a red satchel. Name the stones after a lov-

ing and protective ancestor team. When you place the stones in the satchel, add a teaspoon of magnetic sand, a small amount of Hoyt's cologne and lodestone oil, and a spritz of whiskey. Wear the satchel attached to your bra strap for energy. Feed the lodestones more sand every two weeks.

- *Sea Salt*: Purifies and protects. You can use both pink and white salt with the same intent. I use Kosher salt specifically to remove unsettling vibrations from a place.
- *White Vinegar*: Made from potatoes, beets, sugar cane, and molasses, vinegar is a great cleaner. A mix of one part vinegar and one part absinthe can be poured around the perimeter of your home, spritzed in your car, or spritzed in your workspace to clear any stagnant unappealing energy from your space.

EXERCISE: EGG CLEANSINGS

Eggs can not only be used for cleansings but also to determine if negativity is being sent in your direction.

Needs:

* 1 glass vase, large
* ½ cup water
* ¼ cup Florida water
* 1 egg
* 1 teaspoon liquid black soap
* 1 candle of any color

Instructions:

Fill the vase with the two waters. Wash the egg with the black soap and let it sit out until it's room temperature.

When it's ready, say words of healing over the egg, such as:

I call on the spirit of my lineage, the spirit of my mighty dead—if I have been marked victim, release me from ensuing trauma.

*Strip away all evil deeds and purge from me, physically
and spiritually, the strain of hatred and jealousy whispered my way.*

*Let no deed hide, seeking refuge in the dark, dusty, and
secluded underbelly of my home.*

Release me and make me whole once again.

*Help me determine if I've become the victim of psychic
attack.*

Next, beginning at the top of your head, run the egg over
your whole body to cleanse. Touch your clothes and skin or
hover above. Don't forget the soles of your feet. Every part of
your body must be cleansed.

When done, crack the egg into the water and see what
appears:

* If you see blood or shapes resembling objects of violence such as a gun or knife, someone is sending their
  psychic goons after you.
* If the egg appears as a menacing eye or grimacing
  face, the person is up at night working heavily against
  you.
* If the egg floats or appears to break apart in an elon-
  gated manner, your spirit guides are on the case,
  whipping the daylights out of that energy. You'll need to
  perform the egg cleanse daily for the next three days to
  ensure you're completely rid of the troublemaker.
* If the egg appears to have tentacles, know your physical
  body is fighting against the energy, but the trauma is still
  on your heels.
* If the egg shows you positive images of a dove, an
  ancestor, a spiritual symbol, a deity, or an angel, you're
  on a great path and your support group is strong, not

just with your ancestors but with the deities you love and trust.

When finished, toss the egg and water into the street. Repeat the cleansing as needed.

Showered with Joy and Spirit

These next two rituals are dedicated to giving thanks and celebrating joy. They will uplift you and the spirits and ancestors that have helped you along your journey. The first exercise asks you to write a thank you note to Spirit; consider including this particular work in your regular rituals. The second ritual uses essential oils and other ingredients you've seen in past chapters to help build up your self-esteem as you go out into the world and do the hard work of hurdling challenges. You have a right to your story. Now tell it.

EXERCISE: DAILY NOTE TO SPIRIT RITUAL

Thank you notes to spirits show your appreciation for their assistance in all the work you've done and will do. You'll thank them for giving you hope, and for promising your life will ooze with stability.

Needs:

* 1 pen
* 1 sheet of paper of any kind, such as parchment, stationery, lined paper, or printer paper
* 1 cast-iron cauldron or fireproof container

Instructions:

These are intended to be daily notes you write by hand. Use a standard letter of appreciation. Begin with something like: "Dear Universe, I thank you for…" List at least one idea daily.

Think about ideas that fill you with hope and promise. Thoroughly explain those avenues you're happy to be shedding

through hard work and perseverance. Close the letter with love and list your name in full.

Burn the letter before bed in a cauldron. As the letter burns, repeat the following affirmations:

I am worth loving.
I was born with a purpose in mind.
I must live to fulfill each day's purpose.
The world is a better place because I exist.
Money will not break me because money didn't make me.
I returned to tell the story of my ancestors.
My truth is sacred.
No one will hijack my reality.
I deserve to be liberated, not gaslighted into submission.
This is my life, not reality tv, and I live it for me, not for
    social media.
Never will I give away to anyone the freedom to be me,
    whatever that me evolves into.
I have the right to change my mind and edit my story.

The next day, sprinkle the ashes in a park or wooded area. Repeat the letter writing each morning before you leave the house. Try to do this daily, or as frequently as possible.

EXERCISE: HOLDING MYSELF IN HIGH ESTEEM

After doing this ritual, watch how your esteem begins to sprout into clarity and a deeper understanding that who you are is enough to satisfy your wildest desires.

Needs:

* * 1 scarf, orange, brown, or yellow
* * 3 drops each:
    * – lemon oil (boosts mood)
    * – cinnamon oil (raises your vibration)

- grapefruit oil (raises mental clarity, joy, and balances emotional outlook)
* 1 pillow with case
* 1 picture of you as a younger person (*Note: If the oldest picture you have is only from five or ten years prior, that works too.*)
* 1 piece of carnelian (attracts wealth and success enhances confidence, positivity, and joy)
* 1 orange satchel big enough to hold the picture and gemstone

Instructions:

Place the drops of oil onto the scarf and put the scarf inside the pillowcase. Next, place the picture of you and your carnelian into the orange satchel. Put the filled satchel between your mattress and box spring (or just under your mattress if you don't have a box spring).

Before bed remind yourself that self-esteem is the value you place on yourself. It's not the ideas and motivations others try to hold you to. It's all in how you see yourself—Who are you? What are you trying to become, to own, to reach deep inside that has been impossible to touch? Then, repeat these mantras:

I am worthy of being whole.
Each day I strive to become a better version of the person I was the day before.
As I breathe, the world recognizes my desire to grow.
As my growth widens, my heart space opens to new opportunities.
No one will hold me back. I deserve to be overjoyed.
Love is at the seat of all my dreams coming true.
I haven't maximized my fullest potential, but I'm on my way.

I am transforming as I speak.
I call on the energy of my ancestors to rebuild my self-
    worth.
As I sleep, I transform.
As I sleep, I am reborn.

When you're done, drift off to sleepy land. Repeat this work each night for a month. Your self-esteem will soar as you continue writing your story.

Juju on The Fly

My goal for these final workings, the previous one and the one that follows, is to send you off with a blessing of encouragement for your future Hoodoo endeavors. The last working helped to build up your self-esteem. This final work assists you in holding fast to your dreams, even in the face of judgment and doubt. It encourages you to be patient and above all to always be kind to yourself so you reap a multitude of soul-stirring rewards.

When I was a ninth grader, my English teacher assigned our AP class a writing assignment that would count for 80 percent of our overall grade. We were tasked with writing a sixty-thousand-word manuscript. It had to be a mystery with a complex web of deception. I wrote *Tale of the Black Veil*, a macabre story reminiscent of Edgar Allan Poe. In my story, a psychiatrist is left at the altar after his fiancée finds out that he forged his degrees. In a rage, the man studies newspapers for photos of newly engaged women whom he then stalks and kills. At the scenes, he always leaves a black lace veil covering their decapitated heads. In an even bigger twist, the man counsels many of the murdered victims' families.

My teacher was so astonished with my story—all eighty thousand type-written words of it—that she announced in front of the entire class, "There's no way on God's green earth that a Black girl from uptown New Orleans wrote such a compelling work of art." She then made me look up the definition of plagiarism in the dictionary. The class stared in horror as she detailed what my suspension would entail: sixteen typewritten, twelve-page, single-spaced reports on books by her favorite mystery authors. Afterward she wrote me up and marched me to the principal's office. As we walked, she said the principal was dating her cousin. This meant she had his ear, and he wouldn't push back if she removed me from AP English.

This teacher, however, hadn't met my mother in her truest form. At Back to School night, the teacher had seen a gentle woman whose smile could light up a room. But when suggested that I be reprimanded with suspension, my mother lost her shit. She threatened to involve her attorney if they suspended me or kicked me out of AP. She also told them about watching me write until well past midnight every evening for weeks. Some nights she had to physically remove the typewriter from my room. In the end, I wasn't suspended, and I earned an A for my paper and an A in the class.

The weekend after I was exonerated, we went to Mrs. Delacroix so I could get prim and proper for my upcoming debutante ball. My mother told Mrs. Delacroix all about her run-in with socioeconomic prejudice. They kept sucking their teeth and answering each other with "that bitch was tripping hard."

Later, as my mother napped under the dryer, Mrs. Delacroix handed me a six-five domino. She told me to carry it in my purse alongside my lucky bean. This would help me overcome the sadness I felt after my teacher's humiliating attack and attempt to thwart my hopes of becoming an author one day.

The Hoodoo Mrs. Delacroix imparted etched my dreams in my memory until the day they finally grew legs. In my second year of college, my boyfriend and future husband introduced me to a writing mentor of his. My husband, others, and I became founding members of the NOMMO Literary Society, and that's when my writing career took off.

I still have the domino.

EXERCISE: RECIPROCITY IS REWARDED WITH GREAT PATIENCE

In Hoodoo, dominos are often carried around along with stones, playing cards, and statues of saints. They are used as divinatory tools as well as a way of taking one's luck on the road. Some folks use their pocketed domino as a reminder to say a prayer during the day in praise of an ancestor or saint, thereby increasing the efficacy of any spiritual work brewing on the home front. Some just use it as a talisman or amulet to increase their power over a situation, or as a reminder to protect their sacred space.

In the following ritual you'll use a domino and a lucky bean to help attain your dreams. They will assure you daily that whatever is for you is already yours in the making.

Needs:

* 1 six-five domino
* 1 fava bean as your lucky bean
* 1 small coin purse

Instructions:

Place the domino and lucky bean inside the coin purse. With the purse still open, whisper to the bean and domino the dream that's heavy on your heart. Repeat in detail the goal you're dying to achieve against all odds, then close the purse and place it in your pocket or handbag. Keep doing this daily until the domino and bean speak back inside your dream space.

When that dream manifests, thank the purse and its contents, then place the closed coin purse on your ancestral altar. Offer the purse to someone dear to your heart when their time is ripe, and let them know they're already on their divine path of sweet satisfaction. The purse, with the domino and bean, will manifest the rest.

Conclusion

We are all magickal beings inhabiting a shell of flesh and bone. I grew up on Chitimacha land, where I learned that my ability to conjure is innate. It's up to me when and how I choose to awaken my magick, just as it's up to you to decide the most opportune moment to awaken your magick.

The world we live in oftentimes disapproves of our association with magick. We learn early that magick is evil, demonic, or satanic. However, times are changing, and people are realizing that a life outside of organized religion won't end in their mental, physical, or spiritual demise. These same folks are searching to find the Goddess or God within. Black, Brown, White alike are increasingly turning to palm readers, dousing rods, bones, tarot, reiki, sound therapy, conjure, witchcraft, indigenous spirituality, holistic medicine, metaphysics, and esotericism. The Church and its figureheads, with their centuries-old dogma, are left to watch in awe as people become their own preachers, teachers, and healers.

In recent years the social climate has opened the door for people to explore what words like *salvation, death, spirituality, God,* and *spiritualism* mean in our lives. We're learning how to handle individual pain and finding healing methods tailored to the specific traumas we're living through. People can no longer be silent about their sexuality or their belief systems. We've finally been given time to sort through truths that speaks passionately to both our third eye and our heart's chakra.

Weaponizing Our Conjure

Between 1936 and 1940 (with supplemental interviews in 1970), Harry Middleton Hyatt collected five volumes of conjure in his *Hoodoo Conjuration Witchcraft Rootwork*. This Anglican minister often recorded tales of conjuration unbeknownst to the participants on a concealed telephone.

Many Black Hoodoo practitioners believe that because Hyatt was White, his interview subjects likely only gave him half-truths. Our kinfolk did this to teach the next generation that to succeed against unlawful odds, you have to move in secret. I bring up Hyatt because a lot of what the world understands about Hoodoo stems from his work. Many believe conjure is just a wicked form of inflicting pain, and that its practitioners, being people of color, are heinous and vengeful without reason.

The reality is that Hoodoo magick isn't hocus pocus ranting into an abyss of crapola. Hoodoo magick is as much therapeutic as it is esoteric. It's what happened when African Americans chose liberation over subjugation and married it to magick, not out of obligation but necessity. And isn't necessity the mother of invention?

Conjure teaches us to acknowledge that our interaction with Spirit can happen without a middleman. We can each transform our existence on our own terms. The ability to manipulate Spirit allows us to understand the world's challenges in layman's terms. We can meditate and connect the dots between our nature, our aura, our spirit, and our soul space. We learn to honor Goddess and God, and to not blame deity for teachable moments. After all, what doesn't kill us makes us even more magickal seekers of liberation.

Remember, there's no Hoodoo bible, no rule book. Nowhere in the world will you find a definitively agreed explanation of precisely how to Hoodoo for everyone. Hoodoo is very much dependent on your region, your ancestral lineage, and the comingling of other cultures that have traded ideas with Black and Brown peoples.

How Hoodoo Healed My Life

Living in America has become a dangerous game. It hasn't been easy for any of us.

I contracted Covid-19 in 2020, and I honestly thought I was going to die. I saw death reaching for my ide (a beaded bracelet encased inside a copper bangle), trying to break it. In her anger she flung herself into the darkness, disappearing into the shadow of night. I heard her clawing at my bedroom window. She whispered my name, and I reached for my black tourmaline, the mojo, and juju bags. Clutching my spiritual accoutrements tightly I called out to the spirit of my grandfather, who astrally appeared flanked by two Dobermans. They howled as he sang Babalú-Ayé's orin. As my grandfather massaged my crown chakra, he beseeched me to calm down. His caress made me realize Death couldn't take what I didn't freely offer.

Shortly after, a box came in the mail. The package, labeled "Say More," contained a deck of cards divided into four groups representing the elements: air, fire, water, and earth. The deck is meant to open discourse about menopause, aging, and self-care, and invoke compassionate wisdom in honor of the shifting women go through physically, spiritually, and psychologically throughout life. My sistah friends Omisade Burney-Scott and Catherine Balsam-Schwaber created the cards.

As Hoodoo would have it, one evening I found myself filling a glass with water and adding nine drops of bluing along with three drops each of frankincense and myrrh oil. Then I lit a blue candle and placed a mirror in front of me. I closed my eyes and pulled a card from the water portion of the deck. The card I pulled challenged me to prioritize and redistribute my energy in such a way that made me rethink the day.

I sat there considering the story of the day, the title I'd give it and its moral. I decided to light some Palo Santo incense to clear the debris of other people's words from my mind. I decided my own narrative hadn't been written enough on this day. It was at that point that I realized that every day should be about rewriting, deleting, and shredding what no longer fits my life. I'm the author of my story.

I took a magnolia leaf and, in marker, I wrote, "I am editing my today on tomorrow." Then I placed it inside a blue satchel along with an earth card, and I held it close to my heart.

I still carry that satchel with me, meditating with it at stopping points along the way. Inside is a reminder to make my story top priority no matter what crazed-out insanity is going on around me. My life demands my participation as a main character, not a supporting cast member. I am a necessity; I come with value no amount of money can buy.

My Wish for You

I hope this story and these words encourage you to understand that the magick within you is your right. No one should ever make you feel ostracized for choosing to color outside the spiritual lines. We're all trying to find peace in a world riddled with pain and confusion. Hoodoo magick has helped me find peace and write my own story. Each day I live I challenge myself with a reset ritual. I encourage you to share a sacred piece of your soul with those you love often—reset, resist, and liberate. The Universe is waiting for the most authentic version of you ever known to humankind. Nobody will ever honor your self-worth better than you can. Let's not disappoint ourselves, our ancestors, our destiny, or our Universe.

Ase to all my lovely keepers of the Calabash.

Acknowledgments

I must first acknowledge the entire publishing team at Llewellyn for giving me the platform to spill the beans. Llewellyn's professionalism, warmth, and complete trust in my ability to deliver my truth is deeply appreciated. I thank my husband, Nadir, and my children, Nzingha, Kambui, Camara, Naima, and Sekou for their love and support and their willingness to listen to my rewrites. My husband told me so many times to just write the book. Finally I picked up my set of fountain pens and legal pad after legal pad until words became phrases, and phrases became the energy at your fingertips. Nadir is right most days of the week, but let's not tell him I said so.

My mother has always supported my writing endeavors with the cheer, "That's right, do it, baby!" Mama introduced me to spiritualism. For a moment in our human evolution, we live as three—the mother carries the daughter who carries the ovaries that house the eggs that will one day become her children. My mother Patricia Ann Coulter Dean's womb has carried the seeds of Hoodoo, allowing me to flower my own path. I'm truly blessed to have thrived through her red rains.

I'm thankful for Heather Greene, acquisitions editor at Llewellyn. From our first conversation about tarot's popularity in communities of color, I was delighted by your interest and acceptance of how tarot plays a major role in my Hoodoo practice.

I am thankful for Anitra Budd's patience and dedication to ensuring that through her editing process, my authentic voice danced on every page.

I thank the band of prolific writers at NOMMO Literary Society. This New Orleans–based writing workshop provided a safe space for my esoteric literature to be heard. I also extend gratitude to the cadre of female writers who, unbeknown to them, have shaped my truth. This list includes writers of stories, poems, and African culture, remarkable womenfolk like Zora Neale Hurston, J. California Cooper, Lucille Clifton, AI, Iya Ifalola Omobola, Iya

Luisah Teish, Lilith Dorsey, Stephanie Rose Bird, Najah Lightfoot, Iyalosa Apetebii OlaOmi Osunyemi Akalatunde, Michele Elizabeth Lee, Professor Yvonne Chireau, Katrina Hazzard-Donald, Sherry Shone, Tayannah Lee McQuillar, and Denise Alvarado. Ladies, I love you for being comrades, mentors, and highly potent fire starters.

Bibliography

Allardyce, Carolanne. "Rituals and Ceremonies in Death and Dying." Awaken, January 1, 2021. https://awaken.com/2021/01/rituals -and-ceremonies-in-death-and-dying/.

Anele, Uzonna. "5 Appalling Ways Enslaved African Men Were Sexually Exploited by Their Slave Masters." Talk Africana, December 17, 2018. https://talkafricana.com/5-appalling-ways-enslaved-african-men-were -sexually-exploited-by-their-slave-masters/.

"APA Dictionary of Psychology." American Psychological Association. n.d. https://dictionary.apa.org/trauma.

Atske, Sara. "The Internet and the Pandemic." Pew Research Center: Internet, Science & Tech. Pew Research Center, April 28, 2022. https://www .pewresearch.org/internet/2021/09/01/the-internet-and-the-pandemic/.

Buckland, Raymond. *Buckland's Book of Spirit Communications*. 2nd rev. and expanded ed. Woodbury: Llewellyn Publications, 2004.

Carrellas, Barbara. *Urban Tantra: Sacred Sex for the Twenty-First Century*. New York, NY: Ten Speed Press, 2017.

Chaffey, Dave. "What Happens Online in 60 Seconds in 2021?" Smart Insights, June 28, 2021. https://www.smartinsights.com/internet -marketing-statistics/happens-online-60-seconds/.

Chow, Andrew R., and Josiah Bates. "Black Vietnam Veterans on Injustices They Faced: Da 5 Bloods." *Time*, June 12, 2020. https://time.com /5852476/da-5-bloods-black-vietnam-veterans/.

Cruse, Harold. "Revolutionary Nationalism and the Afro-American." Indianapolis: Bobbs-Merrill, 1960.

Curtin, Philip D. *Two Jamaicas: The Role of Ideas in a Tropical Colony, 1830–1865*. Westport, CT: Greenwood Press, 1968.

Davis, Shanice. "Princess Nokia Talks Infusing Santería in Her Music." Vibe, December 14, 2016. https://www.vibe.com/features/viva/princess-nokia-talks-santeria-473957/#!

Deren, Maya. *Divine Horsemen: The Living Gods of Haiti*. London, UK: Thames and Hudson, 1953.

Duignan, Brian. "Gaslighting." In *Encyclopedia Britannica*. Chicago, IL: Encyclopedia Britannica, 2002.

Folley, Aris. "Kanye West Says Harriet Tubman 'Never Actually Freed the Slaves' at Rally." *The Hill*, July 20, 2020. https://thehill.com/homenews/campaign/508048-kanye-west-says-harriet-tubman-never-actually-freed-the-slaves-during-first/.

Funeral Guide. "Death Rituals around the World: Different Funeral Traditions." Funeral Guide, May 24, 2018. https://www.funeralguide.com/blog/death-rituals-around-the-world.

GirlTalkHQ. "Artist Princess Nokia Is the Intersectional Feminist & WOC Advocate the Music Industry Needs." GirlTalkHQ, November 23, 2017. https://www.girltalkhq.com/artist-princess-nokia-is-the-intersectional-feminist-woc-advocate-the-music-industry-needs/.

Holloway, Joseph E. "African Crops and Slave Cuisine." Rice Diversity, September 19, 2009. http://ricediversity.org/outreach/educatorscorner/documents/African-Crops-and-Slave-Cuisine.doc.

Hurston, Zora. "Hoodoo in America." *The Journal of American Folklore* 44, no. 174 (1931): 317–417. https://doi.org/10.2307/535394.

Jones, Jae. "Antebellum South: Sexual Abuse against Enslaved Women on the Plantation." Black Then, February 12, 2020. https://blackthen.com/antebellum-south-sexual-abuse-against-enslaved-women-on-the-plantation/.

Kai, Maiysha. "'I'm Exercising My Freedom': Janelle Monáe Talks Liberation in Instyle's Badass Women Issue." *The Root,* July 11, 2019. https://
www.theroot.com/i-m-exercising-my-freedom-janelle-monae-talks
-liberati-1836256843.

Kaiser, Shannon. "What Is Grounding?" Spirituality+Health, April 11, 2020.
https://www.spiritualityhealth.com/articles/2020/04/10/what-is
-grounding.

Kearl, Holly. "81 percent of Women and 43 percent of Men Have Experienced Sexual Abuse in USA." Stop Street Harassment, last modified
February 21, 2018. https://stopstreetharassment.org/2018/02
/newstudy2018/

Lawrenson, Emily. "Online Trolls and Cyberbullies: What's the Difference?"
Qustodio, November 23, 2021. https://www.qustodio.com/en/blog
/difference-online-trolls-and-cyberbullies/.

"The Legend of the Black-Eyed Pea." Civil War Family, December 31, 2013.
https://www.civilwarfamily.us/2013/12/the-legend-of-the-black-eyed
-pea.html.

Light, Alexander. "The Spiritual Strength of Hair—Yogic Perspective."
Humans Be Free, February 19, 2018. https://humansbefree.com/2018
/02/the-spiritual-strength-of-hair-yogic-perspective.html.

Mandel, Leah. "How 5 Women Use Religious Traditions to Navigate Modern Life." *The Fader*, November 9, 2017. https://www.thefader.com
/2016/12/08/women-religion-fashion-faith.

March, Evita. "A Psychological Profile of Online Trolls Shows High Self
Esteem and a Penchant for Sadism." *The National Interest.* The Center for
the National Interest, September 17, 2020. https://nationalinterest.org
/blog/reboot/psychological-profile-online-trolls-shows-high-self-esteem
-and-penchant-sadism-169047.

May, Kate Torgovnick. "Death Is Not the End: Fascinating Funeral Traditions from around the Globe." Ideas.ted.com, October 1, 2013. https://ideas.ted.com/11-fascinating-funeral-traditions-from-around-the-globe/.

Midland Health. "7 Surprising Benefits of CBD Oil." Midland Health Testing Services, August 26, 2018. https://www.midlandhealth.com/General-Health/7-Surprising-Benefits-of-Cbd-Oil.

Mineo, Liz. "Orlando Patterson Explains Why America Can't Escape Its Racist Roots." *Harvard Gazette*, June 4, 2020. https://news.harvard.edu/gazette/story/2020/06/orlando-patterson-exp.

Newman, Amy. "Buddhist Death Rituals and End of Life Traditions." LoveToKnow, February 24, 2022. https://dying.lovetoknow.com/burial-cremation/buddhist-death-rituals.

Osofsky, Gilbert, ed. *Puttin' On Ole Massa: The Slave Narratives of Henry Bibb, William Wells Brown, and Solomon Northup.* New York: Harper Torchbooks, 1969.

Overall Motivation Team, The. "65 Anton Lavey Quotes on Success in Life." Overall Motivation. Last modified June 12, 2021, https://www.overallmotivation.com/quotes/anton-lavey-quotes/.

Ponder, Catherine. *The Millionaire from Nazareth: His Prosperity Secrets for You!* (Millionaires of the Bible Series). Camarillo, CA: Devorss & Co., 1979.

Reece. "6 Signs You Are Addicted to Social Media." Anti-Dose, July 30, 2020. https://addictioncounsellors.co.nz/6-signs-addicted-to-social-media.

Root Staff, The. "Myth-Busting the Black Marriage 'Crisis.'" *The Root*, August 18, 2011. https://www.theroot.com/myth-busting-the-black-marriage-crisis-1790865391.

"Sade." Marshall Arts Ltd. Accessed April 17, 2023. https://marshall-arts.com/sade/.

Singh, Deva Kauer. "Improve Your Vitality and Meditation with Long Hair." MrSikhNet, September 4, 2007. https://www.mrsikhnet.com/2007 /09/04/improve-your-vitality-and-meditation-with-long-hair/.

Smith, Earl, and Angela Hattery. "Black Men, Vietnam, Drugs & Prison." Smith & Hattery, February 14, 2016. https:// smithandhattery.com/black-men-vietnam-drugs-prison/.

Spanos, Brittany. "Janelle Monáe Frees Herself." *Rolling Stone*, April 26, 2018. https://www.rollingstone.com/music/music-features/janelle-monae -frees-herself-629204/.

Spielberg, Steven, dir. *The Color Purple*. 1985; Burbank, CA: Warner Bros., 2011. Blue-ray Disc, 1080p HD.

"This Is the Toll That Everyday Racism Takes on Black Men in America." World Economic Forum, July 2, 2020. https://www.weforum.org /agenda/2020/07/george-floyd-racism-opportunities-life-expectancy/.

USAFacts. "Men Are Likelier to Die Each Year than Women. Black Men Have the Highest Mortality Rates." USAFacts, July 1, 2021. https:// usafacts.org/articles/men-die-more-often-than-women-black-men -are-the-hardest-hit/.

Uwumarogie, Victoria. "Pastor Cal Says Black Men Auditioning for MAFS Might Prefer White Women, but 'White Women Don't Prefer You.'" *Madame Noire*, July 18, 2018. https://madamenoire.com/1033090 /pastor-cal-mafs/.

"The Vicious Cycle of Exhaustion and Nightmares." Cleveland Clinic, December 14, 2022. https://my.clevelandclinic.org/health/articles /14297-nightmares-in-children.

Vojinovic, Ivana. "Heart-Breaking Cyberbullying Statistics for 2023." Data-prot. Last modified April 7, 2023. https://dataprot.net/statistics /cyberbullying-statistics/.

Walker, Alice. *The Color Purple*. Orlando, Fl.: Harcourt, 2003.

Walton, Alice G. "Social Media Taps into Our Most Primal Urge: Talking about Ourselves." *Forbes Magazine*, June 30, 2012. https://www .forbes.com/sites/alicegwalton/2012/06/29/facebooks-share-button -taps-into-the-wiring-of-our-brain/.

To Write to the Author

If you wish to contact the author or would like more information about this book, please write to the author in care of Llewellyn Worldwide Ltd. and we will forward your request. Both the author and the publisher appreciate hearing from you and learning of your enjoyment of this book and how it has helped you. Llewellyn Worldwide Ltd. cannot guarantee that every letter written to the author can be answered, but all will be forwarded. Please write to:

Mawiyah Kai El-Jamah Bomani
℅ Llewellyn Worldwide
2143 Wooddale Drive
Woodbury, MN 55125-2989
Please enclose a self-addressed stamped envelope for reply,
or $1.00 to cover costs. If outside the U.S.A., enclose
an international postal reply coupon.

Many of Llewellyn's authors have websites with additional information and resources. For more information, please visit our website at http://www.llewellyn.com.